Schools Council
Research Studies

Mass Media
and the
Secondary School

A report from the Schools Council project
on Mass Media and the Secondary School at
the Centre for Mass Communication Research,
University of Leicester

Schools Council
Research Studies

Mass Media
and the
Secondary School

Graham Murdock
Guy Phelps

Macmillan

First published 1973

SBN 333 14845 2

Published by MACMILLAN EDUCATION LTD
Basingstoke and London

The Macmillan Company of Australia Pty Ltd
 Melbourne
The Macmillan Company of Canada Ltd
 Toronto
St Martin's Press Inc
 New York
Companies and representatives throughout the
world

Printed in Great Britain by
Hazell Watson & Viney Ltd
Aylesbury, Bucks

Foreword

The Centre for Mass Communication Research was established by a grant from the Television Research Committee—a Home Office Committee—at the University of Leicester in October 1966 to study the influence of television and other media on the lives of young people. It was expected, however, that in due course the Centre would receive support from and establish cooperative working relationships with other interested bodies, and that eventually a comprehensive research programme would be developed in which media institutions and communication processes would be studied within the relevant wider social contexts.

The first project at the Centre to be sponsored by an outside body is reported here. Preliminary discussions with the Schools Council actually predated by some months the opening of the Centre in the autumn of 1966, and began at the Schools Council Conference on the Educational Implications of Social and Economic Change at the University of Nottingham in July 1966. There the possibility that the Centre might make some contribution to the Council's policy of 'bringing to the attention of teachers new knowledge about outside factors which impinge on the educational process' was discussed.

Several meetings (in which Philip Taylor, Professor of Education at the University of Birmingham, and J. G. Owen, then Joint Secretary of the Schools Council, played a prominent part) and many letters later a research outline was finally approved and work on the four year project started in September 1967, with James Learmonth as research officer and Guy Phelps as research assistant. It was agreed that the first of the four years should be an exploratory or feasibility year in which the whole problem area could be thoroughly examined with a view to preparing a final research design by the end of the year. Work on the research proper started in September 1968 and, in September 1969, Graham Murdock took over from James Learmonth as research officer in charge of the project.

In the preparatory discussions with the Schools Council there was an underlying assumption that the school influenced—or at least tried to influence—taste and leisure-time preferences in several areas. It was also assumed that this influence could be exerted by both direct (e.g. lessons) and indirect (e.g.

teachers' attitudes, etc.) methods and processes. It was the problematic nature of these relationships and processes that provided the backcloth for this research exercise, and the first research outline called for an examination of:
(a) the ways in which mass media impinged on the school situation, and
(b) the relationships between children's use of, and attitudes towards, the media on the one hand—and teachers' attitudes towards the media on the other.

As the project got under way, as the pilot exercises were carried out, as staff changed and—perhaps above all—as the Centre developed its own approach to mass communication research in various areas, the emphasis in the research approach changed. As a result, the relationship between secondary schools and the mass media was examined not in isolation but as part of the much larger question of 'the relationship between the social structures and cultures sponsored by educational institutions and those offered by the leisure environment'. It became the main aim of the study to determine the extent to which the differences in patterns of social relationships and systems of communication between schools on the one hand and leisure environments on the other are complementary or contradictory.

This developing policy to study the media (or, for that matter, any other institution or process) within the appropriate wider social contexts has some interesting implications. As Murdock and Phelps argue, curriculum change, as conventionally defined, certainly has its place, but far more important is the need to think in terms of possible changes in the structures of schools and in the basic cultural assumptions of our educational system. Until we think like this, until we accept the possibility of using media-based activities as part of a general attempt to create links between school and the wider worlds of work and leisure, until we appreciate that the media offer a complex system of meanings and forms of expression, and until we can relate teaching to life experiences, we run the risk of alienating a sizeable section of the adolescent school population. As I see it, the main difficulty in studying the problems of our society is to get people to adopt this wider perspective.

The Schools Council is to be thanked for its full support of our research which is lucidly, and at times provocatively, reported in the pages that follow. No strings were attached to the grant and there was no interference at any stage, which made it possible greatly to extend the scope of the research originally envisioned. There is a great deal more to be done, and we now know what form the main research thrust should take. It is to be hoped that the Schools Council and other bodies will continue to give attention and support to the research approaches described and recommended in this report.

James D. Halloran
Professor and Director
Centre for Mass Communication Research
University of Leicester

Contents

Appendices

Tables and figures

Tables

M.S.—I*

Figures in Appendices

Notes on tables and abbreviations

Only the main tables have been included in the body of the text, the remaining tables being placed in Appendix 4. Tables are presented in a standard format, based on the following principles:

1 Percentage figures are always rounded off to the nearest whole number, except in cases where the figure is exactly ·5. Hence, percentages do not always add up to exactly 100. The numbers replying (*n*) to the questions on which percentage tables are based are indicated at the bottom of tables.

2 Where arithmetic means or correlation coefficients are presented, figures are rounded off to the first decimal place.

3 Where tests of statistical significance have been used, the following notation is employed: One star (*) indicates that the observed relationship could have occurred by chance no more than five times in a hundred; two stars (**) indicates that the relationship could have occurred by chance no more than once in a hundred, and three stars (***) that the relationship could have occurred by chance no more than once in a thousand. (*NS*) indicates that the relationship between the figures is not statistically significant. In addition, we have attempted to present the results in terms of diagrams and graphs.

Details of how the research was planned and carried out, and of the measures and techniques employed, are given in Appendices 2 and 3. A more general discussion of the ideas and assumptions underlying the research can be found in Appendix 1.

Acknowledgements

We would like to thank Miss J. D. Browne, Mr F. H. Sparrow, Mr Paul Fordham and Mr Maurice Plaskow at the Schools Council for their help and encouragement at various stages of the research. We also are greatly indebted to James Learmonth who worked on the project during the first two years, and whose ideas have contributed much to the final outcome. We would also like to thank our colleagues at the Centre for Mass Communication Research for the very considerable help which they have given us. In particular we would like to thank Adrian Wells, Paul Croll and Richard Dembo for their assistance with sampling and computing problems, and the Director, Professor James Halloran, for his unfailing interest and enthusiasm. Our thanks are also due to the education officers in the various regions and cities, without whose help we would not have been able to set up the sample. Most of all we owe an enormous debt to all the headmasters, teachers and pupils who took part in the study, particularly to those who agreed to participate in the second and third stages. Their generosity and interest provided us with a constant source of ideas, insight and encouragement throughout the project.

The Schools Council and the publishers are grateful to the following for giving permission for the use of copyright material:

LAURENCE POLLINGER LTD. and the Estate of the late MRS. FRIEDA LAWRENCE, and the Viking Press of New York, for the quotation from *Last Lesson of the Afternoon* by D. H. Lawrence on page xvii;

ARC MUSIC CORPORATION, New York, for the quotation from Chuck Berry's *School Day* on pages xvii and xviii;

CHRIS SEARLE (for Reality Press) for quotation from *Stepney Words Number 2* by Patricia Kirk on page xviii; and

WARNER BROS. MUSIC LTD. for the extract from *Ballad of a Thin Man* on page 16.

Introduction

It is now established beyond doubt that many pupils find school a dull and boring experience, and regard it as an inevitable interruption to the 'real' business of living. The evidence for this is formidable, and is to be found not only in the considerable and growing body of educational research but also in the day-to-day experience of teachers and pupils. For most of the day the pupils' attitude are largely dormant, but as the afternoon draws on they are likely to expend more and more mental energy planning their evening's activities and, consequently, their boredom and lack of interest increases until it reaches its height during the last period, when both pupils and teachers are waiting for the final bell. D. H. Lawrence, once a secondary school-master himself, has described very well how this situation may look to the teacher.

> When will the bell ring, and end this weariness?
> How long have they tugged the leash, and strained apart,
> My pack of unruly hounds! I cannot start
> Them again on a quarry of knowledge they hate to hunt, . . .
> What does it matter to me: if they can write
> A description of a dog, or if they can't?[1]

This poem expresses one particular response to the situation, matching indifference with indifference, but there are a wide variety of other possible responses, based on a whole range of attitudes concerning the relationship between schools and aspects of the outside environment, particularly the mass media. The exploration of this variety in teachers' attitudes and responses forms the first part of this study.

The situation of the last lesson, as it appears to a number of pupils, was brilliantly captured in the lyric of an early 'rock and roll' hit, Chuck Berry's *School Day*,† in which he described the sense of release from routine and boredom that accompanies the final bell.

> Soon as three o'clock rolls aroun'
> You finally lay your burden down,

† *School Day* by Chuck Berry © 1958 Arc Music Corp. used with the permission of the publisher; all rights reserved.

Close up your books, get out-a your seat,
Down the hall an' into the street.
Up to the corner an' 'round the bend,
Right to the juke-joint you go in.

Drop the coin right into the slot
You gotta hear somethin' that's really hot.[2]

This song was written at a time when the cultural environment in which the majority of young people grow up was rapidly changing. For the first time adolescents were beginning to emerge as an autonomous grouping, distinct from children and adults. Of course, the problem of youth and of the 'generation gap' had been frequently discussed in the past, notably by Socrates and Shakespeare, but never before had the activities of adolescents been the subject of continual and almost obsessive attention. Following the rise of rock and roll in 1956 and the boom in record sales which accompanied it, adolescents became big business, and magazine publishers, radio and television producers, dance hall proprietors, and later clothing manufacturers adjusted their operations to cater for the emerging teenage market. Pop music was the pivot of change, and consequently, these adolescent-oriented sectors of the entertainment media can be collectively characterized as the 'pop media'.

Since the early days of rock and roll, the pop media, and pop music in particular, have developed at an ever increasing rate and in a number of directions and have become a central part of many adolescents' out-of-school activities. However, it is not the case that previous styles have been cancelled out by newer developments. Rather, recent styles have been added to the existing stock so that today's pupils are presented with a considerable range of choice. (The development and present range of the pop media will be considered in more detail during the discussion of the results of the pupils' study.) Surprisingly, the ways in which pupils have come to terms with the rapidly expanding pop media have never been adequately dealt with in previous research and, in a number of studies, they are hardly even mentioned. The second part of the present research therefore attempts to provide some information in this neglected area. In particular, we have tried to go some way towards determining to what extent the pop media are a central part of pupils' cultural experience and to explore the nature of the relationships between their involvement in pop and their commitment to school.

When does boredom start
When does boredom stop
From 9 till 3.40 the boredom goes on
You can't wait till the end of the day
To get out and do something you want.
Why are so many people bored with school?[3]

The deceptively simple question posed in that last line by a girl from a London East End school (very much like 'Dock Street'—one of the schools in this study) is, in fact, the central question facing anyone actively concerned about the present state of secondary education. It raises a whole series of other questions about the present organization of schools and about the content of the curriculum, and this study is an attempt to contribute information and ideas which may be helpful in answering these questions.

References

1   *The Collected Poems of D. H. Lawrence* (quoted in), (London Martin Secker 1932) p. 76.

2   Berry, Chuck *School Day* (Rock and Roll hit song), c. 1958.

3   *Stepney Words Number* 2 (quoted in), (Reality, c/o 20 Princelet Street, London E.1. October 1971) p. 6.

Part I:

The teachers' study

1 Teachers, pupils, and the mass media: the experiental gap

It is now generally recognized that there is a sizeable gap between the life experiences of many teachers and the everyday lives of many of their pupils. This gap is primarily a result of differences in social class background. It is still to a large extent true that many teachers follow a circular route from the middle class home and the grammar school classroom to the college or university lecture theatre and back again to the classroom. Consequently, many of their reference points are drawn from within the predominantly middle class world of the education system itself.

Some students may gain a glimpse of certain aspects of working class life in a particular area through renting cheap flats and bedsitters or by working in a factory but only very occasionally do they manage to get inside the experience and see the situation as it looks to those who will live in that environment. A recent survey revealed that the majority of those teaching for their first year in schools where over half the pupils came from working class homes had fathers in non-manual occupations. It is thus not surprising that by far the most frequently mentioned problem was 'unfamiliarity with the children's social background'.[1] Pupils rapidly recognize the fact that the life experiences of many of their teachers are markedly different from their own, and they may come to resent it, as the following extract from an interview with a pop-singer illustrates: 'When I was asked to leave, the headmaster told me I was just a spiv and nothing more. But he was so middle class, and what did he know about the ordinary person's life, dashing off to Rotary Meetings in his Rover.'[2] Nor is this gap necessarily reduced where teachers are themselves from working class backgrounds. Indeed, as several commentators have pointed out, these teachers may tend to compensate for the insecurity they feel in their new professional role by becoming even more strongly attached to what Patrick Creber calls the 'anxious and cautious suburban values' than their colleagues from comfortable middle class backgrounds.[3] In the final analysis, therefore, most teachers end up sharing the basic values and life style of the middle class.

The main aim of the teachers' survey was to find out how mass media were being used in the classroom, and consequently only a few very basic questions were asked concerning teachers' own leisure time contact with the mass media. Nevertheless, even from this relatively limited information, it is clear that teachers' media preferences tend to reinforce rather than reduce the experiential gap between them and many of their pupils.

Table 1 presents the profile of teachers' newspaper reading revealed by our questionnaire and compares it with the known profile for the general population derived from contemporary readership surveys.[4]

Table 1   Teachers' newspaper reading compared to the general population (figures in percentages)

National daily newspapers	General Population	Teachers
Daily Mirror	37	3
Daily Express	27	12
Daily Mail	14	11
Daily Sketch	8	1
Sun	8	3
The Daily Telegraph	9	29
The Times	3	14
Guardian	2	30
Local evening newspaper	43	21
National Sunday newspapers		
News of the World	39	2
The People	39	4
Sunday Mirror	35	3
Sunday Express	27	23
The Sunday Times	9	40
The Observer	6	42
Sunday Telegraph	5	10
Numbers replying	30 580	1310

Note: The survey was completed before the Daily Mail was merged with the Sketch and before Mr Rupert Murdoch took over the Sun.

The most immediately striking thing about Table 1 is that teachers' reading is weighted towards newspapers which are generally classified as 'highbrow' or 'heavy'—the *Guardian* and *The Daily Telegraph* on weekdays and *The Observer* and *The Sunday Times* on Sundays—whereas the reading of the majority of the general population is confined to the high circulation 'popular' papers. Thus, on weekdays almost two thirds (64%) of the general population read either the *Daily Mirror* or the *Daily Express* as against only 15% of teachers and on Sundays 78% of the population read either the *News of the World* or the *People*, compared with 6% of teachers.

By and large, then, teachers' choice of newspapers serves to widen rather than reduce the experiential gap between themselves and their pupils, as most teachers do not read the newspapers which are an integral part of the home environment of the majority of their working class pupils.

As one would expect, teachers at different types of school do differ somewhat in their newspaper reading habits. Thus, grammar school teachers tend to have less contact with the popular papers than teachers as a whole. Only 9% read either the *Daily Mirror* or the *Daily Express* and only 6% the *News of the World* or the *People*. Among secondary modern teachers, on the other hand, 23% read either the *Daily Mirror* or the *Daily Express*, and 9% the *People* or *News of the World*. It may well be that these differences reflect the differences in the social class and educational background of teachers in various sectors of secondary education but, in the absence of further information, this must remain a conjecture. However, even in secondary modern schools, there is still a considerable gap between the newspaper reading of most teachers and the families of most pupils.

Another point of interest in Table 1 is that only 21% of teachers read their local evening paper as against 43% of the general population. Again, in the absence of firm evidence, we can only offer a tentative explanation of this discrepancy. Local papers are a very good expression of that sense of 'the personal, the concrete and the local' which Richard Hoggart[5] argues is at the heart of working class life. Teachers, on the other hand, are unlikely to possess this sense of place to the same extent for two reasons. Firstly, teaching as a career means that, for the majority, promotion usually means a geographical move, and hence their attachments to the area in which they work are likely to be weaker than for someone who has lived their whole life in the same place. Secondly, many teachers tend to identify themselves as intellectuals—the producers and distributors of ideas—and consequently they tend to be 'cosmopolitan' rather than 'local' in their outlook. They are more interested in the doings of the cultural and political elites than the local flower show or the Saturday match.

Table 2 Percentage of teachers and pupils having a TV set at home

	Teachers	Pupils
	83%	98%
n	1310	1071

Table 2 shows that, whereas 98% of the pupils we studied had a television set in their homes, only 83% of teachers did. This figure of 83% does, of course, conceal the differences between teachers at different types of school and at various ages. Marginally fewer grammar school teachers (81%) have a television set than teachers at either comprehensives (85%) or secondary moderns (86%), but generally age is the more important factor. Thus, only 69% of teachers under 25 had a TV compared with 81% of those aged 26 to 35, and 91–92% of those older than 35. These differences are obviously related to the material circumstances of young teachers. For a newly qualified teacher in a bedsitter or flat, or for a young teacher starting a family, purchasing or renting a television is a luxury. However, the fact that almost a third of the teachers under 25 had little or no contact with this part of their pupils' media experience is significant, for in other respects it is the younger teachers who might have the best chance of bridging the experiential gap between themselves and their pupils. Their relative unfamiliarity with television, however, makes the establishment of common ground that much more difficult.

Table 3 Teachers' and pupils' television viewing: mean hours per week

	All teachers	Teachers under 25	Pupils
Mean TV viewing hours per week	10·0	8·6	13–20+

Table 3 shows that most teachers watch television far less than many of their pupils. According to one recent study, 11- and 12-year-olds watch an average of 20+ hours of television a week,[6] although another study of the same age group indicates that there are important sex differences and that, although boys watch over 20 hours, girls tend to watch for an average of only 14 hours.[7] Also, television watching decreases with age, so that one study of fourth years put boys viewing at 16 hours and girls at 13 hours.[8] Our own study revealed a considerable range in pupils' television viewing habits; some watched very little and others watched a great deal. However, we found that about a third of third year pupils, both boys and girls, claimed to watch more than 4 hours a night, which adds up to almost 30 hours of television a week, which is three times the teachers' average. Furthermore, this gap is even greater between these pupils and the youngest teachers, who watch only an average of 8·6 hours a week.

However, television is only one component of adolescents' media experiences. A potentially more important area for many pupils is pop music, and it is at this point that age differences exert their most powerful influence.

The experiential gap between teachers and pupils is not only due to differences in the life styles of social classes, it is also a consequence of the enormous changes in the range and content of adolescent experience. One of the most respected authorities on the subject of adolescence, Margaret Mead, has recently emphasized the importance of these changes by saying that . . .

the generation gap has not got anything to do with parents and children. The generation gap is between all the people born and brought up after World War II and the people who were born before it.[9]

According to this argument, the complex social changes attendant upon the Second World War drove a wedge between the generations and opened a gap which subsequent social developments have served to widen. Among these developments, one of the most far reaching has been the rapid rise of the 'pop media', centred on pop music. As will be argued later the often expressed idea that pop music is the basis of a more or less homogeneous set of values, symbols, and means of expression, a 'youth culture', which all adolescents share and which serves to cut them off from adults, is a far too simplistic summary of a complex process of historical change. Nevertheless, it contains a grain of truth. Of course adolescents had listened to the popular music of the day before the mid 'fifties: indeed they were often a major audience. But it took the new technology of the portable record player and the transistor radio to make pop music an omnipresent and integral part of the texture of adolescent experience.

Table 4 Percentages of teachers in various age groups claiming to listen to pop music 'very often' or 'fairly often'

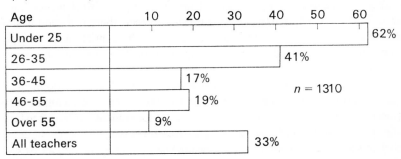

Age	10	20	30	40	50	60	
Under 25							62%
26-35					41%		
36-45		17%					
46-55		19%					
Over 55	9%						
All teachers				33%			

$n = 1310$

Table 4 illustrates the extent to which listening to pop music is a 'youthful' activity. Whereas almost two thirds (62%) of teachers under 25 claim to listen to pop 'very' or 'fairly' often, this proportion falls to 41% among the 26-35 age group, and then drops sharply to between 17% and 19% among middle aged teachers, falling finally to 9% among those nearing retirement. This stepped pattern is an illustration of Margaret Mead's argument that the generation gap is between all the people born and brought up after World War II and the people who were born before it. The teachers in the under 25 group were the first generation to grow up entirely in the post war world—they were the first to have what we might call a 'contemporary' adolescent experience. They grew up with commercial television, they went through secondary schools organized under the 1944 Act, and they were teenagers at the time of the British pop 'explosion' of the mid 1960s. Similarly, among those aged 26 to 35—born before or during the war—there must be many who remember the era of 'rock and roll'.

Those born in the 1930s or earlier, however, had a substantially different experience of adolescence, and so cannot draw upon their memories as a means of understanding and interpretation. Thus, the young teachers, particularly those born after 1945, are potentially in the best position to bridge the experiential gap. Unfortunately, however, although young teachers share certain experiences with their pupils by having grown up in the post war period, they are nevertheless still separated by differences arising from their social class background.

The findings of the pupils' study clearly indicate that adolescents' pop music preferences are strongly differentiated by social class. The tastes of the majority of working class pupils were confined to the routine pop music of the Top Twenty and to the main Negro styles (Tamla Motown and Jamaican Reggae), whereas many middle class pupils largely rejected this 'mainstream' pop and preferred the various minority styles, generally lumped together under the umbrella heading of 'underground-progressive' rock music. These include the work of the singer-songwriters such as Bob Dylan, individual instrumental improvizations of performers such as the late Jimi Hendrix, together with various attempts to fuse elements from pop with elements drawn from jazz and contemporary concert music. Further, there is a good deal of evidence to suggest that this basic social class differentiation in taste for pop music has existed since the beginning of the modern pop music industry.

Although we have no direct evidence from the teachers' questionnaire, it seems reasonable to assume that the tastes of the majority of young teachers (mostly from middle class homes and former college students) will tend to lie in the direction of the 'underground-progressive' end of the pop spectrum, unlike that of the great majority of their working class pupils. Thus, it can be seen that an interest in pop *per se* will not necessarily form an adequate basis for improved relationships between teachers and pupils; it may have just the opposite effect. A dramatic example of such a clash in pop preferences can be found in Evan Hunter's best selling novel, *The Blackboard Jungle*,[10] which is set in the early 1950s before the rise of 'rock and roll'. One of the climactic scenes of the book occurs when the central character, a young middle class teacher in a New York slum school, attempts to engage the attention of his class by playing them a selection of his favourite records. Unfortunately, his taste is for jazz while theirs is for the latest records in the Top Twenty (in this case Perry Como and Tony Bennett). Far from mutually benefiting from an interest shared, the class degenerates into violence as the pupils smash the teacher's record collection. While this incident is somewhat sensationally presented, it does illustrate the point that youth, goodwill and a record collection are not always enough. The average Reggae record is as far away from many of the songs of Bob Dylan as it is from the poetry of Keats.

More important than such differences in preference between pupils and teachers is the fact that, as Table 4 clearly shows, two thirds of teachers have little or no contact with any form of pop music. This lack of interest in one of the principal components of many pupils' out-of-school experiences is certainly a very shaky foundation on which to attempt to erect an experiential bridge.

Type of school also plays a part in determining the extent to which teachers have contact with pop music. 71% of grammar school teachers claim either that they never listen to pop, or that they do not listen often, compared with 66% of teachers in comprehensive and secondary modern schools. This relative lack of contact with pop on the part of most grammar school teachers does not, however, prevent them from having opinions on the subject. As part of his grammar school study, Ronald King asked teachers to rank, in order of their approval, sixty possible leisure activities in which pupils might engage. Reading worthwhile books was ranked first and listening to classical music tenth, while listening to pop records and wearing fashion clothes were disapproved of and ranked forty-fifth and fifty-first respectively.[11] This high valuation of elitist cultural activities and the concomitant disapproval of the entertainments provided by the mass media has been a continuing strand of educational thought since the beginning of modern mass education. In the present context it takes on a special significance. Grammar school pupils are not usually seen as a 'problem' in the sense that they very seldom manifest their discontent in open acts of violence or vandalism. However, as will be shown later, a number of grammar school pupils have little commitment to the values of their schools, and exactly because pop is ignored and disapproved of by many of the teachers it becomes an ideal focus and expression of their disengagement and opposition. Indeed, it is often grammar school pupils who display the greatest degree of involvement in the 'pop media'.

Even from the little information available about teachers' personal leisure-time contact with the mass media, it is clear that many have only limited knowledge and experience of those sectors of the mass media which form part of the accepted background of many of their pupils—popular newspapers, television and pop music. Teachers appear to opt for those sectors of the mass media generally classified as highbrow, and consequently to avoid those sectors usually categorized as purely 'entertainment for the masses'. As a result, mass media experiences may tend to aggravate rather than reduce the gap between teachers and pupils.

References

1 Department of Education and Science, 1971 *Reports on Education Number 68.*
2 *Melody Maker* March 27 1971, p. 21.
3 Duane, Michael, 1972 'Freedom and the State System of Education' in *Children's Rights* Panther Books, pp. 223-4. See also Hannan, Charles et al, 1971 *Young Teachers and Reluctant Learners* Harmondsworth, Penguin Books, p. 22. Creber, J. W. Patrick, 1972 *Lost for Words* Harmondsworth, Penguin Books, p. 21.
4 Joint Industry Committee for National Readership Surveys (JICNARS) *National Readership Survey*—1969 Vol. 1, Table 1. (Figures for the general population are taken from.)
5 Hoggart, Richard, 1959 *The Uses of Literacy* Harmondsworth, Penguin Books, p. 20.
6 Ackroyd, G. L., 1971 Children's Uses of Mass Media *Bulletin of the British Psychological Society* Vol. 24, No. 85, p. 337.
7 Learmonth, J. W., 1966 *Adolescent Self-Image and Television Programmes* (unpublished MA Thesis, University of Cambridge).
8 Curr, W. et al, 1964 'Patterns of Behaviour in Secondary Modern Schools' *Educational Review* Vol. 16, No. 3.
9 Mead, Margaret, 1971 'Future Family' *Transaction* Vol. 8, No. 11, p. 50.
10 Hunter, Evan, 1955 *The Blackboard Jungle* London, Panther Books, ed. 1958, pp. 141-3.
11 King, Ronald, 1969 *Values and Involvement in a Grammar School* London, Routledge and Kegan Paul, pp. 68-9.

2 Teachers at school: views of the job

The discussion in this chapter is based on replies to the first question on the teachers' questionnaire, which asked teachers to rank six aspects of their job in order of their relevance. The idea for this question, together with some of the aspects listed, came from the earlier research of Musgrove and Taylor.[1] The orders in which various groups of teachers ranked the six aspects provided are presented in Table 5.

Table 5 makes it clear that teachers as a whole tend to see their job primarily in terms of giving instruction in particular subjects and inculcating certain moral values. That is, teachers tend to define themselves first in terms of the curriculum and then in terms of the patterns of value and meaning contained in the school's 'official culture'. This 'school centred' definition of the teachers' role necessarily assigns the forms of knowledge and experience derived from everyday out-of-school life a low priority. Thus, the two aspects of the job that require an active engagement with the outside environment—'education for citizenship' and 'education for leisure'—are ranked fifth and sixth respectively. This basic pattern is repeated if teachers' replies to the question are considered in terms of the proportion placing each of the six aspects in the top quartile of the scale, indicating that they saw them as being 'very relevant' to their job. Whereas the great majority of teachers consider 'subject instruction' (82%) and 'moral education' (75%) to be a 'very relevant' part of their job, only 52% place 'education for citizenship' in this category and only 33% see 'education for leisure' as being 'very relevant'. The order of teachers' priorities is thus very clear, but where does it derive from?

Table 5 reveals a high correlation between the order of priorities of teachers as a whole and the priorities of grammar school teachers. The only exceptions lie in their evaluations of 'social education' and 'education for citizenship'.

Thus, it can be argued that the definitions of the teacher's role contained in what might be called the 'grammar school ethos' still appear to exert a considerable influence on the outlook of teachers in other sorts of schools. In her well known study of grammar schools, *The Living Tradition*, Frances Stevens describes very well how in teachers' minds, hard work, intellectual achieve-

Table 5 Teachers' rankings of six aspects of their job

Job Aspect	Rankings							
	All Teachers	By type of school			By subject taught		
		Grammar	Comprehensive	Modern	English	Science*	
Subject instruction	1	1	1	2	1	1	
Moral education	2	2	2	1	2	2	
Education in human relationships	3	3	4	3	3	5	
Social education	4	5	3	4	4	4	
Education for citizenship	5	4	5	5	5	3	
Education for leisure	6	6	6	6	6	6	
Numbers replying	1310	529	370	411	321	305	

* 'Science' is defined here as biology, chemistry, physics or general science.

ment and moral and cultural training are inextricably bound up in a composite ethos.

Teachers think of the individual's development chiefly in terms of intellectual perception, skills and knowledge; of preparation for a higher education or for particular employment; of the maintenance of moral and cultural standards and of the training of character.[2]

Further, as Frank Musgrove points out, it is this basic view of the job which continues to pervade the thinking of the majority of teachers. From the results of his study he concludes that teachers in all types of school 'saw their work primarily in intellectual and moral terms, placing greatest weight on instruction and moral training'.[3] Nevertheless, there are some differences of emphasis.

In most cases the pupils who enter the grammar school world come from middle class homes which have already taught them the appropriate modes of speech and behaviour. Pupils who come from working class homes however may not always be familiar with the customary procedures, in which case the school may undertake a certain amount of social education (in the sense of teaching basic manners) by way of 'compensating' for the home environment. As one grammar school mistress put it, 'If the parents will not or cannot teach table manners then I shall. A girl must have some social graces'.[4] Not surprisingly, this idea of compensating for a poor home environment is considered more important among teachers in comprehensives and secondary modern schools, who rank it 3rd and 4th respectively, as against the 5th ranking assigned to this aspect by grammar school teachers. Similarly, in secondary modern schools where there is likely to be the greatest gap between the basically middle class world of the school and the working class world of the majority of pupils (especially those who are not taking examinations), teachers rank moral education above subject instruction. These are relatively minor variations of priority, however, and the fact remains that teachers in all types of schools assign 'education for leisure' the lowest ranking.

The type of school at which they teach is only one factor, albeit a very important one, in helping to form teachers' definitions of their job. Another important factor is the subject in which they specialize and, if the rankings given by the two main subject groupings—English and science teachers—are compared, some interesting points emerge.

English teachers rank 'education in human relations' relatively highly (3rd), while science teachers assign this aspect a comparatively low rank (5th). This difference in priorities arises out of the different way in which English and science teachers define their subjects, a consequence of their differential positions within the social structure of schools. Whereas science and mathematics teachers spend between 50% and 69% of their teaching time teaching their main subject (depending on the type of school), the corresponding proportions for English teachers is between 34% and 53%.[5]

Thus, at the very centre of his definition of his job as a specialist in English, the English teacher is faced with a considerable degree of uncertainty. While, on the one hand, the training that most English teachers receive encourages them to define themselves as specialists in that corpus of literature which is widely held to be the principal repository of the 'cultural tradition', in the school situation they are often expected also to assume the responsibility for educating pupils in human relationships, which inevitably means some attempt to handle the mass media. Many English teachers are thus pulled in two directions simultaneously, and must inevitably make some attempt to come to terms with the situation. Basically they have two options. Either they can define their job quite narrowly as teaching basic linguistic skills and handing on the 'literary tradition', or else they can see themselves more broadly as specialists in social communications including the mass media. Now, since the act of writing or speaking English can be regarded as a fundamental piece of social behaviour in its own right, it is relatively easy for English specialists to broaden the definition of their job to include teaching about human relationships. Thus, not only may English teachers teach 'social studies' as well as English, they may also teach 'human relationships' as part of their English lessons. In this case, in the words of one grammar school English master:

the English lesson . . . becomes . . . a 'social laboratory', a place and a time for developing the capacity for personal relationships and thought and feeling through activities of expression and communication.[6]

However, this more open ended approach to the teaching situation is only one possible outcome of the diffuseness of the English teacher's role and the difficulty of defining the subject matter of English. The other possible outcome is suggested by the fact that, whereas science teachers rank 'education for citizenship' third (in the sense of helping pupils to understand the modern world), English teachers rank this aspect only fifth. This seemingly simple difference of priority could be taken as an indication that, in the face of the ambiguities in their situation, a number of English teachers tend to erect a barrier between the classroom and the world outside and to fall back on a definition of their job which stresses the transmission of literary values. Science teachers do not need to be defensive, since not only is their basic subject matter relatively unambiguous, but they also spend the majority of their time teaching it. Furthermore, scientists tend to see the environment which contemporary technology has created, including the mass media, as a vindication of their subject rather than a threat to it. Consequently, it is not really surprising that teachers of science may be a little more willing than English teachers to dismantle at least part of the barrier between the world of the classroom and the world outside.

References

1   Musgrove, F. and Taylor, P. H., 1969 *Society and the Teachers' Role* London, Routledge and Kegan Paul.
2   Stevens, Francis, 1960 *The Living Tradition* London, Hutchinson, p. 103.
3   Musgrove, F., 1969 op. cit., p. 63.
4   Stevens, Francis, 1960 op. cit., p. 95.
5   DES, 1968 *Statistics of Education: Special Series No. 1* London, HMSO, Table 15, pp. 60, 84, 94, 96.
6   Shaw, Robert, 1971 'Meaning in English at the Leeds Modern School' in G. Summerfield and S. Tunnicliffe, eds. *English in Practice: Secondary English Departments at Work* Cambridge University Press, pp. 139–140.

3 Teachers' perceptions of the influence of the mass media on their pupils

You walk into the room
With your pencil in your hand
You try so hard
But you don't understand
Because something is happening here
But you don't know what it is,
Do you, Mr Jones?   (Bob Dylan)[1]

The questionnaire form provided teachers with blank spaces in which they were invited to write in their own words the various ways in which they felt the influence of the mass media was reflected in the general behaviour and school work of their pupils. Of the total of 1310 teachers who returned the questionnaire, 834 filled in these open-ended questions. Although these questions yielded a considerable range and diversity of replies, closer examination reveals that the majority of answers are expressions of the same dozen or so basic points.

Teachers' perceptions of the influence of the mass media on pupils' behaviour

It is evident from Table 6 that some teachers at least have recognized the growing importance of the pop media in the lives of their pupils. Thus, the most frequently mentioned effects of the mass media observed by teachers in their pupils' behaviour are preoccupation with pop music and fashion and identification on the part of some pupils with the ideas and life style of media personalities to the extent occasionally of imitating their mannerisms, particularly their catch-phrases. However, if the actual comments from which the figures in Table 6 are derived are examined, it becomes apparent that the elements of pop culture which teachers have noticed are relatively superficial —coloured tights, a snatch of conversation overheard when walking into a class, a cheeky catch phrase.

My lot talk a great deal about 'pop' records among themselves often 'humming' the latest tunes as they enter the classroom. (General studies master, mixed Comprehensive)

The intelligent cheeky pupils are full of topical catch phrases, e.g. at the moment 'sock it to me.' (History master, boys' Grammar)

Table 6 The most frequently mentioned effects of mass media on pupils' behaviour: all teachers

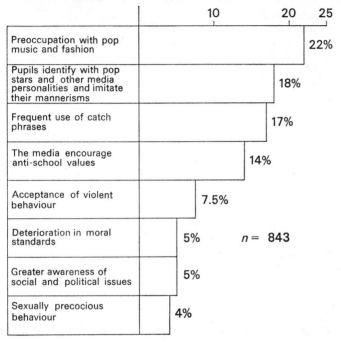

	10	20	25
Preoccupation with pop music and fashion			22%
Pupils identify with pop stars and other media personalities and imitate their mannerisms		18%	
Frequent use of catch phrases		17%	
The media encourage anti-school values		14%	
Acceptance of violent behaviour	7.5%		
Deterioration in moral standards	5%		
Greater awareness of social and political issues	5%		
Sexually precocious behaviour	4%		

$n = 843$

Note: Figures show what percentage of the teachers who answered the question, mentioned each of the main effects

The teachers who have noticed the rise of pop—and it is important to remember that they are in a minority—are thus mostly in the position of Bob Dylan's Mr Jones. They have walked into something which they do not really understand. Teachers rarely seem to look beyond a particular incident in an attempt to see pop as an integral part of the pupil peer groups which make up the school's 'informal' social structure. Comments such as the following from a classics master in a boys' grammar school, were comparatively few and far between:

My form (a lower sixth) talk about pop music a great deal; anyone who doesn't is regarded as being eccentric, e.g. the only boy in the form with a deep interest in classical music is, to a certain extent, a 'social reject'.

It is significant that this remark should have come from a grammar school teacher. Table 7 shows that marginally more (25%) teachers in grammar

Table 7 The effects of mass media on pupils' behaviour most frequently mentioned by teachers: by type of school and subject taught

| | Type of school | | | Subject taught | |
	Grammar	Comp.	Mod.	English	Science
Preoccupation with pop music and fashion	25	22	20	27	17
Pupils identify with pop stars and other media personalities	12	17	18	19	8
Frequent use of catch phrases	13	22	18	23	16
The media encourage values which run counter to those of the school	15	12	15	11	9
Acceptance of violent behaviour	4	7	12	8	6
Deterioration in moral standards	5	4	7	3	11
Greater awareness of social and political issues	8	4	4	5	4
Precocious sexual behaviour	4	5	5	5	1
Numbers replying	297	254	292	261	141

Note: The figures show the percentages of teachers in each group who mentioned each of the main effects.

schools are likely to notice their pupils' preoccupation with pop than teachers in either comprehensives (22%) or secondary moderns (20%). In the case of pupils' identification with pop personalities however this trend is reversed—the pupil study shows that grammar school students are often the most highly involved in pop. But the majority of these grammar school pupils live a Jekyll and Hyde existence and therefore although a number are 'mental drop-outs' in the sense that they do not accept the values and definitions of the 'school culture', only rarely do they reveal their disengagement or opposition in overt behaviour. Most settle for a quiet life by mechanically performing the rituals of school life while at the same time orientating themselves around their pop based leisure activities. In comprehensive and secondary modern schools, however, school rejecting pupils are much more likely to express their opposition openly and so it is not really surprising that more teachers in these schools (17% and 18% respectively) should have noticed the influence of pop on pupils' behaviour.

The extent to which teachers are likely to notice the effects of pop seems influenced more by the subject taught than by the type of school. Table 7 shows that English teachers are much more likely than science teachers to mention pupils' preoccupation with pop, their identification with pop stars and their use of catch phrases. Again, this is not really surprising, for it is in English lessons that the assumptions of curriculum culture come into head-on collision with the pupils' experience of the pop media. English and pop offer pupils two contrasting modes of understanding and expressing emotional experience, the one based on linear communication and literary skills, the other on multiplicity and movement. The same problem also crops up in music lessons where the gap between the definitions of knowledge embodied in the curriculum and those derived from everyday experience is again thrown into relief.

The way in which teachers' replies have been categorized in Tables 6 and 7 does not really do justice to the complexity of their responses. Thus, although only 14% of teachers actually stated in so many words that the mass media provided pupils with a culture counter to that of the school, a good number of the replies placed in the first three categories implied this. In fact quite a few teachers seemed to have grasped, at least in part, the complex nature of the relationship between involvement in pop and school rejection. Here is a representative selection of teachers' comments:

What does disturb me is that many television programmes are devoted to the 'pop' world, the intrinsic value of which is flimsy, but whose leading figures are elevated socially and financially out of all proportion to their real worth. It is a hard task to compete and cultivate other sets of values. (German master)

Television and pop radio constantly show youngsters that, apparently, hard work is not necessary for a successful, financially rewarding career. Their 'idols' for the most part appear not to have found education beyond 'A' level an advantage. (Biology master)

The teacher frequently finds that what he offers is not in accord with what is presented through the mass media, and may therefore be rejected in favour of values emphasized by pop songs and their creators. (French master)

The beat and repetition of 'pop' and the glamour of the 'cult' is very attractive, and they shut their minds to anything else. (Music mistress)

It is also worth noting that several older, more experienced, teachers recognized that the 'media explosion' of the last fifteen years has significantly altered the situation facing them. Here is how one English master, with over twenty years' teaching experience, put it:

The indiscipline and permissiveness of thought and expression which the mass media have helped to suggest belongs to our society at large, has now begun to find expression in pupils' general behaviour. It is, for me, a pattern which I don't recognize as belonging to the fifties, when mass media did not have so influential a hold.

In view of the continuing public concern and widespread debate about the supposed effects of mass media material—particularly certain television programmes—on children's attitudes and behaviour in the areas of violence and sex, it is perhaps surprising that only 7·5% of teachers mentioned violence, and 5% and 4% declining moral standards and sexual precocity. However, the relatively few who put forward these views did so with considerable force.

In many TV programmes an excessive amount of force is used. Victims repeatedly get up and continue to fight after receiving blows which in real life would maim or kill. Thus, there is inculcated in young people the idea that they must be *extremely* violent to produce results. (Biology master)

With these boys sexual morality is that of the TV and the *News of the World*. There has been a marked hardening of scepticism towards marriage. It is expressed in such questions as, 'Why bother to get married when marriage is only sex, and you can get that at any time'. (Religious Knowledge master)

Occasionally, the issue of morality was explicitly linked to pop.

The children are highly influenced by the 'pop' world. The hero worship of 'pop' people can become 'unhealthy'. Moral standards become lower in 'aping' those 'pop' performers. (Music mistress)

Negativeness was perhaps the most important characteristic of the overwhelming proportion of teachers' responses to the question of the effects of mass media on pupils' behaviour. Only 5% mentioned that the media had given pupils a greater awareness of social and political issues, and this was the only positive category of comment of any size. Thus, although the views expressed by the majority of teachers who answered our question could not be described as extreme, they were nevertheless almost always distrustful, and frequently hostile towards the mass media.

Teachers' perceptions of the influence of mass media on pupils' school work

On the questionnaire schedule there were two questions relating to teachers' perceptions of the influence of the mass media on their pupils' work. First, they were asked to indicate on a four-point scale, which ranged from 'to a great extent' to 'not at all', the extent to which they felt the media influenced pupils' schoolwork. Then, they were invited to describe in their own words the areas in which they particularly noticed this influence. Each question will be taken in turn.

The sort of school work expected from pupils varies considerably, depending on the type of school they attend. In grammar schools most set work is securely anchored in the GCE examination syllabus, and consequently there are reasonably strict definitions of the forms and expression of knowledge considered valid in this context. In comprehensive and secondary modern schools, on the other hand—particularly with groups taking a more open-ended type of examination, such as CSE Mode III, or indeed no examinations

Table 8 Percentages of teachers in various groups who indicated that mass media had a 'great' or 'moderate' amount of influence on their pupils' work

	All teachers	Subject taught		Type of school		
		English	Science	Grammar	Comp.	Modern
%	51	70	48	43	54	59
n	1107	253	291	427	313	367

at all—school work is not so strictly tied to the academic essay and the laboratory report. Consequently, the definitions of valid information and expression are not so clear, and inevitably more elements of their everyday life appear in pupils' school work.

It is therefore not very surprising to find that more teachers in secondary moderns and comprehensives than in grammar schools notice the influence of the mass media in their pupils' work. However, there is greater disparity between different subjects than between different types of schools. Subject work in English, quite often requires the pupil to draw on his own experience to produce a piece of imaginative writing. As images and ideas drawn from the mass media make up a considerable part of some pupils' imaginative experience, it is not surprising that these should surface in their creative work. Subject work in science, on the other hand, is generally much more specific and tends to stress the collection and arrangement of factual information rather than the expression of personal experience. This basic difference is reflected in the figures presented in Table 8 which show that, whereas 70% of English teachers said that they thought the mass media had a great influence on pupils' work, only 43% of science teachers were of this opinion. The differences in the way that these two groups of subject specialists perceived their situation become even clearer in their verbatim comments (presented in Table 9). They illustrate very clearly that science teachers tend to see mass media material in terms of factual information, whereas English teachers stress its effects on pupils' imaginative expression.

Of the science teachers who answered the question, by far the largest proportion (39%) indicated that they thought that the mass media had increased pupils' scientific knowledge.

They gain a good deal of factual content from the more informative and educational programmes like *Tomorrow's World*. (Chemistry master, mixed Modern)

Television science programmes (e.g. *Tomorrow's World*) stimulate interest in a few pupils, and reach more pupils than would be the case with science literature. (Physics master, mixed Grammar)

M.S.—2*

Table 9 The effects of mass media on pupils' work mentioned most frequently by different groups of teachers

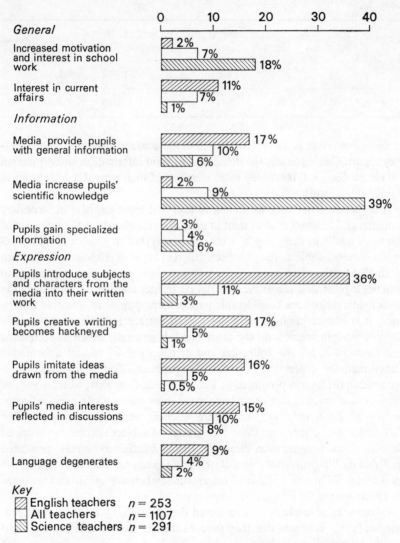

Key
English teachers $n = 253$
All teachers $n = 1107$
Science teachers $n = 291$

Note: The figures show the percentage of teachers in each group who mentioned each of the main effects.

In addition to mentioning this increase in factual information, 18% of science teachers claimed that television programmes like *Tomorrow's World* stimulated pupils' interest in science projects and increased their motivation to find out more.

I feel that *Tomorrow's World* type programmes are stimulating a genuine interest in scientific and technological achievement. (Physics master, boys' Grammar)

Phenomena which have been observed through the mass media, phenomena which would not normally be brought to the attention of the child, promote enquiry as to the 'whys' and 'wherefores'. (Chemistry master, mixed Comprehensive)

The general tone of the majority of science teachers' remarks was definitely positive and they tended to view the mass media's effects on their pupils in terms of increased scientific knowledge and interest in science subjects. The science teachers tended to regard the mass media, and television in particular, as a valuable extension of their stock of audio-visual aids, giving pupils access to information and illustrations which they could not obtain elsewhere. There were, however, a few dissenting voices.

The pupils acquire a vocabulary of technical words that they do not thoroughly understand, e.g. light years, momentum, solar energy. These words have precise meanings and their everyday usage hampers progress in the subject. (Physics master, mixed Grammar)

References to contraceptive pills, fertilization of human ova in test tubes, etc. gives little information and an unbalanced view. (Biology master, boys' Grammar)

These strictures were typical of those made by science teachers. What makes them remarkable is that they do not arise out of an alternative viewpoint but rather out of a difference of emphasis within the same basic 'information oriented' perspective. Instead of stressing the beneficial effect of the increased quantity of information which the mass media make available to pupils, they argue that much of this information is presented out of context and taken over by pupils without a proper understanding either of its source or its implications. In other words, their principal criticism is that the selections and definitions of knowledge and information provided by the mass media do not always correspond to those provided by the school curriculum. These two sides of the information oriented perspective also found adherents among other subject specialists, particularly those in subjects like history and geography in which factual information plays an important part.

Pupils nowadays are much more aware of Europe and the Europeans because of their exposure to mass media. (Geography master, mixed Comprehensive)

TV ads are often useful sources of geographical information—they remember the jingles, e.g. the recent Maxwell House ad on Brazilian coffee beans. (Geography mistress, girls' Grammar)

There is much half-digested information. Names of people and places in the news are bandied about with, as a rule, little or no understanding of what was involved, e.g. one lad today was talking about 'devaluation' in the 2nd World War. (History master, boys' Grammar)

It is very likely that one of the best known facts of twentieth century history in this school is the failure of Prohibition in the U.S.A. This has come down from the TV series *The Untouchables*. (History master, mixed Comprehensive)

Another interesting difference emerges when the kinds of information stressed by different subject specialists are examined. Table 9 clearly indicates that science teachers are predominantly concerned with scientific information (as described in the last chapter); only 6% mention other specialized information, and only another 6% general information. Science teachers tend to see themselves as specialists in a particular and discrete branch of knowledge; a relatively secure definition of their subjects and of their professional role, provides them with a 'subject centred' perspective on their situation and on the influence of the mass media, in which scientific information is logically in the foreground of attention. English teachers are in a very different position. For reasons stated earlier English teachers are often expected to take responsibility for 'social' or 'liberal' studies. Consequently, they are familiar with pupils' responses in a wider range of situations than science teachers and so their perspective is not so securely 'subject centred'. Hence, 17% of English teachers mentioned that the mass media provide pupils with general information and 11% pointed to an increased interest in current affairs. At the same time, it is very noticeable that, whereas 18% of science teachers said that they thought the mass media had increased their pupils' general motivation and interest in schoolwork, only 2% of English teachers mentioned this point, a lack of positive evaluation indicative of a fundamental difference in perspective. Thus, although some English teachers do mention that the mass media are a source of information, very many more are concerned with the effects of the mass media on their pupils' ability to write English and on their imaginative capacities. By and large then English teachers have an 'expression oriented' perspective on the influence of the mass media which tends to see the media not as the sources of information but rather as providers of alternative styles of expression—alternative cultures. At the heart of this viewpoint is the conflict between the forms of literary expression specified in the curriculum and the forms of expression derived from the direct experience of everyday life and from the mass media. The nature of this conflict is most clearly exposed in pupils' creative work, where they are expected to produce a literary essay from their own experience. It therefore follows that the greatest proportion of English teachers (36%) saw their pupils' introduction of subjects and characters from their media experience into their written work as the most important influence of the mass media, and that 17% and 16% mentioned the related points that pupils' creative writing became hackneyed and that the majority of their imaginative ideas were drawn from the media. Here are two representative comments:

Creative written work bears unmistakeable evidence of TV influence—'original' stories, for example, often read like 'Danger Man' scenarios, and descriptions of emotional experience is often given in terms of 'pop' cliche. Monsters, weird creatures and the switch from future to present to past in time are all too common. (English master, boys' Grammar)

In imaginative writing, many of the situations chosen by the child can be traced to superficial stock treatment of themes seen on TV. Generally speaking, this emphasis tends to lie in the child concentrating on the superficial *action* of the plot, thus neglecting a deeper appreciation of character, relationships or description. Such stories tend to be clichéd in their development and conclusions and usually of the cop and robber TV kind, or Westerns. (English master, mixed Comprehensive)

The ways in which emotions are presented and experienced through the 'pop media' of pop music, comics and certain films and television programmes differ very considerably from the mediations and forms of expression associated with literary modes such as the short story. Disjunctions therefore inevitably arise when pupils are asked to squeeze the new wine of the pop media into the old bottles of conventional literary forms. The same problem may also arise in art lessons, and a number of art teachers described the influence of both the content and style of the pop media on their pupils' art work.

Content:

Art work often shows the influence of pop culture. For example, last year there was a great deal of Art Nouveau Beardsley influence; many children, especially girls, were painting flowing hair and richly patterned clothes and there was great copying of the lettering then prevalent in advertisements. (Art mistress, mixed Comprehensive)

Style:

Visual influence of TV commercials, e.g. looking up out of a crisp-bag. Quite a lot of commercial and photographic imagery. Unusual viewpoints, ambiguities of scale and distortion affect shape concepts while pop show projection techniques, set, decor, pattern and fashion, influence decorative, fashion and design work. (Art master, girls' Grammar)

What is at issue here are two distinctly different ways of seeing and responding to experience, the one rooted in the linearity of the printers' book and the conventions of Renaissance perspective, the other derived from the simultaneous experience of the new electronic media—television and stereophonic records. The first forms the basis for the culture of the school curriculum; the second is an important element in many pupils' everyday cultural experience, and each time elements of this media-based culture find their way into the classroom fundamental questions are raised.

A grammar school art mistress, spoke for many of the English and art teachers in this study when she said that as far as she could see:

The children's concept of art is limited to the 'in gear' or to the portrayal of the cigarette advertisements.

As is shown in Chapter 5, teachers have a variety of ways of coming to terms with this situation. But, before proceeding to a discussion of the ways in which teachers handle mass media material in the classroom, attention must be given briefly to their use of another aspect of the contemporary mass media technology—audio-visual aids.

Reference

1   Dylan, Bob, *Ballad of a Thin Man* (a popular song), 1966.

4 Teachers in the classroom: using audio-visual aids

By far the most important factor affecting teachers' use of audio-visual aids is the extent to which they are available.

Professor Norman Mackenzie recently published the results of a survey of ninety-three Sussex secondary schools in which he found marked differences in the availability of various key pieces of equipment.[1] In these schools he found 200 film strip projectors, 246 tape recorders of varying quality, 109 16mm film projectors, but only 90 television sets and 79 radios. There was not sufficient time to make a similar inventory in the schools used in this study, but there is good reason to believe that, in general, they are worse equipped than the Sussex schools. The recent research of George Taylor, for example, has shown that Sussex has considerably more money available to spend on education than the national average, whereas the levels of expenditure in some of the areas researched in this study, particularly the urban ones, are around or below the national average.[2] Certainly, as regards the provision of books, the areas researched here are less well provided for than the Sussex schools. Recent statistics indicate that, whilst East and West Sussex spend £3·17 and £2·60 respectively on books for each secondary school pupil, the average expenditure of the authorities in our samples was only £2·21. This figure hides even lower spending per pupil by all our urban authorities except those in London. Thus Leeds spends £1·45, Coventry £1·85, Newcastle £1·85 and Lancashire £1·86.[3] All nine authorities within whose jurisdiction our schools lay spent less than the £3·00 per pupil recommended by the Joint Committee for the Association of Education Committees and the National Book League as a 'reasonable allowance'. Thus, if an inventory had been taken of equipment in our study schools, in all probability we would have found that they had even fewer projectors, tape recorders, etc. than Mackenzie found in his Sussex schools. Nevertheless, given that our schools are likely to have less equipment in absolute terms, the relative availability of various types of equipment is likely to be similar to that revealed in the Mackenzie study.

Table 10 shows the percentages of teachers who said that they never used certain audio-visual aids, and the stepped pattern of these replies follows almost exactly the pattern of availability reported by Mackenzie. Thus the most

Table 10 Percentage of teachers claiming that they never use certain audio-visual aids

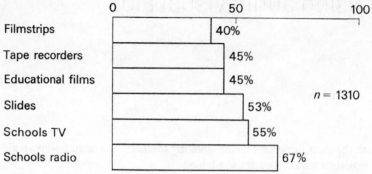

	0	50	100
Filmstrips		40%	
Tape recorders		45%	
Educational films		45%	
Slides		53%	$n = 1310$
Schools TV		55%	
Schools radio		67%	

frequently used audio-visual aids are filmstrips and tape recorders. Similarly, the non-utilization of schools' television and radio broadcasts can be linked to the fact that in practice many teachers have only a very limited access to television and radio sets. As Denis McQuail has pointed out, even if a school has a TV set (and approximately a quarter of British schools still have none) it is more than likely that there is only one set, in an ordinary form room and not in a special room set aside for the purpose. Consequently, there is often an enormous logistic problem simply in getting the right class to the right programmes at the right time.[4] An English master in a mixed comprehensive in a relatively affluent area spoke for a number of the teachers in this study when he said:

I would like to use television and radio a good deal but this is not possible with the limited amount of equipment available—one television set for 1,500 pupils!

The logistic problems arising out of restricted access are further compounded by timetabling difficulties. Quite a few teachers mentioned that the timing of schools broadcasts did not always fit in with the timetabling of lessons.

I should welcome a more enlightened policy for schools broadcasting whereby the timetable would be made more flexible. It is impossible to fit any broadcast into any lessons. (History mistress, girls' Grammar)

The individual master cannot make special pleas for special timetable arrangements. Television and radio sets and fittings are only available at one or two points in the buildings. (French master, boys' Grammar)

Even if the basic logistics of timetabling are overcome, it is by no means certain that schools broadcasts will be used in the most effective way for as Samuel Becker has pointed out

Often the timing works out in such a way that there is not sufficient time in the class period for immediate follow-up discussion or else for preparatory discussion, both essential for adequate utilization of the programme.[5]

Having considered availability and access, there are still considerable differences in the way in which various subject specialists use the equipment available. As Table 11 illustrates, science teachers tend to use films (37%) and filmstrips (36%) far more than teachers as a whole, whilst English teachers tend to make more use of tape recorders (55%), TV (35%) and radio (23%).

Table 11   Percentage of teachers in various groups who claim to use certain audio-visual aids several times a term or more

Audio-visual aid	All teachers	English teachers	Science teachers
Tape recorders	33	55	11
Filmstrips	29	25	36
Schools TV	25	35	21
Educational films	18	14	37
Slides	16	9	19
Schools radio	16	23	7
n	1310	321	305

Evidence thus suggests that tape recorders and filmstrip projectors are likely to be the most readily available pieces of equipment in most schools. In addition, both have the advantage of being mobile so that equipment can be brought to the pupils rather than pupils to the equipment, although there are often problems of inadequate soundproofing and blackout facilities in many rooms. Both tape recorders and filmstrip projectors are relatively cheap to use, in the sense that both filmstrips and tapes can be used a considerable number of times before the quality of reproduction deteriorates to the extent that replacements are required. Nevertheless, the fact remains that there are considerable differences in the frequency with which English and science teachers use films and tapes, and these differences arise out of certain changes in the curricula of the two subjects. Thus, in a number of secondary science courses film loops are no longer an extra but have become an integral part of the course. Similarly, the development of oral skills through the use of tape recordings is increasingly becoming an integral part of many English courses. The frequency with which English teachers use schools radio and television broadcasts is a little more difficult to explain. But the beginnings of an answer can be found in Becker's research, in which he mentions that some of the English teachers he met saw television as an effective way of presenting drama. We have no evidence to support this hypothesis but, in view of the difficulties of presenting drama in the classroom, it seems at least possible that teachers should use radio and television adaptations for this part of the English course. Another possible explanation is that English teachers also use programmes which are nominally categorized as 'social studies', in which case they would have considerably more programmes to choose from in an average week than science teachers, who—as we have already seen—tend to have a somewhat narrower definition of what is relevant to their courses. Unfortunately, we have no information that would enable us to pursue these ideas further.

From his research, Samuel Becker concluded that grammar schools were the least likely to make the necessary arrangements to accommodate schools' television.[6] The findings of this study tend to indicate that grammar school teachers and heads were generally the least likely to use audio-visual aids. Teachers in comprehensive schools, on the other hand, provided the majority of 'once a week' users, while most secondary modern teachers fell in the intermediate categories. The low utilization of audio-visual aids on the part of grammar school teachers can be explained in terms of their definition of themselves as specialists in academic subjects, and the way in which grammar school teaching is securely tied to the formal examination syllabus. As one experienced grammar school French master put it:

> As I see it the English grammar school is geared primarily to grinding children through examinations, and only if they are incapable of sitting these is time allowed for other things—certainly I don't get any time to prepare lessons outside the examination syllabus.

Behind this statement, and particularly the seemingly chance remark that 'other things' can be dealt with only in lessons with non-examination pupils, lies a whole series of assumptions about what counts as valid knowledge and experience in the classroom context, and what is the proper relationship between classroom learning and everyday life. The nature of these assumptions, which are not usually explicitly stated, becomes clearer when teachers are asked to say how they see the relationship between the mass media as an aspect of everyday life on the one hand, and the formal curriculum and classroom teaching situation on the other. The next chapter is therefore devoted to an examination of teachers' replies to questions on this issue.

References

1   Mackenzie, Norman, Jones, Hywell C. and Payne, Trevor, 1970 'Audio-Visual Resources in Sussex Schools' *Journal of Educational Technology* No. 1, Vol. 1, January 1970, pp. 16–34.
2   Taylor, George, 1971 'North and South: The Educational Split' *New Society* No. 440, March 4 1971, pp. 346–7.

3   The Educational Publishers Council, 1971 *Books in School: The Individual Child* London, The Educational Publishers Council, pp. 9–11.

4   McQuail, Denis, 1970 'Television and Education' in: J. D. Halloran ed. 1970 *The Effects of Television* London, Panther Modern Society, p. 185.

5   Becker, Samuel, 1965 *The Utilization of School Television Broadcasts in England* University of Nottingham Institute of Education, Educational Papers No. 3, p. 10.

6   Becker, S., 1965, op. cit., p. 6.

5 Teachers in the classroom: using mass media material

Most commentators on the role of mass media in the classroom have been concerned exclusively with teachers' use of audio-visual aids, and this was discussed in the previous chapter. While it is absolutely essential to assess the impact of such things as schools television broadcasts and, more recently, closed circuit television, it must not be forgotten that the issues raised by research in educational technology and programmed learning are only one aspect of a much wider problem. They deal only with the impact of mass media material produced specifically for the classroom where the process of reception and very often production is under the control of the teacher. This present study addresses itself to another aspect of the situation—the ways in which teachers come to terms with the impact of media material designed for consumption outside school.

Media material in the classroom: the four basic approaches

When describing the extent to which teachers utilize mass media material in their classroom teaching, it is not sufficient simply to say that some teachers introduce such material more frequently than others; there is also the equally important question of the attitudes towards the mass media which underlie these introductions. The frequency with which teachers introduced media material into their lessons were called the 'orientation' dimension. From the replies to the appropriate question in the questionnaire, an overall mean score was computed for the sample as a whole, and the mean orientation scores of particular groups of teachers were then classified as either high or low, depending upon whether they fell above or below the overall mean. The second main dimension in the situation was assessed by means of a Likert-type scale designed to tap teachers' general attitudes towards the effects mass media were having on their pupils. Again, an overall sample mean was computed and the mean scores of particular groups were classified as either favourable or unfavourable, depending again on whether they were above or below the overall mean.*

* Both the 'orientation' and 'attitude' scores are fully described in Appendix 3.

The 'orientation' and 'attitude' dimensions were found to be independent of each other, giving four possible relationships between them corresponding to the four major approaches to handling mass media material in the classroom. These four approaches are represented diagrammatically in Figure 1, and the percentage of grammar, comprehensive and secondary modern schools subscribing to each approach is shown in Table 12.

Fig 1 The four basic approaches

Attitude towards media	Media orientation	
	Low	High
Favourable	Approach 1	Approach 4
Unfavourable	Approach 2	Approach 3

Table 12 Percentage of schools of each type subscribing to each of the four basic approaches

Approach		Type of school		
		Grammar	Comp.	Modern
one } 'Exclusion'		51%	26%	8%
two		29%	16%	28%
three } 'Incorporation'		0%	32%	36%
four		20%	26%	28%
n		35	19	36

Approach 1

Teachers adopting this first approach do not regard the mass media as having a particularly detrimental effect on their pupils and they seldom, if ever, introduce media material into their lessons. This approach found considerable support among the grammar schools in our sample, and just over half (51%) subscribed to it. There may be several reasons for this. First, as has already been noted, grammar school teachers tend to take a narrowly 'academic' view of their subject matter and of their own role; consequently that they tend to regard the mass media as part of a leisure environment entirely separate from the school which has little or no legitimate claim to classroom attention. Secondly, like the French master quoted in the last chapter, the demands of the examination syllabus often leave grammar school teachers with little time for other things. Consequently, media-based lessons come to be regarded as an optional, probably unnecessary and irrelevant addition to the set course work. Thirdly, as suggested already, although a number of academically successful grammar school pupils are alienated from the culture and values of their schools, they tend not to display their disengagement in overt actions such as truancy or open challenges to teachers' authority. Instead they mechanically perform the rituals of school life, while investing their emotional energy in their leisure time activities which often centre on the pop media.

Grammar school teachers increasingly catch glimpses of their pupils' 'other life' but, because these manifestations are generally confined to the breaks and do not spill over into lesson time, they do not present a direct challenge to teachers, who consequently do not feel it necessary to come to terms with them in the classroom. On the other hand, teachers in comprehensives—and more particularly secondary moderns—are more likely to find that their pupils bring various elements of their leisure environment into the classroom. Certainly, teachers in these schools are more likely than those in grammar schools to say that the mass media are effecting their pupils' work. Teachers in secondary moderns as a whole also have a significantly unfavourable general attitude towards the detrimental effect on their pupils of mass media. Coupled with the stress on education as a 'compensation' for environmental influences and the more flexible syllabus structures, this underlying attitude makes media-based teaching more frequent in both comprehensive and secondary modern schools. Consequently, it is not surprising that only 26% of the comprehensives and 8% of the secondary moderns in our sample opted for the policy of exclusion specified by the first approach.

Approach 2
Teachers adopting this second approach also tend not to introduce mass media into their lessons, but in this case the exclusion is underlain by a generally unfavourable attitude towards mass media which are seen as exerting a predominantly harmful influence on pupils' values and behaviour. Not infrequently teachers who subscribe to this approach completely exclude mass media material from the classroom. Not only do they not introduce material themselves, they also resist any attempt by the pupils to do so. Two illustrations of the operation of this approach in practice follow.

The first is Edward Blishen's description of how he reacted to the comic books which his pupils so avidly read:

I tore them up because they seemed the visible (and tearable) signs of the inattention that I could not cure, and also of the forces that made Stonehill Street so reluctant to be educated . . . I remember once tearing up a comic of Dibber's. He scowled and said, just audibly, 'Rat!' . . . Half of the boys I took for art were my enemies because I wouldn't let them copy comic strips. To them comics *were* art. In English lessons it was the same.[1]

The second quotation is from a recent handbook on teaching musical appreciation:

The 'pop' disease is so widespread these days that no child seems to escape it . . . To show disgust at the sounds of those records (and they are undeniably disgusting) will achieve little. Better to keep a calm face and insist on your pound of flesh. It is after all a music period and not 'Housewives' Choice' ... One good defence is to say to the pupil who asks for 'pop': 'What has it to do with a music lesson? Do you ask your English teacher for Superman comics ...?'[2]

The central idea behind this approach is a logical extension of the idea underlying the first approach. Thus the values, experience and forms of expression provided by the mass media are seen not simply as separate and different from those sponsored by the school, but actually opposed to them. This argument that schools are necessarily competing with the mass media for pupils' time, energy and commitment found its most eloquent expression in a slim volume entitled *Culture and Environment*, which F. R. Leavis and Denys Thompson wrote in the early 1930s as a practical handbook for teachers.

Those who in school are offered the beginnings of education in taste are exposed, out of school, to the competing exploitation of the cheapest emotional responses; films, newspapers, publicity in all its forms, commercially-catered fiction—all offer satisfaction at the lowest level, and inculcate the choosing of the most immediate pleasures, got with the least effort.[3]

Underlying this definition is the idea that all cultural artefacts can be ranked in terms of a vertical hierarchy in which things such as poetry, symphonies and easel paintings will be placed towards the top and comics and pop songs towards the bottom. The whole idea of 'high culture' in fact presupposes the notion of a hierarchy based on *a priori* judgements of superiority. The way in which comic books are contrasted with 'art', and the 'disgusting sounds' of pop records with music, in the extracts quoted above, provide a good illustration of the categorizations which result from this essentially elitist conception of culture. To the unhearing and uncaring it is possible that all pop music does sound alike, but then the same is also true of German Baroque chamber music. It takes time, effort and understanding to become sensitive to variations, and unfamiliarity simply breeds contempt. Anyone listening with even a modicum of attention to the range of pop music currently available would very soon be struck by the considerable variety of forms and styles. Certainly, as will be demonstrated later, the pupils studied made quite careful discriminations between different pop styles. However, the definition of the situation underlying Approach 2 ignores these possibilities and stresses instead the absolute difference between symphonies and pop songs, 'high culture' and 'pop culture', and the automatic superiority of one over the other.

One of the main functions of the grammar school is seen in terms of handing on the knowledge and appreciation of high culture to the rising generation of intellectuals, business managers and civil servants. Consequently, it is not particularly surprising that a number of grammar schools (29%) should support an approach which reaffirms this function, and the classification of culture on which it rests, through excluding the alternative forms of expression supported by the mass media from legitimate classroom consideration. Taken together, the exclusion strategies of Approaches 1 and 2 were supported by 80% of the grammar schools in our sample. However, the support for the Second Approach was not nearly as great as the support for the First Approach, which suggests that grammar school teachers are more likely to view the influence of the mass media with indifference rather than overt hostility. This impression was confirmed by the replies to the open-ended questions on the schedule. From these, it was evident that the prevailing definition of the situation among grammar school teachers was that their main task was to get their pupils through the exams and that, because their pupils' involvement in media-based leisure activities very seldom impinged directly on the teaching situation, they felt it could be more or less ignored.

The second approach also had support among a sizeable minority (28%) of secondary modern schools. Certainly, these schools shared—to some extent at least—the same elitist and hierarchical conception of culture as the grammar schools, but their commitment to the Second Approach was also underlined by a further factor which was absent in the grammar schools. The clue to this factor lies in Edward Blishen's remarks about comic books. Faced with the sorts of situations which Blishen and many others have described, there is a considerable temptation for teachers in downtown secondary modern schools to hit out at those elements which pupils bring into the school from their leisure environment—mascara, comics, pop songs, catch phrases—as these provide a convenient and readily available target. As will be argued in the discussion of the pupils' study, these elements often occupy a relatively minor place within the overall configuration of working class pupils' values and activities. Consequently, although reactions such as detentions, confiscations and sarcastic criticism may provide an outlet for a teacher's sense of frustration, they do not begin to touch the central issues behind the situation. On the contrary, they may well exacerbate the problems and increase the degree of mutual incomprehension and hostility. As one girl on the receiving end of this approach put it:

Teachers should try to understand us a bit more; the things we like. If they catch you reading comics like *Jackie*, they throw it in the bin or give you two sides. Especially, Mrs XXX, she takes us for English. She hates me and I hate her.

Approach 3
The schools supporting the Third Approach have the same underlying definition of the situation and unfavourable attitude as the supporters of the second approach. They agree that schools are competing with the mass media for pupils' commitment, but they disagree about the appropriate response to this situation. Instead of excluding mass media material from classroom considera-

tion and concentrating solely on the transmission of high culture, they take the position that teachers must actively combat the countervailing influence of the mass media. Thus, they tend to introduce media material into their lessons quite frequently, in order to expose it to criticism and thereby provide their pupils with some 'defence' against its supposedly harmful effects. Underlying this approach is a particular view of the process of media influence.

According to this view, the mass media can be seen as a series of machines controlled by self-seeking, and occasionally evil, men. These machines send out sounds and images which enter the uncritical minds of the passive audience and turn them into compliant zombies who will willingly accept the implanted ideas, and may even act them out and behave in an antisocial manner. This basic argument is voiced with monotonous regularity in the continuing debate about the relationship between exposure to the media and delinquent behaviour, and stories such as the one entitled 'Peace and Love' song Made Boy a Killer (from which the following extract has been taken) appear quite frequently in the mass circulation press.

Teenager Robert Trimmer's love for a girl turned sour as he listened to the pop record Woodstock. The disc, which is about America's 'peace and love' pop concert, turned Trimmer's mind to hate . . . he decided to kill Miss Randal.[4]

Versions of this same 'zombie' view of media influence have also found their way into school textbooks. Alan Durband, for example, introduces his widely used text, Contemporary English, by arguing that most people

. . . are led like lambs to the slaughter—trained to read and write but defenceless against the clever tricks of those who know how to profit from universal literacy . . . It is where you are off your guard that some of the most damaging blows can be struck.[5]

Although the comparison here is with lambs rather than zombies, the underlying argument, that people are essentially defenceless against the clever tricks of those who control the press, advertising and the entertainment media, is exactly the same.

Proponents of the 'zombie' view quite frequently liken the influence of the mass media to the effects of drugs. Dr Frederick Wertham for example, one of the most widely quoted academic protagonists in the current debate on television and violence, has quite explicitly compared exposure to television violence with the effects of the 'excessive use of the drug phenacetin'. He argues that in the same way that phenacetin 'can cause serious disease by lowering the power of resistance of such organs as the kidney . . . the child whose memory is filled with screen violence may have less psychological resistance to evil influences'.[6] This drug analogy cropped up a number of times among the replies of teachers in this study. This view has an interesting corollary for, if the mass media are seen as a drug that weakens resistance, then logically the teacher's role is to provide some sort of antidote or preventative inoculation.

This basic idea was endorsed by two influential Government reports on education. Thus, in 1938, the Spens Report strongly advocated that pupils should be given 'a defence against the assaults and seductions of the popular press', while the Crowther Report argued that teachers have a duty 'to see that teenagers, who are at the most insecure and suggestible stage of their lives, are not suddenly exposed to the full force of the "mass media" without some counterbalancing assistance.'[7]

In view of the fact that literature is still widely regarded as the epicentre of 'high culture', it is perhaps not surprising that this 'inoculation' approach should find some of its most forceful proponents among teachers of English. Professor Whitehead, for example, echoing F. R. Leavis, has recently argued that English teaching is largely 'a struggle against the environment' created by the 'powerful forces typified by comics and commercials, headlines and hoardings', and that providing pupils with 'some inoculation against the cruder types of emotional bludgeoning to be found in news headlines or advertising slogans' is a necessary part of this struggle.[8] Not infrequently, providing an inoculation against the influence of the mass media is seen not as an end in itself but as a necessary part of a broader strategy aimed at encouraging pupils to move up the hierarchy of cultural experiences and to replace pop music and comics with symphonies and poetry. This strategy was very clearly stated by Matthew Arnold, as long ago as 1869. The aim of disseminating culture, he argued, was 'not to make what each raw person may like, the rule by which he fashions himself' but rather 'to draw ever nearer to the sense of what is indeed beautiful, graceful and becoming, and to get the raw person to like that'.[9]

Various versions of the 'inoculation' approach commanded considerable support from both the comprehensive (32%) and secondary modern schools (36%) in our sample. The probable reasons for this support have already been mentioned—a generally unfavourable view of the mass media, the feeling that the media present a direct and powerful threat to the values sponsored by the school; the stress on education as a compensation for the 'deficiencies of the family and the neighbourhood', and the more flexible syllabus structure. The opposite aspects of these same factors also account for the lack of support for the 'inoculation' approach among grammar schools.

Approach 4
Supporters of the fourth approach also make frequent use of mass media material in their classroom teaching, but unlike the proponents of the 'inoculation' approach, they treat it in a positive rather than a negative way. Thus, Frank Whitehead's stress on media-based teaching as a necessary preventative inoculation against a creeping disease is replaced by Michael Marland's argument that 'the basis of all our teaching must be adding enriching, and encouraging—not deleting, criticizing and inhibiting'[10]. Underlying this sort of

approach is a definition of culture and a view of the process of media influence, which is almost the complete opposite of that behind the 'inoculation'
approach. This alternative view owes a great deal to the work of Richard
Hoggart.

Whereas most commentators are middle class observers taking a bird's eye
view of working class culture, Richard Hoggart writes as an insider, and bases
his widely known book, *The Uses of Literacy*, firmly on his own experience of
growing up in Hunslet in the 1930s. Drawing on this experience, he main-
tains that it was not the case that the traditional rural folk cultures were des-
troyed overnight by the twin processes of industrialization and urbanization
and replaced by a uniform media-based mass culture. Rather, he argues, the
migrant workers brought many of their folk traditions with them to the cities
and, out of the meeting of these remnants and their new experience of the
work situation and city life, they forged a strong and vigorous popular culture
which expressed their distinctive sense of themselves as workers in particular
industries and as people living in specific localities. According to this argument
therefore, the activity of producing a culture ceases to be exclusive to one
particular privileged group and becomes instead, an integral part of the social
life of all groups. Cultures in this sense, are made up of the patterns of beliefs,
values, ideas, and emotions, together with their characteristic forms of expression, through which groups define, interpret and respond to their experience of
social life and social change. Cultures represent a repository and distillation
of the group's common social experience, a series of 'master patterns' of
meaning and expression which permeate the whole texture of family and
neighbourhood life and provide most individual members with their definition
of the situation. Despite the considerable amount of economic and social
change since 1945, these situational neighbourhood cultures continue to provide the basic framework through which many working class people look at
and respond to their social experience.

Far from providing an entirely passive zombie-like audience, therefore,
these people—like others—constantly measure what is offered to them against
the standard of their personal experience and consequently they tend to be
quite selective. As Hoggart puts it;

> The 'common man' . . . is not much deceived; he has some awareness of his
> own difficulties in judging and coping; he has a much more sensitive awareness
> of the fact that he is being 'got at', being 'worked on'. He has suspected 'fancy
> talk' for generations. He can 'see through' most appeals, and is on constant
> watch against being 'taken in'. [11]

This viewpoint leads logically to two further propositions. First, the impact of
media material comes to be seen in terms of a complex interaction rather than
a simple reaction, and the important question to ask becomes; what do people
do with the material they select? rather than, what does the material *do to* the

people who receive it? Secondly, the stress on the essential homogeneity of mass media products is replaced by recognition of the differences between superficially similar sorts of products and between elements within the same product. As Stuart Hall and Paddy Whannel put it in their book, *The Popular Arts*:

> In terms of actual quality . . . the struggle between what is good and worthwhile and what is shoddy and debased is not a struggle against the modern forms of communication, but a conflict within these media.[12]

Instead of falling back on the rigid hierarchical division between the elite culture of the literary tradition and newer media-based cultural forms, which reinforces the gap between middle class and working class life and thought, Hoggart proposes that all cultural artefacts should be ranged along a continuum marked 'authentic' at one end and 'phoney' at the other. 'Our job', he argues, 'is to separate the Processed from the Living.'

> The crucial distinctions today are not those between the *News of the World* and *The Observer* . . . between the 'Top Ten' and a celebrity concert, or between 'skiffle' and chamber music. The distinction we should be making are those between the *News of the World* and the *Sunday Pictorial*, between 'skiffle' and the 'Top Ten'.

> This is to make distinctions between the quality of life in each thing of its own kind—distinctions which require an active discrimination, not the application of a fixed 'brow' or educational scale.[13]

Hoggart's central concern is with the way in which we can use all kinds of communications, the new media as well as traditional literary or oral forms, as a way of 'speaking to each other'. A successful or good cultural artefact is therefore one which embodies a deeply felt and authentic experience and which strikes genuine chords in the audience. Thus he argues, the *Daily Mirror* of 1945 was a better paper than the *Daily Express* because it 'was much more in touch with the prevailing mood' of 'ordinary people', and spoke directly to them about their hopes for the future.[14] This kind of open-ended, relativistic approach leads very rapidly to a complete redefinition of what is meant by culture and, from this, to a reassessment of what counts as valid knowledge in the school curriculum in general and the English lesson in particular. Once the idea of a cultural continuum is accepted, the teacher is necessarily obliged to regard mass media artefacts as potentially valid forms of cultural expression in their own right, and to incorporate them as a necessary and integral part of his teaching. Perhaps the clearest expression of this position, by a practising teacher, has come from Michael Marland:

> It can be said with confidence . . . that no middle-school English course would be complete today without the integration of the newer media into the classroom consideration. Last night's television play and today's newspaper must take their

place in a continuum that ranges from the most trivial of reading matter to the most major literature.[15]

Another statement of the same basic position can be found in a recent article by Robert Shaw, former head of English at a leading Leeds grammar school. He describes the basic aim of his teaching as developing 'a critical awareness of the way language and the other media of communication work', and goes on to argue that:

> The English teacher, traditionally the high priest of culture and entrusted with a special responsibility for communications, has some duty to attempt to introduce the new media of 'popular culture' into the classroom, not simply as audio-visual aids or in . . . artistically acceptable forms, but in. . . representative examples.[16]

A version of this same viewpoint was put to us by a young music mistress in a larged mixed comprehensive school in London:

> I think it is essential that any music teacher today should take account of the vast amount of music the pupils hear through the mass media. I do not mean that entire lessons should be given over to 'pop' but that it should be treated as a branch of music, with an equal right to be enjoyed as much as any other. The teacher must then go on to help the children decide for themselves what they like or dislike *within each type*. (her italics)

The emphasis here is on the teacher being aware of and open to the nature of pupils' everyday cultural experiences and attempting to build bridges between the classroom and the world of leisure. This strategy has recently been endorsed in the report of a Schools Council working party on music and the young school leaver. The report concluded that:

> The school should make every effort, without lowering its own standards or losing its ideals, to bridge the gap between the music offered in an educational context and the music that young people claim as their own and that they spontaneously and actively enjoy.[17]

This was not the first time that this viewpoint had received 'official' sponsorship. Over eight years before, the Newsom Report had argued that cinema and television are a 'unique and potentially valuable art form . . . as capable of communicating depth of experience as any other art form' and that consequently they should be studied 'in their own right' and not simply 'used as visual aids for the presentation of material connected with other subjects.'[18] This in turn served to reiterate and reinforce the policy that the British Film Institute's Education Department, under the leadership of Paddy Whannel, had been pursuing since the mid nineteen-fifties.

Despite such vigorous and widespread advocacy from numerous quarters, this approach was subscribed to by only 20% of the grammar schools, 26% of the comprehensives and 28% of the secondary moderns in the sample. By far the majority of grammar schools (80%) pursued a policy of 'exclusion' while, although the majority of both comprehensives and secondary moderns supported a policy of 'incorporation', most of these opted for Approach Three rather than Approach Four.

With this overview of the various ways in which the schools in this study approached the classroom use of media material, particular aspects of this use, concentrating particularly on the two main groups of subject specialists— English and science teachers, can be given more detailed consideration.

What sorts of mass media material do teachers introduce into their lessons?

Teachers were presented with a list of the major mass media which their pupils would be likely to encounter during their leisure time, and asked to

Table 13 Frequency with which teachers introduce material from various mass media into their lessons (figures in percentages)

Medium	0		50		100
Newspapers		49		27	19
Television		48		22	22
Magazines		38		27	28
Radio	21	19		49	
Cinema	17	26		47	
Pop records	14	20		57	
Comics	5	11		74	

Key

Several times a term or more

About once a term

Never

No response

$n = 1310$

indicate how often they introduced material from these media areas into their lessons. Teachers' replies are set out in Table 13.

The most immediately striking feature of Table 13 is that some sorts of media material are far more likely to be introduced into lessons than others, giving a stepped pattern to the distribution. Thus, while almost half the teachers introduce material from newspapers (49%) and television (48%) at least several times a term, only 14% introduce pop records, which are central to the pop media culture in which many pupils are involved. No one factor satisfactorily explains this pattern; rather it results from the simultaneous influence of a number of factors.

In Chapter 1 we saw that teachers generally tend to spend only a limited time with the major mass media, and that their selections tend towards the 'highbrow'. Consequently, there is a considerable gap between the mass media experiences of many teachers and those of the majority of their pupils. Most teachers' newspaper reading is confined to the 'qualities' whereas most of their pupils, if they read a newspaper at all, are likely to read one of the 'populars'; most teachers watch only half as much television as many of their pupils, and only a third of teachers listen to pop music 'very' or 'fairly' often. Most teachers are therefore faced with a choice, either they draw on their own media experience, in which case many of the examples are likely to be unfamiliar to a good number of pupils, or they encourage pupils to bring their own media experiences into the classroom, in which case they will have to make the effort to bridge the experiential gap. Certainly, there is no economic reason preventing teachers from adopting the second approach.

It is a relatively simple matter to set pupils to watch a particular television programme or listen to a pop music show on the radio and then to follow up the experience with class discussions and various forms of activity. Similarly, a considerable number of newspapers and comics of various sorts can be rapidly accumulated if pupils are encouraged to bring old copies from home. Despite this relative equality of access, the fact remains that newspapers and television —rather than pop music and comics—are most frequently introduced into lessons. Why should there be this difference?

One factor that appears to play a part is the extent to which the teacher is familiar with the material. That is, those teachers who do listen to pop music during their leisure time are very much more likely to introduce pop music into their lessons than those who are largely unfamiliar with contemporary pop. This is also true of television, radio, newspapers and cinema. The more contact a teacher has with these media outside school the greater the likelihood that he will use them in his classroom teaching. However, most teachers are largely unfamiliar with many of the media experiences of their pupils. What factors then determine the approach of a teacher in this position? What decides whether he will attempt to build a bridge between the world of school or the world outside, or whether he will attempt to barricade the classroom against environmental influences?

One significant factor is the kind of training a teacher has received. Those who come into teaching straight from a university generally tend to adopt a narrowly academic view of their role, and consequently are never likely to introduce mass media into their lessons. Teachers from training colleges, on the other hand, tend to have a less exclusive concept of education which does not lay so great a stress on subject teaching, and which leads them to make frequent use of mass media material in the classroom. Not surprisingly, teachers who had both a degree and a teachers' certificate tended to occupy a median position. Among teachers with a more generalized conception of their role, those who assign a high priority to education in human relationships tend to use the media material most frequently, often several times a week. Significantly, those teachers who regard education for leisure as being an important part of their job are most willing to introduce pop music into lessons. But, as noted in Chapter 2, the vast majority of teachers assign education for leisure the lowest priority—a further reason why pop music is so infrequently introduced.

In addition to playing an important part in forming a teacher's view of the job, the sort of training he has received is also an important factor in deciding the sort of school he will teach in. Thus, the majority of degree holders are likely to gravitate to the grammar schools, while the majority of those with certificates will probably teach in secondary modern schools. Once he becomes a grammar school teacher, the university graduate is likely to have the subject-centred values implicit in his academic training further reinforced by the grammar school ethos, which also provides a point of reference for many comprehensive and secondary modern teachers. The grammar school ethos regarding pupils' leisure activities emerges very clearly from the research of Ronald King, quoted earlier, in which teachers regarded reading worthwhile books as the most desirable leisure time pursuit, and listening to pop records or reading comic books as among the least desirable[19]—a further reason why so few teachers introduce either pop records or comic books into their lessons.

Behind this particular evaluation, however, lies a very clear conception of what shall count as legitimate knowledge and experience in the classroom, together with a view of culture which stresses the literary modes of mediating experience. Although, historically, it stretches back to a period earlier than the very beginning of modern education, a recent survey of American High School teachers indicates that this 'literary' perspective is still very powerful. While 6% of the teachers interviewed said that they were willing to discuss 'underground' newspapers with their pupils, only 19% were prepared to discuss contemporary pop music.[20] It may be that the 'literary' nature of newspapers make them more culturally legitimate and also more amenable to handling in terms of conventional critical categories, whereas pop music is a simultaneous, audio-tactile medium.

The effect of a 'literary' view of culture on teachers' willingness to introduce mass media material into their lessons is by no means a simple one however.

Table 14 Frequency with which English and science teachers introduce material from various mass media into their lessons (figures in percentages)

Media	Several times a term or more		Never	
	English	Science	English	Science
Newspapers	67	47	4	29
Television	67	47	8	28
Magazines	41	27	19	36
Radio	27	11	39	64
Cinema	32	6	23	69
Pop records	25	5	35	80
Comics	9	1	58	88
n	321	305	321	305

As Table 14 clearly shows, English teachers are not less willing to introduce media material into lessons; the contrary is the case. For each medium, English teachers are more likely to introduce material than either teachers as a whole or science teachers; but it cannot be concluded from this that English teachers are more favourably disposed towards the media. It is necessary to go beyond simple frequency counts to consider the aims which teachers say they have for using media material.

The aims behind teachers' use of mass media material in the classroom

Teachers were simply presented with a blank sheet of paper and asked to state, in their own words, their aims in introducing mass media material into lessons. Table 15 presents the most frequent replies, for teachers as a whole and for the two main groups of subject specialists. Almost half the science teachers (48%) mentioned that they used mass media material as a bridge between two worlds of experience. Here are a few of their comments:

I aim to link my subject matter with real life situations so that pupils realize the relevance of seemingly isolated problems to practical living. (Maths master, boys' Grammar)

One of the most important things throughout academic training is to bring the subject matter in line with the everyday experiences of the children. If these experiences are not available first hand, mass media is sometimes capable of filling the gap. (Chemistry master, mixed Comprehensive)

Occasionally, this aim was mentioned by English teachers, but they were very much in the minority (18%). Teachers' age also appeared to be an important factor. Thus, whereas 40% of teachers under 35 said that they saw the mass

Table 15 The most frequently stated aims behind the introduction of mass media material into lessons*

General aims	All Teachers	Subject taught	
		English	Science
To relate the classroom to the outside world	31	18	48
To share some common ground with pupils	7	11	4
Media in lessons			
To provide relevant and topical illustrations	23	18	46
To engage pupils' interest	20	16	27
To provide variety in lessons	12	3	11
As a starting point for subject work	14	23	9
Lessons in media			
To provide pupils with a 'defence'	19	36	6
To encourage discrimination and appreciation	19	35	9
To evaluate particular media products	13	29	5
To show how the media work	9	14	4
Numbers replying	820	250	183

* All numbers here are presented as a percentage of the number of teachers who answered this question. Since those who did answer seem more likely to be involved in using media in the classroom than those who did not, these percentages are probably overestimates in terms of the total number of teachers in our sample.

media as a way of bridging the school/environment gap, only 29% of those aged between 35 and 45, and 25% of those aged 46–55 mentioned this as an objective.

Comparatively few teachers (7%) mentioned that one of their aims was to establish some common experiential ground with their pupils and thereby improve teacher-pupil relationships. Paradoxically, English teachers were more likely to mention this as an explicit aim, although there was little or no difference between teachers at various types of school. In nearly every case, however, the prior aim was that of bridging the experiential gap.

The main aim I suppose is that learning should be related to the modern world. A further aim might be to show that 'I am human too' and not above watching telly! (English mistress, mixed Comprehensive)

Television provides a common touchstone of experience that helps us to communicate. When reading a book together in class we can disagree successfully, and this spontaneous aside to the lesson often begins with 'Eh sir, I saw a programme on the telly just like . . .' (English master, mixed Comprehensive)

However, as has already been seen, this kind of receptiveness to the spontaneous intrusion into the classroom of the pupils' everyday experiences is still comparatively rare, and the majority of English teachers—especially the older ones—are more likely to agree with the grammar school English master who said,

I keep the thing strictly limited as far as time goes, finding that discussions about the mass media are singularly barren in contrast to the discovery of great literature.

Turning from general to specific aims, there is a considerable difference between *media in lessons* where media material is simply used as an audio visual aid or an attention-getter, and *lessons in media* where the material is the prime focus of attention. Overall, teachers inclined towards the first type of use rather than the second.

The most frequently cited specific aim in using media material was as a source of relevant and topical illustrations of particular points. This was mentioned by 23% of teachers. Again, there were considerable differences between subjects, with 46% of science teachers mentioning illustration as against only 18% of English teachers.

Quite a few teachers (20%) said that they used media material in order to engage pupils' interest, and often this general aim would be linked to a more specific one—20% of teachers, for example, mentioned using media material as an opening gambit to capture attention, or as a starting point for subject work:

English lessons are 'sold', especially creative English by mod pop records— use of English and development of mood—Beatles' *Eleanor Rigby*—desolation and loneliness. (English mistress; girls' Grammar)

Occasionally, this sort of pragmatic reaction to the immediate situation is elaborated into a long-term strategy in which mass media material is used to sugar the curriculum pill:

The first step is to 'pinch' the children's attention by something they already know about; thus if they are only conversant with films and pop records I have to sell my subject through their interest in these media. (English mistress, girls' Grammar)

Thus, the media become a means to an end, a way of 'selling' the syllabus to the pupils. The idea underlying many of these comments—that mass media material could be a useful panacea which immediately rendered 'difficult' or unwilling pupils quiet and attentive—was put forward in its most extreme form by a teacher in charge of remedial classes in a large comprehensive school.

The words of pop songs are the most interesting thing to remedial classes. They often work better and are calmed by soft transistor radio music while they work.

From Table 15 it can be seen that 'instrumental' aims were mentioned with much the same frequency by teachers of all ages and at all types of schools, but again there was a considerable difference between subject specialists. Thus, science teachers were more likely to mention using media as an attention getter, than English teachers who preferred to use media as a starting point for subject work. Overall, the instrumental uses of mass media material in lessons were more frequently mentioned by science than English teachers, who tended to lay more stress on conducting lessons in media.

A considerable number of English teachers said that their main aim in introducing mass media into lessons was to point out the 'dangers' of the media and to provide pupils with a 'defence'. Of the English teachers who answered our question 36% responded along these lines, and it seems probable that some of those who did not answer would agree with them. This attitude is far more common among English teachers than among teachers of other subjects—only 6% of science teachers answered in this way, and the figure for teachers as a whole is only 19%. The following remarks are typical of this approach to the classroom use of media material:

Study of advertising. Usual aim! To illustrate how manipulatable the unprepared mind could be to subtly stressed anxieties. (English mistress, girls' Secondary Modern)

Often a considerable psychological blow can be delivered by a charities appeal which begins, 'For those with a weak stomach, don't read on'. (English master, mixed Comprehensive)

Many of the phrases which occur in these comments—'the unprepared mind' 'psychological blow', 'manipulatable'—are startlingly similar to those employed by Alan Durband and Frank Whitehead in the extracts quoted earlier. It seemed then that such comments spring from a view of the adolescent audience as captive and defenceless 'zombies'. That this view does not correspond with the real situation will be demonstrated in our discussion of the pupils' study, which shows that most young people approach most products of the mass media with a set of criteria. Nevertheless, the 'zombie' view and its concomitant stress on the need to inoculate pupils against media influence, together with the emphasis on upholding the superiority of literary culture appear to provide the perspective of a number of English teachers.

The viewpoint associated with Richard Hoggart offers an alternative which some English teachers share. They abandon the old vertical hierarchy of cultural artefacts in favour of a horizontal continuum which includes all forms of individual and collective expression. It follows that the relevant discrimination is between the 'processed' and the 'living' within each form, *Eleanor Rigby* versus *Chirpy, Chirpy, Cheep, Cheep* rather than the Beatles against Bach. Most of the 35% of teachers who see their aim in using the media as 'encouraging discrimination' hold this viewpoint.

Before leaving the subject of mass media in the classroom, let us briefly examine the various ways in which teachers today are actually using mass media material in specific classroom circumstances.

Ways in which teachers introduce mass media material into their lessons

From the replies set out in Table 16, it is clear that the most frequently mentioned method of introducing media material into lessons was through planned discussions where the teacher sets aside a lesson or part of a lesson for the specific purpose of discussing the mass media. Altogether 59% of teachers mentioned this method. Sometimes discussion is an end in itself but more often it is either a lead-in to written work or the end product of project work. Here are some examples of the various contexts within which discussions take place.

I played 'pop' or folk records with some interesting point to make, e.g. Bob Dylan's *With God on Our Side*, as an introduction to a group discussion of *War*. (Religious Knowledge master, mixed Comprehensive)

I give four or five boys a week's notice that they will each select an item of news, follow it up and give an account of it, preferably in their own words, at the next lesson. The boy then conducts an open class discussion for about ten minutes. (Current affairs master, boys' Grammar)

I get the children into groups and they compare the same article in the *Times* and *Sun* and assess distortion of fact and to what extent the distortion is allowable—is it in the opinion column, etc. (English mistress, girls' Modern)

Table 16 The most frequently mentioned methods of introducing mass media material into lessons (figures in percentages)

Method of introducing media material	All teachers	Type of school			Subject taught	
		Grammar	Comprehensive	Modern	English	Science
Through discussion planned in advance	59	58	57	63	76	53
Through the evaluation and criticism of specific items	36	31	36	41	75	9
As an illustration of a particular point	27	28	28	24	20	27
By directly exposing pupils to a particular piece of material	25	20	28	29	24	20
As a recommendation, e.g. that pupils should watch a particular television programme	15	17	20	9	13	18
As a basis for project work	13	10	14	15	13	12
Through spontaneous discussion arising out of a lesson or another subject	11	15	9	7	9	17
As a basis for subject work	10	6	13	10	12	2
As an introductory stimulus to a lesson	6	7	4	7	7	5
By means of creative activity involving the producing of media material (e.g. taped interviews)	6	5	5	7	6	3
Numbers replying	743	280	223	240	235	152

We usually plan out a series of typical stereotyped romance situations drawn from magazines like *Mirabelle*. Then we read something like the Vincent-Ingrid first date scene (*Kind of Loving*) and contrast it. (English mistress, girls' Modern)

After planned discussion and evaluation, the next most popular method of introducing media content was as illustration. This was mentioned by 27% of all teachers, particularly those teaching 'fact based' subjects such as science and geography.

I use the mass media as a source of information and statistics and as a visual representation of relative quantities, etc. (Maths master, boys' Grammar)

I use the mass media simply to illustrate the topic under discussion: (1) casual references to films (e.g. California earthquake) when appropriate; (2) reference to forthcoming television programmes that might usefully be watched; (3) references to newspapers for specific things, e.g. weather. (Geography master, mixed Comprehensive)

Finally, it is interesting to note that only 6% of teachers mentioned that their pupils actually created their own mass media material. Obviously, given the general shortage of funds and basic equipment, most of the schools in this study could not afford to finance activities such as film making, but it was rather surprising how few teachers mentioned even relatively inexpensive activities such as producing a class newspaper or magazine, launching an advertising campaign, producing a simulated interview programme on tape, or composing and playing pop songs. However, teachers did mention such media activities as writing scripts for radio and television and stories for magazines and simulating the visual effects on *Top of the Pops* using inks on a clear gelatine film base in conjunction with oils on a heated slide. But these are comparatively rare examples, and, from the results of this study, it appears that the only contact that the great majority of pupils have with media material is confined to their role as consumers and audience members; very few are encouraged actually to produce media material themselves. Without this perspective any understanding of the way in which the mass media work must necessarily remain partial.

This concludes our analysis of the findings of the teachers' study. A general summary of the major points which have emerged can be more fruitfully attempted after looking at the results of the pupils' study. Thus, our summing up has been left until the final chapter of the report, and a discussion of the pupils in the ten study schools directly follows this chapter.

References

1   Blishen, Edward, 1966 *Roaring Boys* London, Panther Books, p. 84.
2   Dwyer, Terence, 1967 *Teaching Musical Appreciation* London, Oxford University Press, p. 115.

3   Leavis, F.R. and Thompson, Denys, 1933 *Culture and Environment: The Training of Critical Awareness* London, Chatto and Windus, 1942 ed., p. 3.

4   *Sun*, Tuesday March 2 1971, p. 21.

5   Durband, Alan, 1963 *Contemporary English: Book One* London, Hutchinson Educational, pp. 13–15.

6   Halloran, J. D., ed. (quoted in), 1964 *Crime, Violence and Television* Television Research Committee mimeo report, p. 36.

7   Board of Education, 1938 *Secondary Education With Special Reference to Grammar Schools and Technical High Schools (The Spens Report)* London, HMSO, p. 223. Central Advisory Council for Education (England), 1959 '*15 to 18*' (*The Crowther Report*) London, HMSO, Vol. 1, para. 66.

8   Whitehead, Frank, 1969 'Why Teach English?' in: Denys Thompson, ed. *Directions in the Teaching of English* Cambridge University Press, 1969, p. 27.

9   Arnold, Matthew, 1869 *Culture and Anarchy* Ann Arbor, 1965 edition, p. 96.

10   Marland, Michael, 1969 *Mainstream* in Denys Thompson 1969 ed. op. cit., p. 86.

11   Hoggart, Richard, 1957 *The Uses of Literacy* London, Chatto and Windus 1959, p. 227.

12   Hall, Stuart and Whannel, Paddy, 1964 *The Popular Arts* London, Hutchinson, p. 15.

13   Hoggart, Richard, 'Culture: Dead and Alive' in Hoggart, 1970 *Speaking to Each Other*, Vol. 1, *About Society* London, Chatto and Windus, pp. 131–2.

14   Hoggart, Richard, 1966 'Mirror for What People?' *New Society* 27 October 1966, p. 657.

15   Marland, Michael, 1969, op. cit., p. 74.

16   Shaw, Robert, 1971 'Meaning in English at the Leeds Modern School' in G. Summerfield and S. Tunnicliffe, eds. *English in Practice: Secondary English Departments at Work* Cambridge University Press 1971, p. 142.

17   Schools Council *Music and the Young School Leaver: Problems and Opportunities* (Working Paper 35) London, Evans/Methuen Educational, 1971, p. 31.

18   Central Advisory Council for Education (England), 1963 *Half Our Future* (The Newsom Report), London, HMSO, pp. 155–6.

19   King, Ronald, 1969 *Values and Involvement in a Grammar School* London, Routledge and Kegan Paul, pp. 68–9.

20   *Life* reported May 26 1969, p. 24.

Part II:

The pupils' study

6 Pupils in school: commitment and disengagement

Introduction

Previous research has indicated that pupils have a general commitment to school, relatively independent of their attitudes towards such specific aspects of their school experience as disciplinary rules, uniforms, individual subjects or particular teachers. The point under discussion, then, is whether pupils actively enjoy being in school or whether they would rather be somewhere else. Our principal measure of school commitment in this sense was an attitude scale constructed expressly for the purpose,* but the age at which pupils wanted to leave school and the extent to which they participated in school-sponsored clubs and teams were also considered as subsidiary indicators. This chapter is devoted to an examination of some of the factors that affect the level of pupils' school commitment.

Social class and school commitment

In the present study the practice adopted by the majority of social researchers has been followed in taking the occupation of the father (or head of the household) as the principal indicator of pupils' social class background. Although this is not an entirely satisfactory way of measuring social class, the bulk of previous research seems to indicate that, in the majority of cases, the broad classifications of occupations into non-manual, skilled manual, and semi-skilled and unskilled manual, does correspond to the conventional social categories—middle class, and upper and lower working class. Thus, referring to pupils as 'lower working class' is a useful shorthand way of saying 'pupils from homes where the father is employed in a semi-skilled or unskilled manual job'. For the sake of convenience and readability, therefore, we have adopted these social class categories when describing the results of our research.

Table 17 presents the mean school commitment scores for each of the main social class groups in the first and third years. If the figures are compared

* The recent debate about the meaning of 'school commitment' and the way in which the attitude scale used in this study was constructed and validated are described in Appendix 3.

Table 17 Pupil's mean scores on the school commitment scale: by year and social class

Year	Middle class	Upper working class	Lower working class	Significance level
First	16·2	15·8		*NS*
	16·2		15·4	*NS*
Third	16·2	14·9		★★
	16·2		13·9	★★★
Significance level	*NS*	★	★★	

Note: A high score indicates a high degree of commitment.

across rows it is evident that, in both years, middle class pupils are more committed to their schools than working class pupils. However, whereas among the first years there is less than one point separating the scores of all three class groups, among third year pupils these differences are large enough to be statistically significant. The reasons for this become clearer when the figures are compared by columns. Thus, whereas the mean scores of middle class pupils in both the first and third years are the same (16·2), the third year means for both working class groups are considerably lower than those for first year pupils.

The same basic pattern of class differences in pupils' commitment to school is also illustrated in Table 18, which shows the percentages of first and third year pupils in the three main social class groups who want to stay on after sixteen.

Table 18 Pupils wanting to stay on after 16: by year and social class (in percentages)

Year	Middle class	Upper working class	Lower working class
First	51% (n = 95)	37% (n = 170)	21% (n = 115)
Third	55% (n = 171)	32% (n = 250)	14% (n = 128)

Comparing across rows again reveals a clear stepped pattern with the percentage of pupils wanting to stay on after sixteen falling symmetrically by social class. This holds for both years, but again the difference between middle and working class pupils is greater among third years than among the first years.

So far then, our results lend support to the argument, that, whereas the majority of middle class pupils actively enjoy their school experience, a sizeable number of working class adolescents feel to a greater or lesser extent alienated from their schools and, if given the choice, would rather be somewhere else. Further, the gap between the committed and the disengaged appears to widen rather than to close as pupils move through their school career. It is now necessary to be more specific, and consider the extent to which the commitment of pupils from different social class backgrounds varies with the type of school which they attend.

Despite the rapid growth of comprehensive schools over the last decade, about two thirds of the pupils now in secondary schools still attend either a grammar or a secondary modern school. Consequently, all three types are included in our sample. Table 19 presents the relevant findings for third year pupils.

Table 19   The rank order of third year pupils' mean school commitment scores: by social class and type of school

Rank	Social class	Type of school	Mean commitment score
1	Middle	Grammar	16·7
2	Middle	Comprehensive	15·9
3	Middle	Modern	15·8
4	Working	Grammar	15·2
5	Working	Comprehensive	14·9
6	Working	Modern	14·1

Taken overall, the results shown in Table 19 suggest that, although within each social class grouping those attending grammar schools have a higher mean commitment than those at comprehensives—and these pupils in turn have a higher commitment than those at secondary moderns—there is still a basic difference between the two social class groupings. Thus, within each type of school, the working class pupils are less committed than their middle class peers. In order to understand this pattern it is necessary to bear in mind both the nature of the selection process and the pecking order of prestige which still characterizes most people's view of the education system.

In order to go to a grammar school, a pupil has to be selected, and there is now a formidable body of evidence which indicates that the various selection procedures operate in favour of children from middle class homes. Consequently, these pupils tend to be over-represented among the grammar school population, while the majority of working class children are allocated to secondary modern schools.[1] This would not affect attitudes particularly were it not for the fact that, in the minds of the majority of pupils and parents, secondary modern schools are seen not only as different from grammar schools but as definitely inferior, with comprehensives occupying an ambiguous intermediate position. Among secondary modern pupils there is a widespread equation of the word 'secondary' with the idea of second best and second rate, and consequently many of these pupils see themselves as failures, 'thickies' who were not bright enough to get in to the grammar school. This sense of failure, of having been rejected and labelled as an 'also ran', reinforces the initial alienation which results from the experiential gap between the basically middle class world of the school and the completely different environment of the working class home and the local neighbourhood. Consequently, the majority of these pupils tend to have a low commitment to school and want to leave as soon as possible. The findings presented in Table 19 and in Table 4.1 of Appendix 4, for example, show that working class pupils in secondary modern schools have the lowest mean level of commitment of any group (14·1) and that among those from lower working class homes only 13% wanted to stay on after sixteen (the new minimum leaving age). Among most middle class pupils at grammar schools the opposite situation obtains. For them, the experience of school is in many respects a logical extension of their home environment and this initial feeling of being 'at home' in the school is further reinforced by the sense of having been successful, of having been chosen. Consequently, it is not particularly surprising that these pupils had the highest level of school commitment (16·7), and that 64% wanted to stay on after sixteen.

Although the selection process operates in favour of middle class children, a minority of working class pupils do reach grammar school. However, unlike their middle class counterparts, they experience a gap rather than a continuity between the world of the school and the environment of the home and the local neighbourhood, and consequently they feel themselves being pulled in two directions.[2] Faced with this tension, these pupils must eventually decide in favour either of the school or of the leisure environment, and there is some evidence to suggest that the latter is more likely.[3] Certainly, the working class grammar school pupils in our sample had a significantly lower mean commitment score than their middle class peers (15·2 as against 16·7 $p < 0.05$). Further, they were much less likely to want to stay on after taking 'O' levels. Thus, whereas nearly two thirds (64%) of the middle class pupils wanted to stay on after sixteen, the proportion among those from upper working class homes was just under a half (46%) and that among the lower working class pupils only 31%. This suggests that the experience of educational success may not necessarily cancel out the effects of the experiential gap between the school and the working class environment. The opposite case of middle class pupils in secondary modern schools provides some further indication that social class background is a more important determinant of school commitment than the experience of educational 'failure' or 'success'. Thus, although these pupils may feel themselves to be to some extent failures, they are nevertheless more likely to feel at home in the basically middle class environment of the school than their working class peers. Certainly, the pupils in this position in our sample had a significantly higher mean commitment ($15 \cdot 8$ as against $14 \cdot 1$ $p < 0 \cdot 01$), and 37% wanted to stay on after sixteen compared to only 13% among pupils from lower working class homes.

The evidence presented so far in this chapter tends to indicate that academically successful pupils from middle class homes will have a relatively high commitment to school. However, even among this most highly committed group there is a significant minority who are to some extent alienated from their schools. One index of this is the fact that over one third of the middle class pupils in both grammar (36%) and secondary modern schools (35%) said that they did not want to stay on after sixteen. In looking for explanations of disengagement therefore, it is necessary to consider not only why so many working class children have a low commitment to their schools, but also why a minority of successful middle class pupils should also feel alienated.

Sources of disengagement

Secondary schools are run by middle class people (the teachers) on behalf of other middle class people (the pupils' future employers). Consequently the underlying values and assumptions of schools are those of the middle class: intellectual ability, individual achievement, deference to authority and seniority, and above all, deferred gratification, living for tomorrow instead of today. A good pupil is therefore one who accepts these values and acts them out by being: punctual, tidy, hardworking, by catching on easily, by not answering back when asked to do something, and by not expecting an immediate reward. Further, research has suggested that this definition of the good pupil is shared by teachers in secondary modern schools as well as those in grammar schools and comprehensives.[4] The majority of middle class pupils expect to enter nonmanual employment and to pursue some sort of career. Consequently they accept the role of 'good pupil' as a necessary dress rehearsal for their adult working life. They accept the restrictions because they expect to reap the benefits later. However, the situation of working class pupils is quite different. They know quite well that they are being prepared for a working life at a factory bench, typewriter or shop counter, and that they are not going to have a career. As a result many of them see no reason to play along with the dress rehearsal. Thus, the fact that working class pupils are expected to behave like middle class pupils, while at the same time not receiving any of the rewards for this behaviour, is the first source of these pupils' disengagement from their schools.

Most working class secondary modern pupils thus have a relatively weak attachment to the middle class values of the school culture. At the same time they recognize that certain sorts of knowledge can be useful in improving their ability to make the best of the situation. By the time they reach the third and fourth years therefore, most pupils will have arrived at an 'instrumental' attitude to school. Their view of education is utilitarian. Many teachers, on the other hand, regard education as being concerned with something more than the bread and butter of everyday life, and consequently they tend to see part of their task as the transmission of culture in the Arnoldian sense of the forms of knowledge—sensitivity and response developed by successive groups of the European intelligentsia. The actual selection from the available tradition and the production of new forms of knowledge is done by writers, publishers, examiners and university dons, but nevertheless, many teachers, particularly those trained in universities, feel themselves to be part of the chain, entrusted with the crucial task of making this tradition of valued knowledge available to all. The core of this 'selective tradition' is literature, for it is the major literary forms, drama, novels or lyric poems, more than anything else that are regarded as the major repositories of what F. R. Leavis has called ' the "picked experience of ages" regarding the finer issues of life'.[5] We therefore arrive at a situation in which pupils who want the school to teach them things they can perceive as being directly relevant and useful in their everyday life, are offered a curriculum which is still 'in general geared to the culture of the highly literate and sophisticated'.[6] The extent of these differences in perspective was brought out very clearly in the results of the Schools Council enquiry into early leaving. Respondents were asked to say which of various school objectives were very important to them. Table 20 sets out the answer for 'studying poetry' and 'learning things which will be of direct use to you in your job'.

Table 20[7]   Relative importance of school objectives (in percentages)

	Poetry	Direct use
Headmaster	32	14
Teachers	20	33
Parents of 15-year- old boy leavers	7	79
15-year-old boy leavers	4	81

It is obvious from these figures that the vast majority of early leavers (who are overwhelmingly working class) have a predominantly 'instrumental' attitude towards school which is very largely supported by their parents. It is also equally obvious that a number of headmasters (32%) and also teachers (20%) give 'instrumental' aims the lowest priority and maintain a considerable residual attachment to 'cultural' pursuits such as studying poetry. This gap between what most working class pupils want the school to teach them and what many teachers feel they ought to be taught is the second source of working class pupils' disengagement.

So far the source of working class pupils' disengagement from school has been considered, but there is a third factor which affects all pupils simply by virtue of the fact that they are adolescents. This is the question of how schools come to terms with adolescents' emotional and sexual development. All schools are basically concerned with preparing pupils for the world of work, not for the world of leisure, and consequently all schooling is based on the central value of deferred gratification, preparing for the future rather than seeking fulfilment in the present. The emphasis is on cognitive skills and self control, and therefore most forms of emotional and physical expression are either penalized (e.g. swearing, fighting and sexual behaviour) or else carefully regulated and controlled through such devices as school uniforms, supervised games periods and segregated play areas for girls and boys. The research reported by J. M. Tanner, however, clearly indicates that during their thirteenth and fourteenth year (i.e. the third year of secondary school) most adolescents are reaching a crucial stage in their sexual and physical maturation, and that consequently the question of emotional and physical expression becomes extremely important to them.

Girls are likely to have experienced the onset of menstruation somewhere about the age of thirteen[8] and, consequently, during their third year they will be coming to terms with their awakening consciousness of themselves as physically mature and sexually desirable. But it is exactly this awareness that is suppressed by the social organization and official culture of the school, as the regulations attaching to school uniforms demonstrate. Whereas teenage fashion clothes serve as expressions of individuality and sexuality, 'projections of our fantasy selves . . . our weapon, our challenges, our visible insults'[9], uniforms serve to deny these functions and to enforce conformity. Most schools in this study, therefore, had rules such as the following, taken from the school rules at Minedale:

The scale of clothing approved by the Governors is useful and modest. School uniform sets the right tone for a school and *prevents individuals from attracting attention to themselves.* (our italics)

Sexual maturation in boys is not marked by a single dramatic event and consequently the height/growth spurt and associated development of physical abilities which occurs around the age of fourteen, tends to assume a more central place in boys' consciousness.[10] Again, in various ways, these growing physical capacities are either suppressed or carefully controlled. Most desks, for example, are designed for 'children' so that many third year boys begin to find it physically frustrating to sit for hours on end at desks that no longer comfortably accommodate them. Nor do school-sponsored sports necessarily provide an expressive outlet, for as Start has shown, pupils who play for the school teams tend also to accept the academic pupil role so that sports become another manifestation of school culture.[11]

Secondary school pupils, particularly those in the third and fourth years, are therefore placed in a difficult position. On the one hand, the acceleration of the maturation process is constantly directing adolescents' attention to body changes and the attendant arousal of emotions, while on the other hand, the organization and culture of the school systematically emphasizes the development of mental capacities, the acquisition of intellectual skills and the necessity of self control and the deferment of gratification. At the same time, during their leisure time, pupils are exposed to cultural constellations which reverse the schools' priorities and stress the immediate and spontaneous gratification of physical and emotional needs.

This tension between the demands of the school and the experience of maturation is particularly acute among grammar school pupils and those at the top of comprehensives. These pupils are placed in a highly competitive situation in which they are expected consistently to display the academic and behavioural attributes of the 'good pupil', and this requires them to concentrate on intellect at the expense of emotion and to express their individuality through academic achievement. For some the strain and the cost of constantly having to achieve a higher and higher academic standard proves too much and they orientate themselves around their leisure pursuits which provide an outlet both for their expressiveness and their individuality. It is no coincidence that the majority of American 'Hippies' had been academically successful in their high school.[12] It is a reaction to living in an academic hot-house.

The third source of pupils' disengagement therefore arises from the fact that most schools make very little attempt to accommodate to or come to terms with their pupils' sexual and emotional development or their search for identity and personal expression. On the contrary, most schools try to exclude these aspects of adolescence, with the consequence that many pupils feel that the teachers do not really understand them and continue to treat them as children. This was a very common cause for complaint among the pupils interviewed.

School organization and the creation of anti-school peer groups

The three sources of alienation discussed above operate, either singly or in combination, to produce pupils who are to some extent disengaged from their schools and who orientate themselves around their out of school activities. Given the fact that these sources of alienation are experienced differentially by pupils from different social class backgrounds and in different types of school, within a particular school, the number of these alienated pupils and the extent and depth of their disengagement is by no means fixed. Rather, it can be controlled to some extent by the school's organization. In particular, the extent of pupils' non-commitment can be affected by the nature of the grouping system employed.

The way in which our study schools divided pupils into manageable teaching groups varied considerably, but beneath the apparent multiplicity of arrangements three basic grouping systems could be discerned. Under the first of these systems, *streaming*, pupils are allocated to a top, middle or bottom group on the basis of their academic ability, as assessed by internal school examinations. However, the same factors influence this internal selection procedure as influence the initial allocation to secondary modern or grammar schools. Consequently, pupils from middle class or skilled working class backgrounds tend to be over-represented among the upper streams, while those from lower working class homes tend to gravitate towards the lower streams.[13] As Brian Jackson put it, streaming is a miniature reproduction within the school of the general structure of the wider education system.[14] The essentially hierarchical nature of this arrangement is often indicated by calling the top group 3A, the middle group 3B and so on, down to the last group. Nor are these categories simply nominal—indeed they often have a very real organizational reality in the sense that pupils in the bottom streams are treated differently from those in the middle and top streams. They may have fewer privileges; for example, they may not take such a large range of subjects and they may be taught by the inexperienced and inadequate teachers. As both Colin Lacey and David Hargreaves have pointed out, these factors tend to reinforce the low-stream pupils' sense of being failures and lead them to have a low commitment to school. Some of our schools, such as Brownhill, recognized this process and attempted to alleviate it by designating the groups according to the initials of the form teacher's name, on the assumption that the children would not recognize the hierarchical nature of the arrangement. The differentials in the distribution of rewards, prestige and privileges however remained unaltered, and consequently there were considerable differences in the level of commitment of pupils in the top and bottom streams (19·3 as against 13·8). The second grouping system, *creaming*, is a variation on streaming, in which the top ability group is 'creamed off' and groomed as an 'express' stream who will sit their GCE or CSE examinations a year early, while the remainder of the pupils are allocated to mixed ability groupings. Finally, three of our schools made no attempt to stream or cream their pupils, and all third years were allocated to mixed ability groupings.

The level of commitment of third year pupils in the various sorts of ability groupings in our study schools are presented in Table 21. The figures in Table 21 suggest a clear and consistent pattern. In those schools which operate a streaming system, the level of commitment in the top streams is in all cases significantly higher than that of the middle and bottom streams. Similarly, in the 'creamed' schools the level of commitment among the pupils in the top streams is significantly higher than that of pupils in the mixed ability group-

Table 21   Third year pupils' mean school commitment scores: by school and ability grouping

Grouping system	School	Ability grouping			Signifi-cance level
		Top	Middle	Bottom	
Streaming	Brownhill	19·3	15·2		★★★
	(inner urban comprehensive)	19·3		13·8	★★★
	Churchgate	16·6	14·6		★
	(suburban modern)	16·6		14·2	★
	Middleton	15·1	13·1		★
	(inner urban modern)	15·1		13·1	★★★
	Minedale (rural modern)	15·1		11·0	★★★
Creaming		Top	Mixed		
	Woolton (inner urban grammar)	17·2	15·1		★
	Northlawns (suburban comprehensive)	15·8	12·2		★★
Mixed ability grouping		Mixed	Mixed		
	Park Road (surburban grammar)	15·4	15·1		NS
	Woodfields (rural comprehensive)	15·2	14·4		NS
	Dockstreet (inner urban modern)	15·3	14·0		NS

Notes: (1) All schools in the sample were assured of anonymity and consequently each has been given a fictitious name. The way in which the schools were selected is described in Appendix 2.

(2) Due to the very small year sizes at Peakside, all third year pupils were taught in one form, and consequently, there is no comparison group.

ings. However, in those schools where all the pupils are in mixed ability groupings, there are no significant differences between the levels of commitment of the various groups. These findings suggest that the more rigorously a school divides the pupils into academic successes and failures, the greater is the likely difference in the commitment levels of the various form groups. This fits in well with Colin Lacey's argument that the more rigorously a school differentiates between pupils on the basis of academic ability, the greater will be the extent of the polarization of pupils into those who are for school and those who are against.[15] The two inner urban secondary modern schools, Dockstreet and Middleton, provide an instructive example.

At Dockstreet, there were no statistically significant differences between the two third year groups used in the study (the mean scores were 15·1 and 15·4) whereas, at Middleton, the mean commitment of the bottom stream (13·1) was significantly lower than that of the top stream (15·1). What appears to have happened therefore, is that the streaming system operated at Middleton has created a 'lump' of alienated pupils in the bottom stream. This hypothesis was confirmed when we came to interview pupils in the two schools. There were of course pupils at Dockstreet who were disenchanted with school, but it was clear from our conversations with them that their alienation was far less complete than that experienced by their peers at Middleton who came from very similar circumstances and who faced almost identical employment prospects.

So far, pupils' disengagement has been discussed as though it were an entirely individualistic response to school experiences. Of course it is true that each pupil must decide for himself what his attitude to school will be, but in most cases this decision will be encouraged and supported by his friends. Therefore, when considering patterns of pupil disengagement, we are primarily concerned with a group phenomenon.

The school's organization largely determines the pattern of pupil peer groups by limiting both the nature and the range of the contacts between pupils. Thus, pupils tend to pick as their friends the people with whom they have most contact and whom they know best, which in effect means their form peers. In all the schools we studied, over 60% of the school friends nominated by pupils came from within the same form, which is in line with the findings of Julienne Ford, Colin Lacey and David Hargreaves.[16] There was no consistent pattern by type of school. Park Road, for example, had the most 'closed' system with 83% of friendship choices being confined to pupils in the same form, while the other grammar school, Woolton, was comparatively 'open' with only 63% of peer nominations coming from within the same form. But the type of grouping system did make a considerable difference. In streamed schools as a whole, 72% of peer choices were confined to the same form—as against 65% in both 'creamed' and unstreamed schools. Thus, it appears that the more rigidly a school sorts pupils into academic successes and failures, the more likely it is that pupils will pick their friends from among their peers in the same form.

Despite the fact that all our study schools were mixed, only about one pupil in ten included a member of the opposite sex among his school friends. Possible reasons for this might be that firstly, most of the schools actively discouraged contact between the sexes by means of such devices as segregated play areas. Secondly, the great majority of the boys themselves preferred single sex groups to mixed groups. Occasionally, girls were admitted to predominantly male peer groups, but mixing almost never seemed to occur the other way round. Such mixing as does take place, therefore, appears to be very much a question of girls being admitted to the boys' world on the boys' terms. Further, this situation was most likely to occur in secondary modern schools and least likely to occur in grammar schools. Romantic attachments do, of course, occur, but judging from the results of this study, they are comparatively rare. Having said that in all our study schools there was a complex network of tightly knit pupil peer groups existing beneath the official organization, it is now necessary to examine the relationship between the kinds of values, activities and roles supported by these peer groups and those sponsored by the school.

In a recent paper, Royston Lambert and his colleagues at the Dartington Research Unit have suggested that there are four basic sorts of relations possible between cultures of pupil peer groups in the school's 'official' culture. These relations they call: supportive, manipulative, passive and rejecting.[17] However, David Hargreaves, in his study of fourth year boys in a northern secondary modern school, has argued that despite the nuances and intermediate postures there were basically two main cultures among the pupil peer groups he studied. The first of these, an 'academic' culture led by the school captain, was supportive of the school's culture while the second was a 'delinquescent' culture led by the school's best fighter, which represented a rejection of the 'official' culture and an inversion of its values.[18] The fact that the school rejecting group at Lumley could be called 'delinquescent' does not, of course, mean that all school rejecting pupils are necessarily on the verge of delinquency. On the contrary, as will be argued presently, school rejectors are involved in a considerable variety of environmental cultures. Nevertheless, Hargreave's analysis provides a way of looking at the situation which had a general applicability and could be usefully employed in a number of our study schools.

Figure 2 represents the third year in a hypothetical streamed school. In line with our previous finding that school commitment decreases symmetrically by stream, Fig. 2 indicates that the proportion of pupils supporting the 'official' school culture also decreases as more and more pupils orientate themselves around one of the major environmental cultures. In the top stream the great majority of pupils are relatively highly committed to school and consequently the majority of the pupil peer groups support the 'official' school culture, and school rejection is confined to a very few. In the bottom stream the opposite situation prevails. The general level of school commitment is low and the majority of pupil peer groups reject the school culture. The middle stream is caught between these two poles and consequently the peer group cultures tend

Fig. 2 Diagrammatic representation of the relationship between the formal and informal school systems in the third year of a streamed school

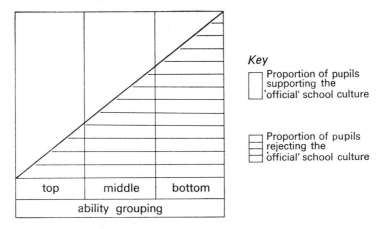

Key

☐ Proportion of pupils supporting the 'official' school culture

▤ Proportion of pupils rejecting the 'official' school culture

to be more or less equally divided between supporters and rejectors. This process is of course most marked in 'streamed' schools, but the results of this present study tend to indicate that it is also evident in 'creamed' schools.

So far it has been argued that a certain proportion of pupil peer groups, especially those in low streams, are likely to reject the assumptions of the school culture and orientate themselves around activities, roles and values drawn from one or other of the main environmental cultures. Having said this, the question arises as to how these peer groups manage to maintain an anti-school culture within the school, given that the school is making considerable efforts to instill in them the values of the 'official' school culture; but of course pupils in school are never entirely cut off from environmental cultures. Recent research has suggested that interest in pop music and a knowledge of the current Top Twenty may play an important part in initiating and cementing friendships between pupils[19] and, although we have no direct evidence, it seems reasonable to suppose that this may also apply to other aspects of leisure activity such as football, motorbikes and fashion. A shared interest in a particular part of the environmental culture may therefore form the basis for a school peer group. In many cases the links between school peer groups and the social context of outside leisure activities are strengthened by the fact that there is often a considerable overlap between the friends a pupil has in school and those with whom he spends his leisure time.

With the exception of pupils in comprehensive schools, the proportion of school friends who are also friends outside school is consistently around 50%. The somewhat higher percentages among comprehensive school pupils

Table 22 Percentages of out of school friends coming from the same school: third years by sex and type of school

| | Type of school | | |
	Grammar	Comprehensive	Sec. modern
Boys	46% ($n = 61$)	61% ($n = 90$)	48% ($n = 140$)
Girls	51% ($n = 67$)	57% ($n = 102$)	52% ($n = 143$)
Total	48% ($n = 128$)	59% ($n = 192$)	50% ($n = 283$)

can be easily explained by the fact that two of the comprehensive schools used in this study were neighbourhood schools which took almost all the children from a certain area, thereby considerably increasing the chances of overlap between school friends and friends outside.

This situation can present a considerable problem for the school. Not only are a number of pupil peer groups formed on the basis of patterns of meaning and expression derived from environmental cultures, but in some cases school time may become an extension of non-school time as individuals continue to act out their peer roles. The 'hard guy' role, for example, may not necessarily end when a pupil enters a classroom; indeed, exactly because the class is likely to include at least some of his outside school peers, the individual is subject to cross pressures. Either he must act in accordance with the teacher's expectations and play the 'good pupil' or he must conform to the expectations of his peers and play the 'hard guy'—he cannot do both. His choice will depend largely on three things: how committed he is to the school culture and to the pupil role, how much he values his position in his outside school peer group, and the general degree of support he is likely to receive from the rest of the form. As has been seen, working class pupils, together with those in secondary moderns and in low streams, are likely to have a relatively low commitment to the school, and consequently school rejectors who act out their peer roles are likely to receive support both from their immediate friends and from most of the rest of the class. This is one possible reason why these pupils are more likely to manifest their disengagement from school in overt behaviour. Middle class pupils, pupils in grammar schools and those in high streams, however, are likely to be faced with a somewhat different situation. In these cases the school rejecting group is likely to be in a minority and the general pupil culture is likely to be pro-school. Consequently, school rejectors may tend to conform outwardly to the pupil role when in class, and are not always seen as being a 'problem'. Nevertheless, the school is still failing to reach them.

Patterns of disengagement at Northlawns comprehensive

The situation at Northlawns, a large purpose-built comprehensive in a North London suburb, illustrates many of the points we have been making in this chapter.

Of the pupils for whom we could obtain information, the majority (75%) came from homes where the father had either a skilled manual job (43%), or else had a lower non-manual job (32%). There were, however, a minority of pupils from both ends of the social scale. Thus, the fathers of 11% of the pupils were employed in professional or managerial positions, and some were very highly paid indeed. A number were successful businessmen who owned their own firms and had moved up to the greener pastures of Northlawns. There was also a sprinkling of diplomats' children. These 'wealthy' families tend to live in an exclusive private development of detached houses. At the other end of the scale, 14% of the Northlawns pupils had fathers in semi-skilled or unskilled manual jobs with a relatively low income, and lived on the nearby council estate.

Technically, at Northlawns, only the top ability group were 'creamed' off and the remaining pupils were taught in mixed ability groupings. However, a number of teachers claimed that the system was a covert form of streaming in the sense that certain forms were regarded by both teachers and pupils as the lowest. Of these, 3N was seen as the bottom form. Given our previous argument about the class bias of selection procedures, it was not surprising to find that all but two of the 3N pupils came from the lower working class 'estate' group, and that the mean commitment level in the form was low (12·2). Conversely, it was no surprise to find that almost all the pupils in 3A, the 'express' stream, came from the wealthy upper middle class families and had a relatively high mean commitment (15·8). In short, the formal organization at Northlawns produced all the conditions necessary for the kind of polarization of pupils depicted in Fig. 2, and this was in fact what had happened.

The pupil peer group culture of 3N was dominated by a group of boys led by Johnny. His response to our initial questionnaire to pupils perfectly illustrates the dominant values of this group. At the end of our questionnaire, we asked the simple question; 'What class or form are you in at school?' The 'official' answer to this was 3N, but Johnny wrote, 'the toughest, of course. We are the boot boys.' That is, he refused to see his form in terms of the school's label as the bottom non-examination stream, and instead he described it in terms of the central value of the peer group culture, its ability to beat other forms in fights. Membership of this group, and his own reputation as a 'hard nut' provided him with a source of self esteem and a view of the school which was completely independent of the 'official culture's' stress on intellectual attainment. The pivot of his particular pattern of meaning and explanation was his membership of the 'boot boys', a large and loosely structured group centred on support for the local football team. Johnny's anti-school values were supported, in varying degrees, by all but two of the rest of the form. Significantly, these two were both from middle class families and consequently their commitment to the pupil role was encouraged and sustained by their parents, one of whom employed a private tutor to give his son extra tuition in mathematics and English language.

The situation in 3A was almost the complete reverse. Here the dominant pupil peer culture was supportive of the school's 'official' values and the great majority of pupils defined themselves principally in terms of the 'good pupil' role. For them leisure activities were secondary—something to engage in after the school's expectations concerning homework, participation in sports teams etc., had been met. For a closely knit group of three girls however, it was the other way round. All three had a very low commitment to school and wanted to leave directly after 'O' levels. Unlike the 3N group, however, they did not act out their disengagement openly within the school. They were well behaved and did the work necessary to pass the examinations. Nevertheless, they were 'mental drop-outs', in the sense that they orientated themselves not around the school but around their leisure time, which was centred on the boutiques and discotheques of London's West End. For them, school was a necessary but regrettable interruption to the real business of 'living'.*

Towards the leisure environment

The example of these two Northlawns groups illustrates the very important point that pupils with a low commitment to school are involved in several distinctly different sorts of leisure environment, and that these differences are related to their social class background, to the kind of neighbourhood they live in, and to their sex. In fact, the two Northlawns groups point to the existence of two major 'environmental cultures', each of which provides meanings, values and forms of expression which pupils may draw upon as a way of articulating their disengagement from the culture of their schools. The first of the cultural constellations is provided by the *pop media*, and the second is provided by the *street culture* of the working class neighbourhood.

* This group is described in more detail in Chapter 10.

Fig. 3 Values transmitted by the pop media contrasted with those sponsored by the school

Values sponsored by the school	Values transmitted by the pop media
work/production preparing for the future mind/intellect self control	play/consumption living in the present body/emotion/feeling physical and emotional expression

From Figure 3 it is evident that the aspects of life which are emphasized by the pop media are those which are devalued or ignored within the schools In the first place, the pop media prepare adolescents for their future role as consumers by introducing them to the notion of continuous and conspicuous consumption. Given that the continued viability of the present production system depends upon a high level of consumption, this aspect of the pop media could be considered as a logical complement to the rehearsal for work roles sponsored by the schools. Secondly, the pop media provide adolescents with a variety of ways of coming to terms with and expressing their developing emotional and physical capacities. To this extent they could be considered a safety valve. However, many teachers regard the situation very differently. They see themselves as responsible for handing on the culture of the 'selective tradition' and in particular, for instilling in their pupils an appreciation of the 'picked experience of the ages', encapsulated in works of literature. Consequently, they see the means of articulation and expression offered by the pop media as a direct threat, and they react with hostility. It is exactly this element of hostility, that makes involvement in the pop media a potential means through which pupils can articulate their disengagement from their schools. If a pupil knows that a particular teacher regards pop music as a series of disgusting sounds, then pasting a picture of a pop star on the front of the appropriate exercise book becomes far more than a gratuitious decoration, it becomes an act of refusal. But the relationship between involvement in pop and commitment to school is by no means a simple matter of either/or. Even though the pop media provide a potential source of oppositional meanings and expressions, it does not necessarily follow that all pupils will make use of this potential.

One of the questions on our first pupil questionnaire asked respondents to list as many records as they could that were in the current top twenty best selling 'single' records of that week. In order to possess this knowledge a pupil would have to have had recent contact with a range of pop based media such as pop radio and teenage magazines. It was therefore reasonable to suppose that a good knowledge of the current hit records was an indicator of a high involvement in pop.* For each form, the resulting scores were ranked and divided into three equal groups—high, medium and low. The same procedure was carried out independently with the school commitment scores derived from the attitude scale. This procedure produced nine possible relationships between school commitment and pop involvement. Leaving aside the 'medium' categories we arrive at the four basic relationships depicted in Fig. 4.†

Fig. 4 Relationships between school commitment and pop involvement

	School commitment	
Pop involvement	High	Low
Low	Group 1	Group 4
High	Group 2	Group 3

A considerable number of middle class pupils in grammar schools and in the top streams of comprehensives (as in the case of 3A at Northlawns) come within *Group 1*. They have a high commitment to their schools and define themselvs principally in terms of the 'good pupil' role, with its stress on individual academic achievement and 'conformist' behaviour. Much of their spare time is taken up with homework and they are significantly more likely than other pupils to be members of a school club or society or to play for a school team. Any time not occupied in school-sponsored activities is likely to be taken up with pursuits such as stamp collecting, astronomy, aero-modelling and reading, which receive the school's approval. They take little interest in the world of pop.

The pupils in *Group 2* also have a high commitment to school, but unlike the 'swots' of Group 1, they are also involved in various areas of pop. They put the demands of the school first, but after they have done their homework and turned out for the school team, they are quite likely to go dancing or listen to records. Through their involvement in these pop-based leisure activities they are able to explore and come to terms with these areas of personal development which the school does little to cater for. In particular, pop provides a useful medium through which to explore the problem of constructing and managing a viable sexual and emotional identity. In this instance, therefore, pop provides a complement to the school's emphasis on the development of intellectual ability. It represents a way of managing the tensions generated by the school's expectation that they should continually improve their level of academic attainment. Perhaps not surprisingly, the Group 2 pupils are drawn from the same backgrounds as those in Group 1.

* This measure is discussed in more detail in Appendix 3.
† This procedure is described in more detail in Appendix 2.

For the pupils in *Group 3*, the activities and forms of expression provided by the pop media represent an alternative rather than a supplement to those sponsored by the school. The trio of 3A girls at Northlawns discussed above fall within this category.

The school-rejecting boys of 3N at Northlawns provide an illustration of the final grouping, *Group 4*. Like the Group 3 pupils these boys had a low commitment to school, but unlike them they were not involved in pop-based activities to any great extent. Although they had the necessary money, their leisure activities were centred, not on the West End discotheques and boutiques, but on the streets, parks and cafés of their local neighbourhood. Certainly, they took an interest in the latest records and in new fashions, and they sometimes went dancing. But, and this is the crucial point, their basic values— group solidarity, physical skill, and 'hardness'—were derived from the wider values of their neighbourhood and not from the pop media. The 'pop media' have in fact overlaid the adolescent 'street cultures' of the local area and, although the pop media extend the range of meanings and expressions available to these youngsters, they do not obliterate or replace these locally rooted patterns.

Pupils from predominantly middle class and suburban areas such as Park Road do not have ready access to street culture activities, both because there are generally fewer meeting places, such as cafés or fish and chip shops, and also because parents and neighbours in these areas do not usually consider the streets an appropriate leisure milieu. (Suburban streets usually contain a number of carefully tended front gardens which are likely to get damaged during a game of scratch football.) Thus, pupils in these areas might be more likely to orientate themselves around pop based activities, such as listening to pop records—which can be engaged in at home—or going dancing, which requires a visit to a dance or disco; they are less likely to spend time in the local streets.

In the case of girls, opportunities to engage in street culture activities are further restricted by the fact that the majority of third year boys (72%) preferred to go around in an all male peer group. The remaining 28%, however, appear to be more open, and quite often half the members are girls. Altogether 48% of third year girls claimed to belong to a mixed group. Generally then, about half the girls (52%) are members of all girl groups and the other half (48%) gravitate towards the relatively few boys' groups who will accept them as members, or else become 'hangers on' of a male group to be occasionally incorporated into activities more or less on sufferance.

The evidence from Northlawns therefore clearly indicates that access to the values and activities supported by neighbourhood street cultures is differentiated firstly by social class and area of residence, and secondly by sex. Generalizing from these results we can suggest that of those not committed to the school-sponsored values the groups most involved in the pop media culture will be those who have the least opportunity to participate in local street cultures. In other words, there is a more or less inverse relationship between involvement in pop and access to street cultures. Thus, we might expect that middle class girls would be the most pop oriented group and working class boys the least, with middle class boys and working class girls occupying intermediate positions between the two.

However, not all working class boys with a low school commitment necessarily participate in the neighbourhood street cultures. Some who find difficulty in making friends and have little rapport with their brothers and sisters gravitate towards activities which can be pursued alone. This sort of individualistic response is very well illustrated by the case of Billy Caspar, in Ken Loach's film, *Kes*. Billy is totally at odds with the school and yet he has almost nothing in common with his older brother and is very much on the margins of the local peer groups. Consequently, he immerses himself in training a kestrel, an activity which totally absorbs his interest and provides him with a source of self esteem and a coherent set of values.

In this chapter it has been argued that schools place children from different social class backgrounds in situations where they experience varying amounts and types of strain, and that their responses to their situation cannot be understood without an analysis of their leisure environments. The next chapter is therefore devoted to examining pupils' leisure-time activities in greater detail.

References

1 Little, A. and Westergaard, J. H., 1964 'The Trend of Class Differentials in Educational Opportunity in England and Wales' *The British Journal of Sociology* Vol. 15, No. 4, pp. 301–16.

2 The dilemma of working class pupils at grammar schools has been graphically described in: Richard Hoggart, 1957 op. cit., and in Jackson, Brian and Marsden, Denis, 1962 *Education and the Working Class* London, Routledge and Kegan Paul.

3 Dale, R. R. and Griffith, S., 1965 *Downstream* London, Routledge and Kegan Paul.

4 Stevens, Francis, 1960 *The Living Tradition* London, Hutchinson; Musgrove, F. and Taylor, 1969 *Society and the Teachers' Role* London, Routledge and Kegan Paul.

5 Leavis, F. R., and Thompson, Denys, 1933 *Culture and Environment: The Training of Critical Awareness* London, Chatto and Windus, 1942 ed., p. 81.

6 Bantock, G. H., 1968 *Culture, Industrialization and Education* London, Routledge and Kegan Paul, p. 23.

7 Williams, Roma Morton and Finch, Stewart, 1968 *Schools Council Enquiry I Young School Leavers* London, HMSO, Figs. 1, 3 and 5, pp. 33, 39 and 42. (adaptation).

8 Tanner, J. M., 1961 'The Course of Children's Growth' in: R. E. Grinder ed. 1969, *Studies in Adolescence* London, Collier-Macmillan, p. 445.

9 Carter, Angela, 1967 'Notes for a Theory of Sixties Style', *New Society* December 14, p. 866.

10 Tanner, J. M., op. cit., pp. 434–5.

11 Start, K. B., 1966 'Substitution of Games Performance for Academic Achievement as a Means of Achieving Status among Secondary School Pupils' *The British Journal of Sociology* Vol. 17, No. 3, pp. 300–305.

12   Yablonsky, Lewis, 1968 *The Hippie Trip* New York, Pegasus, p. 344.

13   Partridge, John, 1968 *Life in a Secondary Modern School* Harmondsworth, Penguin Books, Chapter 5.

14   Jackson, Brian, 1964 *Streaming: An Education System in Miniature* London, Routledge and Kegan Paul.

15   Lacey, Colin, 1966 'Some Sociological Concomitants of Academic Streaming in the Grammar School' *British Journal of Sociology* Vol. 17, pp. 245–62.

16   Ford, Julienne, 1969 *Social Class and the Comprehensive School* London, Routledge and Kegan Paul, p. 38. See also Lacey, Colin, 1966, op. cit. and Hargreaves, David, 1967 *Social Relations in a Secondary School* London, Routledge and Kegan Paul, p. 7.

17   Lambert, Royston, et al. *The Informal Social System: An Example of the Limitations of Organizational Analysis* Paper presented at the British Sociological Association Annual Conference, 1970, p. 6.

18   Hargreaves, David, op. cit.

19   Brown, Roger and O'Leary, Michael, 1971 'Pop Music in an English Secondary School System *American Behavioral Scientist* Vol. 14, No. 3, pp. 401–13.

7 Pupils out of school: spending spare time

The social context: pupils' spare time companions

At the beginning of the interview, pupils were asked to say how they had spent the last Friday and Saturday evenings and the replies showed that about half had stayed at home on each evening and half had gone out (46% on Friday evening and 48% on Saturday evening). Interviewees were then asked to say who had been with them on each occasion. The replies to this question, shown in Table 23, indicate that a good deal of their non-school time was spent either with parents or with friends.

Table 23 The leisure time companions of fourth year pupils (Figures in percentages)

	Friday night	Saturday night
Alone	18%	14%
With parents	25%	29%
With brothers or sisters	20%	19%
With one friend	16%	18%
With a boy friend or girl friend	6%	10%
With a group of friends	33%	25%
n	167	167

Note: The response categories are not mutually exclusive because pupils were asked to note all the people who were with them on each occasion. Consequently, the percentages do not add up to 100.

Table 23 shows that, whereas over half of the pupils who answered the question mentioned being with one or more friends on both nights (55% on Friday and 53% on Saturday), only 25% and 29% respectively mentioned being with parents.

From these figures it appears that, on the two major weekend nights traditionally set aside for leisure, pupils are more likely to spend their time with their friends than with their parents. It is tempting to conclude from these figures that pupils who go out are likely to be with their friends, whereas those who stay in are likely to be with their parents. However, as the figures in Table 24 indicate, such a conclusion would be a considerable oversimplification.

Table 24 Proportion of leisure time spent with parents or friends

| | Pupils who went out | | Pupils who stayed in | |
	on Friday evening	on Saturday evening	on Friday evening	on Saturday evening
Percentage mentioning being with parents	6%	10%	39%	46%
Percentage mentioning being with friends	71%	85%	29%	24%
n	77	80	90	87

The figures in Table 24 suggest that, although the great majority of pupils who went out on Friday and/or Saturday night went out with friends, it is not the case that a comparable majority of those who stayed in spent their time in the company of their parents and, in fact, on both nights a substantial minority of those who stayed at home were with their friends. Thus peers not only appear to provide the most frequent social context for pupils' outside leisure activities, they also have a substantial foothold in the home. This foothold is particularly evident in the case of home based pop media activities. When interviewees were asked with whom they usually watched *Top of the Pops* for example, 22% mentioned parents and 19% friends. In reply to a similar question for listening to pop music on the radio, the proportions were almost equal, 11% mentioning parents and 12% friends. In the case of listening to pop records at home, however, 43% said that they listened with friends and only 2% mentioned parents. Thus, although this latter activity takes place in the home, the social context in this case tends to be provided by friends rather than parents.

The fact that a great deal of pupils' leisure time is spent in the company of friends does not necessarily mean that they get on badly with their parents or are rebelling against them. In fact, as measured by the frequency with which pupils disagree with their parents over various issues concerned with their school life and leisure, the great majority of pupils seem to have quite amicable relationships with their parents. Table 4.2 in Appendix 4 indicates that the level of disagreement between pupils and their parents is generally low (the highest mean score being 9·7 out of a possible 22). It is also remarkably stable, both as regards age and social class. The only statistically significant differences occur in the third year where the difference between boys and girls in both the middle and lower working class groups reaches the 5% level of significance, boys having higher mean disagreement scores in each case. However, these differences are still relatively small, the lowest score being 8·4 and the highest 10·5.

The general pattern of our present findings fits in quite well with recent American research into the relative influence of parents and peers on adolescents' decision about various aspects of their life. Taken together, this research tends to indicate that parents and peers are not direct competitors, but rather that their competence is acknowledged in different areas. The studies reported by Brittain and Kandel, for example, suggest that although peers provide pupils with their dominant reference group in areas such as deciding what new clothes to buy, when it comes to major decisions such as whether to stay on at school, it is the parents who are the more influential.[1] Unfortunately, we do not have any evidence on this last area, but our findings concerning the way in which pupils choose their non-school clothes tend to bear out the American research. When third year interviewees were asked to say where they got their fashion ideas, 41% mentioned seeing what their friends were wearing, 48% said they went window shopping with friends, and only 3% mentioned their parents. When they actually went to buy something, however, parental influences increased somewhat. Thus, 53% said that their mother usually came with them to the shop, but 72% said that one or more friends were with them.

It therefore appears that pupils tend to see their parents and their friends as constituting two relatively independent reference groups, each with its own sphere of competence and influence. It is also clear, however, that when we are talking about pupils' leisure activities and about the influence of the pop media, we are essentially talking about the sphere of influence of the peer group. Before we look at the ways in which various groups spend their spare time, we must first examine the influence of one very important factor—money. Lack of money severely restricts the leisure activities available to adolescents, and therefore exerts a strong influence on the way in which they spend their non-school time. Many of the leisure activities which teenagers enjoy are far from cheap and can quickly swallow up a 50p a week budget. Here are a few examples of prices at the time the fieldwork was done:

Buying a 45 r.p.m. record—50p
Buying a long-playing record—£2·15
Going to a cinema—25 to 60p
Entrance to a discotheque—20p upwards
Entrance to a dance hall—30p upwards
Buying *Jackie* magazine—3½p
Buying *Shoot* magazine—6p
Going to a football match—20p to 30p

Prices like these mean that young people must be very selective indeed and choose carefully between the many options before they lay down their money.

The myth of the 'affluent teenager'

The concept of the 'affluent teenager' is largely derived from a study carried out in the late 'fifties[2], which estimated that young people represented about £900 millions a year of uncommitted spending power. However, this figure is very misleading, for the study defined 'teenagers' as all unmarried people between the ages of 15 and 25. Since about 85% of all those who fall into this category are wage or salary earners, the actual spending power of those who are not in employment will be very much lower than the average, which was calculated to be about £4 a head. In fact, the study guessed that pocket-money for the 800 000 non-employed teenagers would be about £1, but even this modest sum may be an overestimate. Certainly school-age teenagers today tend to receive considerably less than this, as several recent studies have demonstrated. Two surveys of northern towns have shown that pupils there are very far from affluent. A study of 15-year-old school leavers in Sheffield at the end of the fifties found that 63% of boys and 83% of girls had a weekly income of less than 50p, while a quarter of the boys and almost half the girls were getting under 25p.[3] Only 6 children in the whole sample of 200 were given more than £1 pocket money each week. Another study carried out in Bury, Lancashire, in 1962 found that children's spending power was very limited. 89% of 14-year-olds spent less than 50p each week and none spent more than £1.[4] Our own findings suggest that children are only slightly better off than they were a few years ago and that the majority still receive less than 50p a week from their parents.* Only 38% of third form pupils in our sample were given 50p or more spending money by their parents. Column 1 in Table 4.4, Appendix 4, indicates that rural and grammar school pupils tend to come off worst in this respect. One possible explanation is that parents of grammar school pupils are generally more anxious that their children should concentrate on their studies and that the restriction of spending power is used as a simple and effective means of curtailing participation in the many forms of leisure activity which require money. The low level of pocket money in the rural schools may be related to the generally low level of parental income in these areas.

A number of children supplement their pocket money with earnings from part-time employment. A study of fourth year secondary pupils in an inner urban secondary modern in the Midlands, for example, found that 51% had an income of this sort,[5] while a more recent survey of a similar school in the

---

* It is likely that some children supplement their regular pocket money with occasional extra spending money, so that these figures may slightly underestimate total spending power.

North found that, depending on stream, between 26% and 54% of pupils had part-time jobs.[6] Our overall figure, 27%, is rather low by these standards, but refers to third year pupils instead of the slightly older group of the earlier studies. Furthermore, as column 2 of Table 4.4. indicates, pupils in the secondary modern schools in our sample were more likely to have jobs than those in other types of school, particularly those in grammar schools. Secondary modern, and to some extent comprehensive school pupils not only tend to have more pocket money, therefore, but a greater proportion of them also have another source of income outside the family. In addition, as column 3 in Table 4.4. indicates, these children are more likely to earn relatively large sums from their jobs. Pupils from three schools in particular have a high overall discretionary spending power. Two of these are inner urban secondary modern schools (Middleton and Dock Street) and the third is a suburban comprehensive (Northlawns). All three are in areas of high wages (London and the Midlands) relative to the north or rural areas where the other schools are located.

It might be thought that social class would be an important factor with regard to the amount of pocket money that parents give their children, but Table 25 suggests that this is not the case. Class seems to bear little relationship to pocket money, but it does seem to influence the likelihood of young people having spare time employment. Working class adolescents are more likely to have a job, and are also more likely than their middle class peers to earn more than £1 per week. Middle class girls in particular earn very little. In sum it appears that working class children have rather more spending power than middle class children, but only because they are able to earn it. Even the working class children, however, can hardly be called affluent. Of the 634 third year pupils in our sample, only 11 received more than £1·25 pocket money weekly, and of these only 4 were given more than £2. In addition, only 9 children managed to earn over £2 a week, so that the vast majority have very limited financial resources.

Table 25   Pocket money and part time earnings of third year pupils by sex and class

	Boys		Girls		
	Middle class	Working class	Middle class	Working class	
% receiving 50p or more pocket money each week	35%	35%	44%	42%	n = 634
% having a part-time job	29%	35%	20%	25%	n = 634
% of those with a part-time job who earn over £1 each week	33%	48%	24%	49%	n = 170

Table 26 Principal spare time activities of fourth year pupils (Percentages are marked wherever they are 8% or more of the sample)

	Activity	Last night	Last Friday evening	Last Saturday Morning	Last Saturday Afternoon	Last Saturday Evening	Last Sunday Morning	Last Sunday Afternoon	Last Sunday Evening
School or family oriented activities	Doing homework	23%	14%				9%	9%	9%
	Routine Family errands		8%	22%	10%		37%	9%	
	Watching television	32%	35%	16%		35%		27%	41%
	Listening to records		13%			10%			
	Shopping for self			17%	18%				
Peer group oriented activities	Visiting friends		8%			10%		8%	
	Out on the streets	8%			8%	10%			10%
	Going to a dance or discotheque	8%				9%			

n = 167

The general pattern of leisure activities

Given their financial limitations, most pupils must be content to spend most of their time doing things that are free. This is indicated in Table 26 which shows the activities pupils mentioned most often. This material is derived from the series of questions in our interviews where pupils were asked to say how they spent their time during the weekend preceding the interview and on the night immediately before the day on which the interview took place. The table shows the most frequent responses of our fourth form sample, the figures indicating the times when 8% or more of the sample were taking part in these activities.* Although two activities ('shopping for self' and 'listening to records') imply either prior expenditure or preparation for future purchases, the primary characteristic of these eight ways of spending spare time is that they cost little or nothing.

A distinction should be made clear at this point between 'spare time' and 'leisure'. The former may be defined as referring to all the time that is not taken up with school. However, not all of this spare time is totally 'free' as young people usually have a number of obligations to their family and these may consume a good deal of their time. In Table 26, the categories 'routine'—which involves helping around the house and various types of chore—and 'family errands' both figure prominently. Many children also have to spend a certain amount of time doing their homework which, as we shall see, is a prominent feature in the lives of grammar school pupils. Only the time that remains after these 'compulsory' jobs have been done can be truly considered as leisure time. As our table indicates, when the adolescent is free to do what he wants, he is likely to choose peer group oriented activities rather than activities based on the home. Only television, the great provider of free entertainment, challenges the dominance of activities that either include physical involvement in the group, such as visiting friends, hanging around in the streets or doing personal shopping (nearly always with a friend or group of friends), or that are based on peer group values such as listening to records. A number of other peer-oriented activities were mentioned although not often enough to be included in Table 26. These included going to the cinema (7% had been on the previous Saturday night), and playing unorganized sport, usually football (7% on Sunday afternoon). Most of these activities clearly fall into one or other of the two categories we have discussed earlier—'street culture' and 'pop media culture'. These alternative value systems and styles of life dominate the leisure time of many young people, although 'street culture' is confined largely

* Care must be taken in interpreting these findings, since questions like this that rely on detailed recall of past happenings are inevitably rather unreliable. Certain sorts of behaviour are more 'memorable' than others—we know, for instance, that our respondents spend a lot of time listening to the radio at weekends, yet this was hardly ever recalled as part of their weekend activities. While this may indicate the way that radio is used—largely as aural wallpaper—it means that we do not have a reliable estimate of how often the radio is turned on.

to working class teenagers, particularly boys. It is they who spend their time hanging around on street corners, joining the local 'bootboys' at the football match every other Saturday, and playing football themselves on the recreation ground or in empty streets. Nor can this be explained in terms of their being unable to afford to do anything else for, as we have seen, working class adolescents tend to have more money than their middle class peers. The explanation which we would suggest is in terms of the differing social situation of the two groups. We would suggest that activities such as mucking about in the local streets, playing scratch football or going to the local cafe or youth club are rooted in the general pattern of leisure in working class neighbourhoods, and that they might be seen partly as a logical extension of the patterns of childhood and partly as a rehearsal for the adult ambiance of the pub and the club. Middle class adolescents lack this situational base, and consequently they are more likely to gravitate towards leisure activities based on the pop media.

Many pop media activities do involve expenditure, however, and we have some evidence to indicate that they would probably figure more prominently in pupils' leisure activities if they had more money to spend. When we asked interviewees what they would do with a sudden windfall of £5, well over half said that they would spend it on peer-oriented activities connected with the pop media, such as buying clothes or records. A much smaller group elected to spend the money in ways unconnected with 'pop' such as buying equipment for hobbies or presents (4%). Just under a third thought that they would save all or part of the money, either for holidays (11%), for some other large purchase such as a record-player or a motor bike (4%) or with nothing

Table 27 How fourth year pupils would allocate a £5 windfall (figures in percentages)

Item	Boys	Girls	Total
Spending on 'pop' (pop records and fashion clothes)	46%	69%	58%
Other spending	22%	8%	15%
Save	31%	23%	27%
n =	79	88	167

specific in mind (18%). Table 27 shows the percentage of answers that fell into the three broad classifications and demonstrates clearly that a number of adolescents would like to be able to spend more money on items related to fashion and pop music.

The role of the mass media in leisure time

Although financial considerations are clearly limiting the money, and consequently the time, that is devoted to these media, adolescents nevertheless
spend a good deal of time in contact with some sort of 'pop'. Tables 4.5–8 in
Appendix 4 show the extent of this contact as indicated by the frequency with
which they go to discotheques or dances, buy pop records and listen to pop
music on the radio. Briefly, these tables indicate that over 40% of the third
year pupils have been out dancing in the month before they answered our
questionnaire, that over 30% buy at least one record a month, that over 60%
listen to pop radio for more than 2 hours over a weekend, and that over 30%
listen for more than 2 hours on an average weekday evening. These figures
point to the very considerable interest that the pop media hold for a large
number of children of this age. The children in our first year sample tend to
have less contact with pop, although this is partly explicable in terms of their
even poorer financial status. Money is also a constraint on certain of the third
year pupils. Grammar school children who, as has been seen, receive rather less
pocket money than their peers and have relatively few extra earnings, tend to
engage in those activities that demand expenditure less frequently than other
groups. They are less likely to go to dances and less likely to buy records than
pupils at comprehensive or secondary modern schools. However, this financial
constraint does not apply to radio listening. In fact, the chief problem here is
lack of easy access to a radio, and grammar school pupils are fortunate in this
respect, for a larger percentage of them than of other pupils possess their own
radios (Appendix 4, Table 4.9). Not surprisingly, therefore, grammar school
children spend more time listening to pop music on radio during the weekend
than other children (Appendix 4, Table 4.7). The same is not true of weekday
evenings, however, for a further constraint, homework, operates to limit the
time that grammar school children are able to spend in this way. As Table 4.10
in Appendix 4 shows, grammar school pupils not only have homework to do
on more days each week than their comprehensive or secondary modern school
comrades, but they also tend to take longer over it. As a result, some grammar
school pupils who would probably listen for four hours or more, are restricted
to 2 or 3 hours (Appendix 4, Table 4.8). In one way or another, then, children
from all types of school have some degree of contact with the pop media, but
the extent of this contact is affected by such factors as impecuniousness or
having homework.

The fact that pupils have contact with the pop-oriented sectors of the mass
media does not necessarily mean that they are involved in pop to any great
extent. Over 70% of the pupils interviewed, for example, said that they quite
often had the radio on while they were doing something else such as eating
breakfast, helping around the house, or doing homework. In order to gain a
general impression of the extent of pupils' involvement in pop, they were

asked—as part of our original questionnaire—to write down the titles or performers of as many records as possible which were in the current Top Twenty list of best selling 'singles'. Possession of this knowledge presupposes that pupils have paid careful attention to selected radio and television programmes such as *Pick of the Pops* and *Top of the Pops* which give the current 'chart' in full. A pupil who used pop radio as a sort of 'aural wallpaper' or who was only a casual viewer of *Top of the Pops*, would be unlikely to know more than three or four titles. As far as could be ascertained, pupils' scores on this question were not related to factors such as intelligence, memory or general writing ability and consequently one can be reasonably sure that differences in the scores do in fact indicate real differences in knowledge and hence involvement.*

Table 28 Mean number of Top Twenty records recalled by third year pupils: by sex and social class

	All pupils	Social class Middle	Skilled working	Unskilled working	Significance level
Girls	9·6	11·4	9·4		**
		11·4		7·3	**
Boys	6·1	6·5	6·2		*
		6·5		5·3	**
Significance level	**	**	**	**	

Table 28 indicates that the extent of pupils' knowledge of the current Top Twenty depends both upon sex and social class. Middle class pupils are more familiar with the best selling records of the moment than either group of working class children, and within each social class, girls are more knowledgeable than boys. Further, these two factors appear to reinforce each other so that middle class girls are the best informed and are familiar with over half the records in the current chart at any one time, while working class boys are the least informed and know only a quarter of the Top Twenty. If pupils are further subdivided on the basis of the type of school which they attend, even greater differences are revealed. Thus, whereas middle class grammar school girls can recall an average of 13·7 titles, working class secondary modern school boys know only 4·7. These differences can be seen as a reflection of these children's access to street cultures. Because working class secondary modern boys have the greatest access, they will have only a limited involvement in pop. Conversely, because they have little or no access to the masculine peer group

* This item is discussed in detail in Appendix 3.

M.S.—4*

cultures of the city streets, middle class grammar school girls will tend to immerse themselves in the other main area of adolescent leisure, the pop media.

Another indication of the degree to which pupils are involved in the pop media is provided by their familiarity with pop argot*—words which have a particular meaning in the context of pop. We presented interviewees with a dozen of these argot words drawn from disc jockeys' patter and from pop magazines, and asked them to explain their meaning. The results again indicated that grammar school pupils were able to give more correct definitions than either comprehensive or secondary modern children (7·1 as against 6·0 and 4·3 respectively) and middle class children more than those from lower working class homes (6·8 and 5·1 respectively). Although these differences are in the same direction as those revealed by the Top Twenty scores, they are not nearly so dramatic. However, this is scarcely surprising since the commoner pop argot expressions such as DJ, flip and LP have had a very general and comparatively long established currency, whereas knowledge of the current Top Twenty records is much more limited, both in terms of time and place. Almost anyone even casually listening to Radio 1 would hear at least four or five of the commoner argot expressions in the space of an hour or so, but the full current chart is only given at particular times. Hence, listening must be both more selective and more involved.

Television presents a very different case. It is not essentially a pop medium, although certain programmes may display a pop style. Pop music itself is given very little time on television, although *Top of the Pops* is a favourite programme for many children. Watching television is essentially a family based activity, and consequently patterns of viewing tend to differ considerably from patterns of participation in the peer-oriented pop media. Unlike the pop media, the two principal predictors of the amount of time spent with television are type of school and social class. Table 4.11, in Appendix 4, indicates that grammar school children watch less than comprehensive or secondary modern school pupils; as they have more homework, they have less time available to watch television. Only 17% of the third year pupils at the suburban grammar school claimed to watch for four hours or more, as against 60% of the third year pupils at the two inner urban secondary modern schools. This finding is part of a stronger and more general relationship between the amount of television viewed and social class in that, whereas 40% of pupils from lower working class homes claim to watch four hours or more of television on an average weekday evening (when they are not going out), the corresponding proportion for upper working class pupils is 35%, and for middle class pupils 25%. The most fundamental explanation for this pattern lies in differing amenities in the home. In many working class homes the television occupies a central position in the only living room, so that—if they are going to spend the evening at

* This item is discussed in Appendix 3.

home—many working class children have little option but to watch whenever and whatever their parents choose. Middle class children, in contrast, may have another living room and very often their own room as well to which they can retire if they wish to avoid watching television. Secondly, parental pressure to restrict viewing is likely to be stronger in middle class homes because middle class parents generally keep their children under closer supervision and because they more often consider television as a potential danger, a distraction from 'worthier' occupations such as reading or hobbies.

Essentially our findings about the media consumption patterns of young people are in line with the discoveries of others. The television viewing habits were similar to those outlined by earlier researchers in this country and in America.[7] A study of secondary modern school children in 1964 had pointed to the growing interest in pop music, with 87% of 750 pupils saying that they liked it 'very much' and a further 12% liking it 'a little'.[8] That study found a marked growth of interest at age 13, and the 13–14 year olds in our group were certainly much more involved in pop than our younger respondents. A recent British study had demonstrated the attraction of dancing for young people, particularly girls, and comparison with an earlier investigation[9] suggests that there has been an increase of interest in dancing since the mid-fifties, coinciding with the rise of rock and roll. While British surveys of the late fifties tended to find very little radio listening, American studies suggested that radio had adopted a new function as a provider of pop music and had again become very popular amongst teenagers. The present study provides evidence that this adaptation in face of the competition of television has now taken place in this country and that consequently certain radio channels have become primarily a pop medium and attract a considerable number of adolescent listeners.

A general review of the media consumption of young people, as has been attempted here, is valuable as a rough guide to teenage leisure behaviour, but it tends to obscure the activities of sub-groups within the total sample. In the last chapter it was argued that both the range and extent of pupils' media usage will vary depending on their commitment to school and their orientation to the pop media, and four groups were distinguished, each of which reacts to school and to pop in a different way. A brief examination of the out of school activities of children in these four groups will illustrate the extent to which these various attitudes to school and the pop media are associated with different leisure patterns.

Not surprisingly, school based activities such as homework figure more prominently in the daily behaviour of children who are highly committed to the school and its values. Among our fourth year interviewees, 28% of those children highly committed to school had done some homework on the weekday evening before the interview, compared to only 17% of those not so committed. However, degree of orientation to the pop media also appears to be a factor, for only 16% of pop-oriented children had done some homework compared to 30% of those not so oriented. Table 29 shows the proportions of children in each of our four groups who had done some homework. Children in Group 1 were more likely than others to have done homework, while children in Group 3 had only rarely done any. The fact that Groups 2 and 4 lie midway between the two polar groups indicates that high commitment to school in itself does not necessarily mean that a pupil will spend a lot of spare time on homework, and that the competing attractions of pop must also be taken into account. In fact, commitment to school and orientation to pop seem to play a more or less equal part in regulating the amount of time devoted to homework.

A similar point can be made in regard to reading, which can be considered as a school approved occupation. In this case we find that whereas 15% of children highly committed to school had done some reading on the evening before the interview, only 3% of uncommitted children had done so. Again, we find that pop-orientation is also a factor, for while 13% of children with a low pop-orientation had read during the previous evening, only 1% of highly oriented children had done so. Once more this suggests that both factors must be considered before reaching an adequate understanding of reading habits. The reverse is also true of any consideration of the extent to which adolescents use the pop media; so that not only their media orientation but also their school commitment must be taken into account.

Table 29 Effects of school commitment/pop involvement on other spare time activities

School commitment	High		Low	
Pop involvement	Low	High	Low	High
Group	1	2	4	3
Had done *homework* on evening preceding interview	38%	19%	20%	6%
Had played *pop records* on previous Friday evening	0%	11%	7%	26%
Had been out *dancing* on evening preceding interview	0%	0%	0%	27%
Had watched *television* on previous Saturday evening	38%	30%	47%	16%
n =	21	27	15	31

If we examine record playing habits and attendance at dances as giving some indication of involvement in pop, we find a direct reversal of the pattern for homework. Group 3 shows the highest proportion of positive responses to our question on record playing behaviour. Group 1 contained no children who had played records on the night in question, while children in groups 2 and 4 were intermediate. An even more extreme pattern emerges when considering the incidence of dancing, either in discotheques or dance halls. On the evening before interview 8% of our sample had been dancing, but, as Table 29 shows, this activity was confined solely to the Group 3 children who had both a high orientation to pop *and* a low commitment to school.

As has already been seen, television viewing takes up a good deal of adolescents' leisure time, although our evidence suggests that many young people of this age view less often and for fewer hours than many children or adults. Our respondents frequently volunteered that they watched only as a last resort—if it was too dark to be 'mucking about' outside, if their parents insisted on their being at home for a while, or if they could not afford any alternative. Television is not primarily a pop medium, so it is not to be expected that the pattern of viewing would correspond to the patterns of record listening or dancing and, in fact, Table 29 shows that the pattern is more akin to that of doing homework. On the previous Saturday evening very few children in Group 3 had been watching television compared with children in other groups. In this occasion Group 4 provides the highest percentage of positive respondents, which seems to indicate that some children who have little involvement in either school or pop may turn to television as a source of values and social roles.

In summary it can be said that the findings presented in this chapter tend to indicate that adolescents of all social classes, attending all types of schools, are in varying degrees interested in the pop world, but that participation in pop based activities is limited by factors such as shortage of money and the demands of homework and domestic chores. However, it has been suggested that the crucial factor appears to be the way in which pupils come to terms with the competing demands for time and involvement made by the schools and the pop media and, among working class pupils, how they manage the extra alternative offered by the street culture.

So far pupils' involvement in pop has been discussed in very general terms. However, as pointed out in our discussion of teachers' media consumption patterns, pop is not a unitary phenomenon and a number of diverse styles co-exist under this general umbrella heading. Consequently, it is not sufficient simply to say that some pupils are more involved in pop than others, it is also necessary to examine what sorts of pop they are involved in. This forms the subject of the next chapter.

References

1   Brittain, Clay V., 1963 'Adolescent Choices and Parent-Peer Cross Pressures' *American Sociological Review* Vol. 28, No. 3, pp. 385–91. See also Kandel, Denise B. and Lesser, Gerald S., 1969 'Parental and Peer Influences on Educational Plans of Adolescents' *American Sociological Review* Vol. 34, No. 2, pp. 213–22.

2   Abrams, M, 1959 *The Teenage Consumer* London Press Exchange.

3   Carter, M. P., 1962 *Home, School and Work* London, Pergamon, p. 227, abridged as *Education, Employment and Leisure* 1963.

4   Smith, Cyril S., 1966 *Young People at Leisure* University of Manchester, p. 17.

5   Watson, J. D., 1962 *The Use of Leisure* Unpublished Diploma Thesis, University of Leicester School of Education.

6   Hargreaves, David, 1967 *Social Relations in a Secondary School* London, Routledge and Kegan Paul.

7   Himmelweit, H., Oppenheim, A. N. and Vince, P., 1958 *Television and the Child* Oxford University Press, Chapter 8. See also Himmelweit, H., 1962 'Television Revisited' *New Society* Nov. 1, Bristol Joint Standing Committee on the Effects of Mass Media, 1965 *Television Viewing Habits of Pupils in Bristol Schools* pp. 11–16 (pamphlet). Granada T.V. Network, 1961 *What Children Watch* Granada, London, pp. 7–10 and Schramm, W., Lyle, J. and Parker, E., 1961 *Television in the Lives of our Children* Oxford University Press, Chapter 3.

8   Dimsdale, A. G., 1964 'Pop, Schools and Sex' *New Society* Aug. 27.

9   Rust, F., 1969 *Dance in Society* London, Routledge and Kegan Paul.

8 Pupils and pop music

At the present time adolescents have a very considerable range of pop styles from which to choose, each of which has gathered particular accretions of meanings and associations in the process of its development. Therefore, in order to understand the patterns of pop preference and antipathy among particular groups of pupils, it is necessary to trace the social and cultural origins of the major contemporary pop styles.

Sources of contemporary pop music

BEFORE 'ROCK AND ROLL'

The dance bands of the 1940s are the first important source of contemporary pop style. At the beginning of the decade there were over three hundred big swing bands of national reputation in America, and the most successful, such as Tommy Dorsey or Benny Goodman, could gross over half a million dollars a year. Then the bands began to add featured vocalists, who gradually replaced the bandleaders as the focus of popularity. The most successful of these band singers was Frank Sinatra, arguably the first pop star. It was not entirely unknown for material to be written expressly as a vehicle for a particular performer. The Hollywood film industry was based on the star system almost from its earliest days, as was the Edwardian music hall to a great extent. But it was Sinatra's unique blend of relaxed ballad and more swinging up-tempo numbers that set the seal on one dominant modern pop style. The material of the band singers was overwhelmingly concerned with love and romance (83% according to one estimate)[1], performed in a suitably restrained manner. Several singers, however—most notably Johnny Ray—developed a more emotional delivery, sometimes bordering on the hysterical, complete with unrestrained sobbing. Both styles are still in evidence today. The Sinatra formula is characteristic of such performers as Andy Williams and Engelbert Humperdinck, while Tom Jones has developed the more emotional and sexually charged delivery.

In addition to the big bands, white America also produced various blends of British folk music, evangelical hymns and sentimental ballads, collectively known as 'country' music. Country music was centred in Nashville, Tennessee, home of the nationally known radio show, *Grand Ole Opry*, which did much to make country music commercial. Stimulated by numerous singing cowboys, such as Roy Rogers, the vogue for country music, or 'country and western' as it was dubbed, reached its peak between 1949 and 1953 when forty-nine country records each sold over a million copies. This musical source, particularly the style of Hank Williams, was to have a considerable influence on the development of pop.

Apart from these forms of white music was the music of the American Negro, with its own radio stations and record companies. Until the late 1940s the black and white audiences were largely segregated. At this time there were three major currents of black music. There was 'traditional' jazz, developed by musicians such as Jelly Roll Morton and Louis Armstrong, first in New Orleans and later in Chicago and New York. Then there was the emerging 'modern' jazz style which laid the stress on individual improvization rather than ensemble playing. The most influential development in this field was the 'bebop' style pioneered by the saxophonist, Charlie Parker. Lastly, there was the raw, driving blues developed by the singer-guitarists of the Mississippi Delta who had moved north to play in the clubs and bars of Chicago and who, in the process, had added a rhythm section to the basic guitar to form 'rhythm and blues'. The lyrics, however, remained squarely in the blues tradition, dealing directly with sex, drink, suffering and death. This 'rhythm and blues' music is the most important root of contemporary pop.

Two of these streams of black music had small but enthusiastic followings among white adolescents, particularly middle class youth. However, often it was not so much the music which appealed as the life style it represented. Brian Jackson, for example, has described the way in which the myths surrounding 'traditional' jazz musicians such as Louis Armstrong had a very strong appeal to boys in a Huddersfield grammar school in the early 1950s. Through their vicarious leisure time involvement in the supposedly, expressive, hedonistic life style of the jazzman, which they saw as an exaggerated version of the street life of working class Huddersfield, these pupils were able to satisfy their need for the sort of expressiveness which the school was denying them.[2] The New York college 'dropouts' who constituted the core of the American 'Beats', went one stage further and attempted to live out the myth by adopting what Norman Mailer called the 'white Negro' life style. Taking Charlie Parker as their model and incorporating elements of the hobo way of life, they systematically attempted to construct a hedonistic style based on marijuana, promiscuous sexuality and free, fast travel across America.

The early postwar period also saw the emergence of two further styles of behaviour, one American, the other British. From 1946 onwards, groups of nomadic motorcyclists emerged in California. One such group, later to become the 'Hell's Angels', gained a great deal of publicity in 1947 when they caused considerable damage to property in a small town near San Francisco.

This, and other similar incidents, provided the basis for the 1951 film *The Wild One*, starring Marlon Brando. This film was banned in Britain, but the black leather jacket sported by Brando in the movie was copied in numerous films which followed and the leather jacket became the symbol of the British 'Rockers', now known as 'Greasers'. It was only much later that the cut down Levi denims actually worn by the 'Hell's Angels' gained currency among some sectors of British 'bikers'.

The other major source of style emerged among the young working class males of South and East London and was based on the Edwardian fashions which emanated from Saville Row in the immediate postwar period. Despite their novel appearance, however, the values of these 'Edwardians' or 'Teddy Boys' as they were dubbed in the press, were firmly rooted in the local cultures of working class London. Their attachment to 'flash' and to 'hardness', for example, represented a direct continuation of the ethos of the earlier 'Wide boys', 'spivs' and 'cosh boys'. Similarly, anyone who was familiar with the numerous accounts of working class life in Victorian London, would have been aware that the street clashes between rival groups of 'Teds' were not quite such a novel phenomenon as many of the press reports implied.

'ROCK AND ROLL' AND AFTER

By the beginning of the fifties in America it was obvious to the major white record producers that the newly emerging affluent teenagers constituted a potentially lucrative market. At the same time it was also clear that the monotonous diet of standards from Hollywood and Broadway hits—plus the occasional commercial cowboy song—was not the right material to reach this audience, while the sort of performers who favoured these songs were generally too old to appeal to younger listeners.

The breakthrough came in 1952 when a Cleveland disc-jockey, Alan Freed, began to broadcast Negro rhythm and blues records on his radio shows for white adolescents. His audience reacted instantly and Freed's show became an overnight success. The white record companies immediately began to look round for young white performers who could handle such material, although the resulting 'cover versions' were invariably watered down, as both lyrics and music were regarded as too earthy for adolescent consumption. The Decca company signed a contract with a group called 'Bill Haley and his Comets' whose record, *Rock Around the Clock*, became the best selling single record of 1955. The record's success was greatly helped by the fact that it was used as the theme music for the film *Blackboard Jungle*. This film, which was about leather jacketed 'teenage hoodlums' in a New York high school, attracted a good deal of publicity and firmly associated the new rock and roll music with the steadily rising juvenile delinquency figures. This image was further reinforced by the disturbances in cinemas which accompanied the showing of Bill Haley's own film, *Rock Around the Clock*. These disturbances followed a familiar pattern. First, sections of the overwhelmingly adolescent, and working class audience would attempt to dance to the music in the theatre aisles. This attempt would be stopped by the 'bouncers' and this sparked off retaliatory vandalism among the audience during which seats were slashed and fittings such as fire hoses torn out. These incidents gained a good deal of publicity and served to cement the association between Bill Haley and rock and roll and the violence and vandalism of the 'Teds'.

By this time however record producers had come up with a whole host of new performers. Two of these were particularly important, Elvis Presley and Pat Boone. In 1957, for example, Pat Boone's *Love Letters in the Sand* was placed second on the number of copies sold, while Presley's *Heartbreak Hotel* of 1956 reached the top of both black and white hit parades, a hitherto unachieved feat. Pat Boone was the archetypal clean cut all-American boy who sang mainly romantic ballads and cleaned-up rock and roll songs, while Presley was the singing Marlon Brando, complete with mumble, leather jacket, smouldering sexuality and contempt for authority. He was the perfect synthesis, the country boy become 'white Negro'. According to James Coleman's study, however, the largest sector of American adolescents (45% of girls and 43% of boys) favoured Boone, while only 21% of boys and 17% of girls favoured Presley.[3]

When assessing the impact of rock and roll, it is important to bear two things in mind: firstly, that rock and roll served to reinforce already existing behavioural styles rather than initiate new ones; secondly, that a considerable sector of the adolescent audience rejected raw rock and roll (already itself, of course, a refinement of Negro rhythm and blues) and its performers, and preferred the 'teenage crooners'. For example, in order to retain popularity, Britain's most successful rock and roll star, Cliff Richard, rapidly dropped the sulky sub-Presley image of his first film *Dangerous Charge* and became much more the 'boy next door'. The basic subject matter of pop songs at this time remained romantic love but general formulations such as *Love is a Many Splendoured Thing* were replaced by more specific adolescent-oriented songs such as *Teenager in Love, Teenage Crush* and *Teen Angel*.

Seeing the initial success of rock and roll in appealing to youth, other sectors of the mass media were not slow to capitalize. Hence, at the height of the rock and roll boom of 1956–7, three new magazines, *Romeo, Mirabelle* and *Valentine*, were launched in Britain, dealing exclusively with teenage romance and pop music. Television, too, tried to adapt itself by producing a number of rock and roll shows and had the good fortune to find a producer, Jack Good, who understood the music. The shows for which he was largely responsible, *Six Five Special* and *Oh Boy*, went a long way towards finding a visual style which fitted the music. More often than not, however, pop was slotted into an already existing formula. The BBC's long running *Juke Box Jury* programme, for example, was a variant of the conventional panel game.

At the same time that rock and roll was introducing adolescents to the basic styles of rhythm and blues, other elements of Negro music were also surfacing in Britain. In 1956, Lonnie Donegan, the banjo player with Chris Barber's traditional jazz band, made a record of *Rock Island Line*, a traditional blues originally recorded by the Negro singer, Hudie Ledbetter. Donegan's simple version performed on guitar, bass and washboard met with unexpected success and started a boom in home made performances of traditional work songs, gospel songs and country blues, collectively known as 'skiffle'. This skiffle craze had three important effects. Firstly, it initiated a renaissance of home made music as adolescents all over the country began to form skiffle groups. Secondly, it drew attention to the traditional jazz bands themselves and led to the 'trad jazz revival' of 1960–62. Thirdly, it stimulated interest in the original styles of Negro music from which skiffle had been derived. This interest, however, was generally confined to the art students and Beats, and centred in a very small number of specialized London clubs.

Another important development in the late 1950s was the growing interest in folk music, sparked off by the Kingston Trio's 1958 hit recording of a ballad from the American Civil War, *Tom Dooley*. Again this 'folk revival' initiated interest in traditional folk music and laid the grounds for the later development of the Greenwich Village folk singers, particular Joan Baez and Bob Dylan. Baez's first LP (1960) included mostly traditional ballads, while Dylan's album released two years later drew heavily on the country blues and on the political songs of the legendary hobo, Woody Guthrie. Dylan went on to write and record songs which dealt with the political issues which American college students were then involved in, particularly Civil Rights. In Britain the music of Baez, Dylan and their followers appealed mainly to those adolescents who also liked trad jazz and probably supported the Campaign for Nuclear Disarmament and were, as Frank Parkin has pointed out, overwhelmingly middle class and grammar school educated.[4] Their 'uniform' comprised jeans, long jumpers and duffle coats, rather than black leather jackets or Italian suits.

Thus, at the beginning of the 1960s in Britain, three major groups of adolescents could be distinguished on the basis of their musical preferences. At one end there were the working class groups comprising the successors of the 'Teds' and the newer 'rockers' who supported the sort of rock and roll performed by Presley, Little Richard, Gene Vincent, etc. At the other end there were the mainly middle class Beats, art students, grammar school sixth formers and 'politicos' whose interests lay in traditional and modern jazz, blues and folk music. In the middle there was the great mass of adolescents who enjoyed the 'mainstream pop' offered by the Top Twenty.

DEVELOPMENTS IN NEGRO MUSIC

The appropriation by white producers of rhythm and blues as the basis of rock and roll had deprived Negroes of 'their' music. They responded by emphasizing the gospel elements which had always been present to some extent in much black music, producing two new forms, 'soul' and 'ska'. Soul music is basically a blues lyric performed within a gospel framework, and hence it represents a fusion of two hitherto separate Negro traditions, the secular and the sacred. The most well known soul singers include Ray Charles, Otis Redding and Aretha Franklin. Ska represented the same secular-sacred fusion in the Jamaican context, in this case, a mixture of calypso with the rhythm of the pocomania cults. The ska beat is basically the blues beat reversed. Instead of the stress falling on the second and fourth beat in each bar, it falls on the first and third.

By far the most popular Negro style with white teenagers, both in Britain and America, is the music produced by the 'Tamla Motown' label, a Negro-owned record company based in Detroit. 'Motown' music is characterized by an insistent, and more or less equal, stress on all four beats in the bar, which makes it excellent to dance to. Indeed much of its success is traceable to its continuing popularity in the discotheques.

An important function of popular music has always been to provide an accompaniment to dancing, whether it be the waltz, the foxtrot or 'jiving' to rock and roll. The dances which developed in the 1960s, however, differed from previous styles in that they were generally performed without a partner. The first solo dance to achieve widespread acceptance and popularity was the 'Twist', pioneered by the Negro singer, Chubby Checker. The Twist gave way to other dance styles such as the 'Shake' but the essential breach had been made and dancing without a partner, or at least without bodily contact, became the norm. The increasing popularity of partnerless dancing was also related to changing sexual mores. Previously, dance halls had been one of the few places where young people could establish close physical contact; with increasing tolerance of physical expression in public places, this function had been largely cut away.

Black music is still popular today, largely because it is good to dance to and satisfies the continued demand for records with a steady and distinctive beat. Ska in particular is strongly favoured for this reason and, known now as 'Reggae', is very popular amongst working class adolescents.

THE RISE OF BRITISH POP

Until 1963, with the exceptions of the 'Teddy Boys' and the skiffle craze (itself American derived), British pop and fashion were imitations of the major American styles, suitably adapted for local conditions. In that year, this pattern was broken and Britain originated its own pop styles. The factors that precipitated the rise of British pop were many and complex, but economic forces were inevitably among the most important.

In the early 1960s the British economy reached its peak of postwar prosperity and this had two important effects. First, there was an expansion in the production of leisure goods, particularly cheap transistor radios and portable record players. Then, there was an expansion in the adolescent market for these goods, as the postwar 'bulge' babies reached adolescence with a relatively large amount of discretionary spending power at their command. By 1962 adolescents were better equipped than ever before to support a boom in the pop record industry. Unfortunately, the industry did not at first have a suitable product with which to exploit this situation. A new impetus was needed to enliven the by now rather tired formulae of mainstream pop. The situation of the record companies was made more acute by the fact that they had just made the complex technological turnover from the old shellac 78 r.p.m. records to the vinyl 45 r.p.m. singles. Increased sales were essential to cover the costs of this capital investment.

The impetus was finally provided by the British groups, headed by the 'Beatles' and 'Rolling Stones'. The emergence of these groups was both sudden and spectacular, but their styles had been germinating over a long period of time. Although both John Lennon and Paul McCartney were grammar school boys, and the former had also been to art college for a short time, the Beatles began as a local Liverpool group playing for a predominantly working class audience. Originally a skiffle group, they soon became rockers complete with slicked back hair and leather jackets and a basic rock and roll style to match. Onto this they grafted a considerable number of different musical influences until, after several years in the beat clubs and dance halls of Merseyside and Hamburg, they finally evolved their own version of rock and roll. The Rolling Stones on the other hand emerged from a middle class background, playing versions of Negro Soul and rhythm and blues records to audiences of Beats and art students in the small jazz and blues clubs of Soho and the London suburbs.

The Beatles and the Stones thus represented the two main minority styles which the record industry had largely submerged in romantic ballads and processed instrumentals. The British groups restored the basic elements of pop and brought rock and roll and rhythm and blues out of the clubs to which they had been confined. The record companies were not notably quick to realize that this was an important new development but, when they did, a boom in record sales immediately followed. This sparked off a chain reaction in other sectors of the media.

BBC radio had been several years behind in its appreciation of musical changes, and had largely ignored rock and roll until 1958 and the introduction of *Saturday Club*. With the exception of the commercial station Radio Luxembourg, therefore, radio in 1964 was still dominated by 'light' music and family oriented request shows. This 'BBC approach' to pop was challenged by the 'pirate' radio stations, led by Radio Caroline, which started transmitting non-stop up-to-date pop from a ship anchored off the southeast coast, over the Easter weekend of that year. The constant music and American-style patter of the young disc jockey contrasted sharply with the rather staid presentation of the two major BBC pop programmes—*Easy Beat* and *Saturday Club*. The pirates were legislated out of existence in 1967, but their unprecedented success forced the BBC to review its policy, resulting in the creation of Radio One, which re-employed many of the young 'pirate' disc jockeys and attempted to repeat the formula of the 'pirates'—even including jingles and advertisements for other BBC programmes.

The British pop explosion also had an effect on the visual style of television. The most important show in this respect was Rediffusion's *Ready, Steady, Go* (*RSG*), launched in the summer of 1963. This was the first programme to make any real advance on Jack Good's efforts, and it did for television what the pirates had done for radio, by creating a style and atmosphere that perfectly reflected the mood of the moment. It also did much to disseminate nationally the new styles of music, fashion and dance then emerging in London. Not the least of its advantages was its young commère, Cathy McGowan—in George Melly's words 'the prototype dolly', the perfect mixture of trendiness and 'girl next door'.[5] *RSG* faded with the decline of the groups, but its style continues as the basis for BBC 1's long running pop show, *Top of the Pops*, which remains the most popular show with teenagers. Magazine publishers got into the act as well and, in 1964, three new magazines (*Jackie*, *Rave* and *Fabulous 208*) were launched to cater for the new 'dolly bird' readership. Of these, *Jackie* was the most successful in finding the right balance between the sort of romantic stories pioneered by the 'love comics' of the 'rock and roll' era and the greatly enlarged interest in the new pop stars and fashion clothes. According to one survey, *Jackie* devoted 30% of its space to romantic stories (often with pop settings), 27% of its space to pictures and stories about pop stars, and 12% to fashion.[6] This mixture of romantic story magazine, fan magazine and fashion magazine continues to be very successful, and *Jackie* remains by far the most widely read magazine among adolescent girls.

Not only did the years 1963–5 see Britain producing a new style of pop music, but another important adolescent grouping—the 'Mods'—also appeared in this country. In some respects the Mods were heirs to the Teddy Boys. Like the Teds, they were originally working class London boys and the essence of their style lay in its fetishistic attention to clothes and appearance. Girls were secondary and tended to underplay their femininity by wearing clumpy shoes and cropped hair. But the Mod differed sharply from the Ted in that his clothes were only one part of a distinctive pattern of life that centred on the newly established and proliferating boutiques of Carnaby Street and the King's Road and the discotheques of London's West End. Mod pop groups such as 'The Who' and the 'Small Faces' appeared, projecting a sartorial elegance and panache on the stage which matched the mood of their audience.

The Mod phenomenon represented the final stage in the transformation of the concept of fashion which the Teds had initiated. For a considerable time fashion had applied almost exclusively to women's dress, and traditionally new styles had been dictated by a small number of Parisian designers and disseminated by the wealthy few who could afford one of the limited number of 'originals'. Only after a suitable time lag would styles permeate to the High Street chain stores. This system had now been short-circuited. Young designers like Mary Quant and John Stevens got their inspiration from the kids on the streets and the new styles immediately became available in the boutiques. Only later did they become accessible to the affluent middle aged.

Inevitably there were conflicts when the Mods came into contact with other adolescent groups, particularly the rockers whose values and leisure style were entirely different. Friction culminated in the well publicized seaside 'battles' of 1964 and 1965 between factions of these two groups. However, the days of the Mods were numbered and they finally faded as the dominance of British pop groups came to an end in 1966 in the face of new developments.

THE EMERGING 'UNDERGROUND'

The term 'underground' refers basically to those young people who see themselves as constituting an opposition to mainstream forms of social organization and cultural expression which is in the process of developing alternatives to these forms. The contemporary underground first emerged in San Francisco in the mid 1960s, where it was made up of an uneasy coalition of the radical students of Berkeley and the old established Beat community, later to evolve into the 'Hippies'. From the beginning, pop music was a central component. The music evolved by the underground musicians, however, marked a distinct development over previous styles. In the first place, the lyrics began to deal with a range of subjects hitherto excluded from pop and confined to blues and folk music. These included drug experiences, sexual deviation and political radicalism. In the second place, the music itself became much more complex in an attempt to simulate the experience of LSD use, which formed one of the central components of the Hippie life style.

The underground first became visible in Britain in the summer of 1965, when, with almost no prior publicity, thousands of young people packed the Albert Hall to hear the American Beat poets, led by Allen Ginsberg, read their poetry. Soon afterwards, the first British underground paper *International Times* was produced, the San Francisco groups became known, and the 'arts lab movement' got under way. Underground pop music had two distinct segments, the songs of the singer-songwriters, and what came to be called 'progressive rock'.

The singer-songwriters, led by Dylan, extended the trend for public poetry into musical performance. They concentrated mainly on expressions of personal experience, occasionally interspersed with an individual comment on a public event. The most successful of these singer-songwriters include Tom Paxton, Leonard Cohen, James Taylor and Joni Mitchell. 'Progressive rock' is an umbrella heading which includes almost any attempt to experiment with new musical styles within a pop framework. One of the basic trends in this area of pop is the growth of individual improvisation around a basic theme in the manner of modern jazz. The most notable guitarist improvisers included Jimi Hendrix and Eric Clapton of 'Cream', both of whom based their music on the blues. The other trend in progressive rock is the attempt to create fusions between pop and other music styles such as jazz, folk and concert music, and to experiment with extended instrumentation including electronic sounds. However, it would be a mistake to see these developments simply as an expression of new demands from audiences and performers. Indeed, they would not have been possible without two very significant developments in the technology of the recording industry. Long playing records which give the performer a much longer time module in which to develop his musical ideas had been produced since the late 1940s, but only in the mid-1960s did they assume any great importance. By the end of the decade they were outselling 45 r.p.m. singles, which had been the staple product of the industry since their introduction. Secondly, the development of multi-track recorders and stereo record players makes possible both the production and consumption of more complex textures of sound.

The underground is largely the prerogative of middle class adolescents and students. Many working class groups resent the apparent intellectualization of pop and have reacted against it. The 'skinheads' who emerged in London in 1969 represented a reassertion of the basic values and interests of the male working class peer group—cleanliness, toughness and fighting ability. Their overtly 'masculine' uniform of heavy boots, short hair, turned-up jeans and braces contrasted sharply with the more sexually ambiguous Hippie styles. They gravitated towards Negro pop music and particularly towards Jamaican Reggae which offered a total contrast to progressive rock. Not only did its intrinsic merits—simplicity and a good dancing rhythm—appeal, but it also fitted in with the skinheads' already existing patterns of values and preoccupations.

THE CONTEMPORARY SITUATION

Thus, at the present time, pupils have a very considerable range of pop music styles available to them, each of which is associated with distinct dress styles, leisure activities and values. The symbols and meanings carried by pop are the touchstones of adolescents' attitudes. There are basically three main clusters of pop style; 'mainstream pop', 'underground–progressive rock', and the various Negro styles.

Mainstream pop accounts for the majority of Top Twenty records and hence it is the sort of music most often heard on radio and television. Within this general mainstream category, however, there are a number of substyles. There are performers such as Andy Williams, Tom Jones and Engelbert

Humperdinck, whose styles derive from the 1940s band singers. Then, there are the solo singers who began in either the rock and roll era (e.g. Cliff Richard) or at the time of the British groups (e.g. Cilla Black, Lulu) and have now become 'all round entertainers' with their own family television shows. There are also the pop groups such as 'Marmalade', 'Middle of the Road', etc., who perform the standard processed material of 'Tin Pan Alley'. The lyrics of mainstream pop are still predominantly concerned with romantic love themes and are usually performed in a mechanical way with relatively simple instrumentation or orchestral arrangements. The performers themselves are usually ideal 'next door' types and, as such, the majority have adult approval. Mainstream pop is still to some extent tied to the flagging mythology of 'Swinging London' and the economics of built-in obsolescence. In the same way as the Top Twenty survives on musical gimmicks, mainstream fashion depends on fads such as 'hot pants'. Each product is designed for a maximum immediate appeal followed rapidly by a loss of interest so that the next fad can take its place. Finally, the great majority of the Negro pop music available in Britain, particularly the music of the 'Motown' company and the various 'soul' labels, also falls under the heading of mainstream pop.

Underground progressive music also has a number of subcomponents. There are the songs of the singer-songwriters, Bob Dylan, Donovan, James Taylor, Leonard Cohen; the virtuoso guitarists such as Johnny Winter, improvising around a blues theme and employing amplification and feedback; the groups such as Led Zeppelin, playing so-called 'heavy rock' which is basically rhythm and blues based, but with an extended lyric range; there are those artists experimenting with new fusions between pop and other musical forms such as jazz (Blood, Sweat and Tears), folk (Fairport Convention), country music (The Band, The Byrds) or contemporary concert music (Soft Machine); and finally there are the individual innovators such as John Lennon and Frank Zappa, who are experimenting with almost every known musical and lyrical combination. Underground progressive music is distinctly different from mainstream pop. It stresses individual expression and improvisation rather than processed presentation, and its lyrics often deal directly with sex, drugs, and social and political problems rather than simply with romantic love. Similarly, there is no set pattern of fashion in which one particular style is 'in' at a particular time, rather individuals are free to raid the entire storehouse of past styles in the same way as the music draws on almost every musical form. 'Do your thing' eclecticism is at a premium. The perceived 'expressivity' of underground progressive styles tends to appeal to the predominantly middle class pupils, who at an earlier period would have supported blues, folk or trad jazz.

These three categories are not entirely distinct, for it is characteristic of pop to integrate 'cleaned up' versions of minority styles into the mainstream. This certainly happened to 'Motown' and soul music and at the present time it is also happening to both underground and Reggae music. Nevertheless, when our research was carried out, pupils tended to see considerable differences between the various categories of music and their performers.

Pupils' patterns of pop music preferences

Information on pupils' pop music preferences was obtained in two ways. During the interviews they were asked to say what sorts of pop they particularly liked and to give reasons for their choice. In addition some pupils were also played a tape containing $1\frac{1}{2}$ – 2 minute extracts from twelve recent pop records. After listening to each extract pupils were asked to indicate how much they had liked or disliked it by putting a tick on a five point scale. Then, for each of the first eight extracts, they were asked to rate the record on each of nine bipolar adjective pairs. The extracts were selected to represent most of the major varieties of pop music currently available. For example, the tape included examples of mainstream records by white performers (e.g. The Brotherhood of Man, Creedence Clearwater Revival and the Beatles), examples of the major Negro styles (e.g. 'Motown'—The Jackson Five, Soul— Aretha Franklin, and commercial Reggae—Owen Gray) together with records by singer-songwriters such as Leonard Cohen and Simon and Garfunkel, and examples of blues-based progressive rock (e.g. The Rolling Stones and Johnny Winter). Basically, we wanted to see how pupils reacted to records which they had not heard before but which belonged to a recognizable general pop style. Thus, we deliberately selected LP tracks and the reverse side of single 45 r.p.m. records—neither of which are played very often on the radio. Pupils were asked as part of the test to say how often they had heard each of the records before, and their replies clearly indicated that the overwhelming majority were unfamiliar with the particular examples we played them. As will be shown, however, they were able to classify the records into general stylistic groups.

For this work with the music tape a sample consisting entirely of fourth formers was used who, it was felt, could handle this sort of complicated question more easily. A random selection of groups from schools was used—some were in form groups, others were groups specially made up of pupils who had completed our interview schedule. Altogether a total of 104 boys and 107 girls completed the test. Our consideration of the results of this tape test will begin with a discussion of the pupils' evaluation of the first eight extracts.

In order to tap pupils' evaluation of the records, a modified form of the research technique known as the 'Semantic Differential' was employed.* For each of the eight records pupils were given a sheet on which were printed nine pairs of descriptions, e.g. simple–complicated. Each descriptive pair was presented in the form of a five point scale: very simple, quite simple, can't decide,

* This technique and the construction of the music test is fully described in Appendix 3.

quite complicated, very complicated. Pupils rated the record by putting a tick somewhere along the five point scale for each of the nine descriptive pairs. Each scale point was assigned a numerical value between 0 and 4, with the 'can't decide' category scoring 2. The nine descriptive pairs were not completely independent of one another; on the contrary, they were designed to tap four basic dimensions of classification which previous research had indicated were important. These dimensions are:

'activity–potency' (constituted by the descriptive pairs, 'exciting–unexciting' and 'gentle–powerful')

'understandability' ('easy to understand–hard to understand' and 'simple–complicated')

'evaluative' ('beautiful–ugly' and 'interesting–boring')

'novelty' ('old-fashioned–up-to-date' and 'original–unoriginal').

Differences between the resulting scores can be analysed in a number of ways and in this study two methods have been employed. The simpler of the two consists of computing various mean scores. Thus, for each record, a total mean score can be calculated from all the answers of all the respondents. In addition, other means can be arrived at by subdividing the respondents or by breaking down respondents' replies into scales or factors, each of which has its own mean score.

The second analytical method employed attempts to measure the distance between concepts in semantic space. If two concepts are close together in semantic space it can be concluded that they have similar meanings for the group making the judgement. In order to measure this distance, researchers have developed the 'D' statistic, D representing the distance apart of the two concepts in semantic space. A low D score shows that the two concepts are perceived as similar in meaning. In our case D scores can be used to build up a concrete picture of the respondents' semantic space in respect of the various pop records. In actuality this representation will have an unlimited number of dimensions, but in general it can be reproduced with adequate accuracy in two dimensions.

From the analysis of the mean scores, it was apparent that the major dimensions which pupils employed when rating and classifying the records, were those of 'understandability' and 'activity potency'. The mean scores of each of the eight records on these two dimensions are presented in Fig. 5.

This diagram shows that the records seem to fall into distinct clusters. At one end are the Rolling Stones, Aretha Franklin, and the Jackson Five which are all rated high on activity, but relatively low on understandability. These records all feature what may be called a 'black' sound. Two of the three are by black performers and feature the distinctive Negro styles of 'Motown' and soul, while the music of the Rolling Stones draws heavily upon black influences, particularly urban blues. Quite different from this group is the cluster

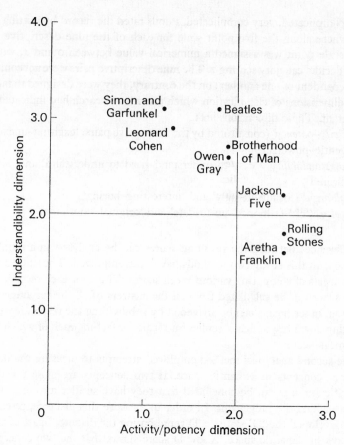

Fig. 5 Mean scores of records on the 'understandability' and
'activity–potency' dimensions

comprising Leonard Cohen, Simon and Garfunkel and the Beatles, who are all
white performers. Both Cohen and Simon and Garfunkel base their music on
the relatively simple musical structures of folk music and the particular
Beatles record used was also folk-influenced. Also, in all three of these records,
the lyrics took precedence over the music. Between these two poles lie the
records by Owen Gray and the Brotherhood of Man. The Beatles and the
Jackson Five lie nearer this pair than do the other records and these four are
in fact the records which would be most likely to appear in the best-selling
charts.

A very similar pattern emerged when the Difference Scores were calculated,
as illustrated in Fig. 6. The double lines represent low D scores, indicating
that the two records were perceived as similar by the respondents. The single
lines are rather longer, showing that the records are only perceived as being

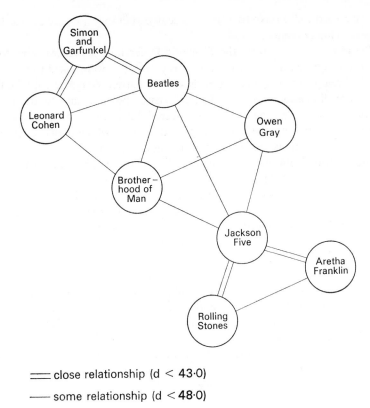

══ close relationship (d < **43·0**)

── some relationship (d < **48·0**)

Fig. 6   Diagrammatic representation of difference scores

similar to a certain extent. If two records are not joined by any lines, it indicates that they are perceived as being different from each other. Once again the three basic groupings of records are distinguishable, with the Beatles and the Jackson Five again tending towards the central pair. The fact that the four records in the centre of the diagram are related to some extent to both the activity and understandability clusters tends to indicate that they may have elements which appeal to several sorts of record buyer. Of them all, the Beatles' record has more relationships than any other, which may provide some clue to their enormous popularity and success. The basic pattern is thus reasonably clear. There appear to be two distinct and separate clusters of records, the black 'active' records and white 'easy to understand' records, with those records which have elements of both lying at various points in between. This pattern remains largely unaltered when respondents are subdivided into those who are highly pop oriented and those who are not. Both groups produce patterns very similar to that illustrated in Fig. 6, but those who are not keen pop fans tend to differentiate less clearly between different sorts of records. The three basic clusters remain, but they are perceived as being more closely related.

The results derived from the Semantic Differential schedules were confirmed during the interviews when fourth year pupils were asked to say why they had nominated particular records as their current favourites. Again, the two major dimensions appeared to be, 'activity–potency' and 'understandability'. Thus, of the 140 pupils who answered this question, 36% mentioned the record's beat, 22% the lyrics and 30% the way in which both the musical and lyrical elements combined to produce an overall sound.

The situation is not quite as simple as this, however, for cutting across the activity/understandability dichotomy is the mainstream/underground division which it has been argued is an important characteristic of the contemporary pop scene. From pupils' replies to the first question on the tape test schedule, which asked them to indicate on a five point scale how much they liked each record, it was evident that they also recognized this division as an important one.

Due to the fact that the tape test had to be fitted into an ordinary school period, it was usually possible to play only the first eight records. A total of fifty-four pupils did complete the liking scale for the first ten records, and from the factor analysis of the resulting scores we derived the clusters shown in Table 30.

Factor analysis enables us to see to what extent the elements within a correlation matrix, in our case records, co-vary together and are associated in coherent clusters or factors. Each factor is defined in terms of the items with the

Table 30 Principal clusters of records liked (varimax loadings—decimal points omitted) (*n* = 54)

Record	Cluster 1	2	3	4
Aretha Franklin	72	31	07	−04
Creedence Clearwater	71	24	15	20
Brotherhood of Man	61	−36	−09	−35
Owen Gray	60	−19	23	17
Jackson Five	59	−08	−43	−07
Rolling Stones	12	76	14	02
Johnny Winter	−08	78	−15	−02
The Beatles	−05	20	−77	−12
Simon and Garfunkel	−05	−24	−80	29
Leonard Cohen	08	01	−08	89
% of total variance accounted for	26·10	14·40	13·69	10·18

highest loadings and like the values of correlation coefficients these loadings may vary between $+1$ and -1. Because of the small sample size involved, very great care must be taken in interpreting the results of the factor analysis. Nevertheless, the basic pattern is reasonably clear and unambiguous.

Three of the five records with high loadings on the first cluster are by Negro performers; Aretha Franklin's soul record; The Jackson Five's contemporary 'Motown' offering, and Owen Gray's commercialized Jamaican Reggae. Further, although the other two records with high loadings are by white pop groups, they both draw heavily on Negro styles; blues in the case of Creedence Clearwater and 'Motown' and soul in the case of the Brotherhood of Man. As their titles suggest, the lyrics of these Cluster 1 records deal with various aspects of romance and love, viz. *Come Back Baby, Girl What You Doing to Me,* and *Living in the Land of Love.* The only exception is the Jackson Five record which is concerned with another staple subject of pop—the problems of being an adolescent. However, as we saw from the results of the Semantic Differential schedule, the lyrics of these records are generally seen as less important than the beat and rhythm. In all cases the Cluster 1 records follow a standard and predictable musical arrangement. Taken overall, therefore, we can place these records on the 'mainstream' side of the dividing line.

Cluster 2 is defined by the high loadings of the Rolling Stones record and the record by the American blues guitarist, Johnny Winter. As in the Cluster 1 records, the emphasis here is on the overall sound and rhythm which is based in both cases on the basic structures of urban blues. However, unlike the records in the first cluster, both the Rolling Stones and Johnny Winter feature extensive individual improvisation rather than simply following a standard formula. Earlier in the chapter, it was argued that improvisation was one of the characteristics of underground rock music, and from the interviews it was clear that this opinion was widely held by underground supporters in our sample. We can therefore place the Cluster 2 records on the 'underground' side of the line.

The highest loading factors on Factor 3 are those by the Beatles (-77) and Simon and Garfunkel (-80) which tends to indicate that this cluster revolves around the intelligibility of the lyrics rather than the musical sound itself. However, the fact that the Leonard Cohen record has a very low loading on this factor indicates that it is not a general white lyric cluster. A clue as to why this might be so can be found in the records themselves. Both the Beatles and Simon and Garfunkel records employed supplementary instruments including strings, whereas Leonard Cohen accompanies himself on the guitar alone. Also, both the Beatles and Simon and Garfunkel have had hit singles and are played frequently on Radio 1. Cohen, on the other hand, is only known through his LPs and has received relatively little publicity. Once again, it was clear from the interviews that pupils attached considerable importance to these factors, and on that basis placed Simon and Garfunkel and the Beatles (while they were still a group) on the 'mainstream' side of the line, and Leonard Cohen on the 'underground' side.

Our results tend to suggest that pupils classify pop records along two major dimensions—'activity/understandability' and 'mainstream/underground'. We therefore arrive at the four basic taste clusters shown in Fig. 7. Of the two

Fig. 7 A summary of pupils' classifications of pop music: the four basic taste clusters

	Mainstream	Underground
Activity–potency (Negro based music stressing beat and rhythm)	*Cluster 1* Aretha Franklin (soul) Jackson Five ('Motown') Owen Gray (Reggae) Brotherhood of Man Creedence Clearwater	*Cluster 2* 'Heavy rock' (Rolling Stones) Progressive urban blues (Johnny Winter)
Understandability (music performed by whites stressing the lyrics)	*Cluster 3* The Beatles Simon and Garfunkel	*Cluster 4* Individual singer-songwriters (Leonard Cohen)

divisions, that between the mainstream and the underground is by far the most important. In the interviews it was frequently found that pupils' preferences embraced both activity and understandability records, but that these preferences were generally *within* either the mainstream or underground groupings.

Having sorted out these basic taste clusters, it is possible now to go on to examine which groups of pupils each attracts, using these four basic groupings as a way of classifying the information on pop music preferences obtained during the interviews.

Both because some of the ways in which respondents have been subdivided leaves us with rather small numbers, and because in most cases the underground supporters were very much in the minority, we have included clusters 2 and 4 under the general umbrella heading underground music. Let us look first at the effects of age.

Table 31 shows that, while the proportion choosing a Negro pop record as their favourite is almost exactly the same in both years, the fourth years are more likely to nominate an underground record and correspondingly less likely to select a mainstream white pop record. When the actual distribution of choices is compared, the difference between the two years is statistically significant at the 5% level as measured by chi square ($\chi^2 = 7\cdot58$). Between the second and fourth years, then, a number of pupils reject the routine pop music of the Top Twenty and gravitate instead towards the underground; Who, then, are these underground oriented pupils?

Table 31 Pupils' favourite pop records: by year group and type of music (figures in percentages)

Type of music	Year group	
	Second	Fourth
Mainstream white pop	65%	49%
Negro pop	25%	24%
Underground-progressive	10%	28%
n	58	140

Table 32 shows that just over 50% of pupils from both middle class and lower working class backgrounds opted for mainstream pop. However, while the great majority (41%) of the rest of the lower working class pupils chose a Negro pop record as their favourite, the majority of the remaining middle class pupils (42·5%) selected an underground record. The underground music supporters are thus more likely to be middle class than working class. These findings fit in very well with those recently reported by researchers at the University of Michigan on the basis of a large scale survey of American high school pupils. They found that pupils from middle class homes were more

Table 32 Fourth year pupils' favourite pop records: by social class and type of music (figures in percentages)

Type of music	Social class	
	Middle	Lower working
Mainstream white pop	52·5%	51%
Negro pop	5·0%	41%
Under-ground-progressive	42·5%	8%
n	40	37

than twice as likely as pupils from working class homes to list 'protest' songs as their favourites (i.e. records which deal with taboo subjects such as drugs). Working class pupils on the other hand were very much more likely to nominate mainstream Top Twenty records.[7] Our present findings also lend support to our earlier argument that because middle class pupils are largely cut off from the situational working class street cultures, they will tend to turn to pop as a source of those values, roles and meanings which the school under-values. Working class pupils on the other hand are able to derive their alternative meanings from street peer groups rooted in the situational cultures of working class neighbourhoods; and consequently, for them, pop music is likely to be either something which is part of the taken for granted background of group activities, or else part of the small coin of social exchange. Either way, interest or involvement is not likely to extend beyond the current hits. More light can be thrown on this question if pop preferences for groups with high and low commitment to school and high and low orientation to pop are considered.

Table 33 Fourth year pupils' favourite pop records: by level of school commitment and degree of involvement in pop (figures in percentages)

School commitment	High		Low	
Pop involvement	Low	High	Low	High
Group	1	2	4	3
Mainstream white pop	48%	48%	48%	24%
Negro pop	24%	24%	28%	27%
Underground-progressive	28%	28%	24%	48%
n	13	26	13	29

Despite the small number of respondents involved, Table 33 indicates that the pop oriented school rejectors of Group 3 are more likely than pupils in other groups to nominate an underground pop record as their favourite. In fact, whereas in Groups 1, 2 and 4 almost half the respondents (48%) nominated a mainstream record as their favourite, among Group 3 pupils this situation is reversed and underground records receive the greatest proportion of the nominations (48%). If we leave aside the Negro pop choices and concentrate on the crucial distinction between mainstream and underground records, when the actual distribution of nominations in Group 3 is compared with the distribution within the other three groups taken together, we find that the difference in the allocation of nominations between the two main categories of records is statistically significant at the 5% level as measured by chi-squared ($\chi^2 = 5 \cdot 025$).

In addition to being asked to choose their favourite record, interviewees were also asked to give reasons for their choice and to say what it was about that particular record which appealed to them. The replies most frequently given by various groups are presented in Table 34.

Again the numbers here are small and care must be taken in interpreting the results. Nevertheless, a clear pattern emerges. Among the non-pop oriented school rejectors of Group 4 the greatest proportion mentioned the beat and the overall sound of the records as their main reasons for liking them. In fact almost all of the pupils in this group nominated the hit record of the moment—

Table 34 Reasons given by selected groups of fourth year pupils for liking favourite records (figures in percentages)

School commitment	High		Low	
Pop involvement	Low	High	Low	High
Group	1	2	4	3
Good beat	8%	46%	45%	36%
Good overall sound	58%	37%	45%	21%
Lyrics are saying something meaningful	18%	19%	9%	40%
Original record	—	23%	—	18%
Good to dance to	18%	12%	—	21%
Like the performer	18%	19%	9%	25%
n	11	26	12	28

Note: Percentages do not add up to 100 for two reasons, (1) minor response categories have been excluded, (2) respondents could give more than one reason.

Ride a White Swan by T. Rex as their favourite. Only one person, mentioned either the words of the singer as a reason for this choice. Among the pop oriented rejectors of Group 3, on the other hand, it is the lyrics which are most frequently mentioned and, in fact, the difference between Group 4 and Groups 1–3 is statistically significant ($\chi^2 = 5 \cdot 195$ $p < 5\%$). Group 3 pupils are also more likely than other groups to mention that they admire the performer or that the record is good to dance to, although these differences are not statistically significant. These findings lend further support to our earlier argument. They suggest that, whereas the predominantly street culture oriented pupils of Group 4 appear to use pop music to provide a pleasant and lively background, the Group 3 pupils, for whom pop music provides an important source of meanings and expression, tend to select records primarily for their lyrics, and to a lesser extent because they admire the performer or because the music gives them the opportunity to express themselves physically through dancing. Which of these takes precedence depends on the record in question. From the interviews it was evident that, although pupils tend to make a clear distinction between the two main clusters of underground music represented by Leonard Cohen and the Rolling Stones, liking for one does not necessarily exclude liking for the other, and in fact the two are usually closely associated. Thus, when asked to name their favourite record, the Group 3 pupils frequently mentioned both 'activity' music such as Jimi Hendrix and Led Zeppelin and also 'lyric' music such as James Taylor, Joni Mitchell and Bob Dylan. When asked to select one record some picked one sort and some the other, but nearly all admired both. Before leaving the music itself let us add a word about dancing.

We saw in the last chapter that the Group 3 pupils were the only ones who had gone out dancing on the evening preceding the interview and figures in Table 34 indicate that these pupils are more likely than others to give dancing as a reason for choosing records. A clue as to why this should be can be found in a recent study of middle class American adolescents. The most frequently mentioned reason which these young people gave for going dancing at a disco-theque was that it gave them a chance to express themselves physically. Boys said that dancing gave them a sense of physical release and of sexual arousal, and girls mentioned physical release and a feeling of being seductive as their main reasons.[8] Thus, according to this study, middle class adolescents appear to use fast, frantic partnerless dancing to pop music as a means of establishing contact with their physical and emotional capacities, which fits in with Eldridge Cleaver's remark that the first modern pop dance style, the 'Twist', gave white adolescents 'a new awareness and enjoyment of the flesh, a new appreciation of the possibilities of their bodies'.[9] These findings are also in line with our argument that, because middle class pupils—particularly girls—are cut off from the opportunities for physical expression afforded by the roles and activities of street cultures, they will tend to turn to pop as an alternative source of such opportunities. This argument receives some further support from the fact that none of the non-pop oriented school rejectors had been dancing on the evening before the interview and none of them mentioned dancing as a reason for choosing a record as their favourite.

This concludes our analysis of pupils' pop music preferences and their perceptions of pop singers will be examined.

How pupils see pop stars

At the end of the interview, pupils were presented with a modified form of a type of psychological testing known as the Repertory Grid, which required them to say in what ways various pop performers resembled each other or differed from one another. In this way it was hoped to gain some insight into the repertoire of constructs which pupils use when classifying pop stars into various groups.* From the results of the Grid Test it was clear that pupils categorized pop stars not only in terms of the type of music they performed, but also in terms of their general appearance and self-presentation on stage, and their overall life style. Further, cutting across all of these three main dimensions of classification there appeared to be an underlying division in terms of conventionality/unconventionality which represented an extension of the mainstream/underground division into the area of appearance and life style. These various divisions, together with the most frequently mentioned constructs within each category, are presented in Fig. 8.

In most cases these three dimensions were seen as congruent so that, for example, Cliff Richard was clearly perceived as being on the conventional and

* The Grid Test is fully described in Appendix 3.

Fig. 8 Pupils' classification of pop stars

	Conventional	Unconventional
Music	Mostly 'commercial' music	Sings what he likes
Appearance and self presentation	Subdued, doesn't jump about—smart, well dressed, suit type, short neat hair	Goes wild on stage, dressed how he likes— scruffy, weird clothes, hair all over the place
Life style	Respectable, quiet, doesn't take drugs	Always in the news, not respectable, takes drugs

Mick Jagger as on the unconventional side in all three dimensions. In several cases, however, there was a degree of ambiguity as certain performers were perceived to be in some respects on one side, in other respects on the other.

At the end of the Grid Test, pupils were asked to say which of the eleven pop performers presented to them they thought their parents might approve of, and which they might disapprove of. From these replies we computed a net score for each of the performers with a range of +100 to −100.* A high positive score indicates that a large number of pupils said that their parents approved of a particular singer while a high negative score means that a large number said that their parents disapproved of that particular performer. These scores are presented in Table 35.

The adverse publicity which accompanied Sinatra's rise to fame, and the activities of the 'Clan' has died away and now, at least in the pupils' eyes, he is classified with Val Doonican as someone on the wrong side of forty who has short hair and wears suits or carefully tailored casuals, and whose mixture of ballads and carefully arranged upbeat numbers appeals mainly to parents.

The singers in group one, Val Doonican and Frank Sinatra are seen as conventional in all respects, and represent a continuation of the styles of the big band 'crooners' who were popular at the time that many of the pupils' parents were themselves adolescents.

The second group, consisting of Cliff Richard, Engelbert Humperdinck and Tom Jones, are also perceived as being highly conventional and represent what we might call 'respectable pop' singers, who have graduated from adoles-

* The *net scores* were arrived at as follows. Pupils' replies for each singer were given a numerical value. If they said that their parents definitely approved of a singer he scored +1, definite disapproval scored −1, and if respondents said that their parents neither approved nor disapproved, the score was zero. The perceived level of parental approval/disapproval of the various singers among various groups of pupils was arrived at by adding the scores together and dividing by the number of respondents in order to facilitate inter-group comparisons. Finally, the net scores were multiplied by one hundred to give whole numbers.

Table 35 Net scores of pupils' perceptions of their parents' attitudes towards selected pop performers (all interviewees)

		Performer	Net score	
Perceived degree of parental approval	High	Val Doonican	+48	Group 1
		Frank Sinatra	+44	
		Cliff Richard	+33	Group 2
		Engelbert Humperdinck	+30	
		Tom Jones	+20	
	Low	Elvis Presley	+08	Group 3
		Stevie Wonder	+0·9	
Perceived degree of parental disapproval	Low	Donovan	−19	Group 4
		Ringo Starr	−30	
	High	John Lennon	−50	Group 5
		Mick Jagger	−60	

cent pop star to family entertainer and have their own programmes on television appealing to both parents and pupils. Due to his somewhat frantic and sexually charged performing style, Tom Jones is perceived as receiving less parental approval than the other two, but this is counterbalanced by the fact that he wears a suit together with his well publicized family life and homely Welsh background.

Both Stevie Wonder and Elvis Presley are perceived as being on the borderline of parental approval and it is not difficult to see why. Despite the fact that he now sings mostly ballads and has a large adult following, Presley is still remembered principally for his early rock and roll hits and for his leather clothes, slicked-back greasy hair, and his sexuality. Stevie Wonder has a similar dual image. On the one hand his ballad-style records and neat and tidy appearance command adult approval but, on the other, he is one of the most successful of the Tamla Motown singers and, as such, associated with the sort of fast, loud, Negro-based music which many pupils see their parents as disapproving of.

Both Donovan and ex-Beatle, Ringo Starr, display the external trappings of youthful rebellion such as long hair, and consequently pupils tend to see them as being unconventional and therefore to some extent disapproved of by parents. However, the power of this unconventional appearance is to some extent counteracted by other elements. Ringo Starr, for example, is presented in the mass media as essentially a quiet, shy, family man who married the girl next door, and Donovan is to some extent legitimized both by his appearances as a guest artist on a number of respectable pop shows, and by the fact that little is known about his ideas or life style. In the case of both John Lennon and Mick Jagger, however, pupils perceive no disjunctions in the three

dimensions and consequently they tend to see both these performers as overwhelmingly unconventional and hence as being unreservedly disapproved of
by parents. Firstly, both are associated with the sort of loud pop music that
most antagonizes parents. Secondly, both have a public image which extends
beyond unconventional dress to embrace an anti-establishment life style. A
number of pupils for example, mentioned Jagger's affair with Marianne
Faithful and his trial for possessing drugs, and Lennon's experimentation with
LSD, his association with Yoko Ono and his Toronto 'sleep-in' for peace, as
reasons for their parents' disapproval. Having established that interviewees
were able to give a clear picture of how they thought their parents saw these
various pop performers, the pupils' own preferences will now be examined,
and it is at this point that some interesting differences emerge. Table 36 shows
the net liking scores of fourth year pupils from middle class and lower working
class backgrounds.

Table 36 Fourth year pupils' degree of liking or disliking for selected pop
performers: net scores by social class (overall rank order in brackets)

Performer	Social class	
	Middle	Lower working
Donovan	+28 (1)	+07 (5)
Stevie Wonder	+15 (2)	+44 (1)
John Lennon	00 (5)	−17 (10)
Elvis Presley	−06 (7)	+27 (2)
Mick Jagger	−13 (8)	−22 (11)
Tom Jones	−15 (10)	+20 (4)

From Table 36 it is evident that pupils' evaluations of pop performers vary
considerably according to their social class background. Basically, lower working class pupils tend to like singers who are associated with mainstream Negro-
based pop and whose personal style they perceive as matching that of the
music—Stevie Wonder, Elvis Presley and Tom Jones—who, as we have seen,
are all in varying degrees perceived as receiving parental approval. Donovan is
liked to a small extent, but the two other underground performers, John
Lennon and Mick Jagger, were greatly disliked and ranked tenth and eleventh
respectively.

Among middle class pupils the best liked performer is Donovan, who
represents a sort of licensed rebellion confined to stylistic aspects such as long
hair and casual clothes, and is associated with the singer-songwriter cluster of
underground music. Opinions were equally divided on John Lennon, giving a
zero score. Overall more respondents disapproved of Jagger than approved,
yielding a negative score, but the degree of disapproval among middle class
pupils was not as great as among lower working class pupils. Stevie Wonder

was liked by middle class pupils, but not to the same extent as among those from lower working class homes. Further, among middle class pupils, the other two 'mainstream-activity' singers, Presley and Jones, were disliked, and in fact Jones was ranked last. In summary then, it appears that in terms of the groups shown in Table 35, whereas the preferences of lower working class pupils are concentrated in Group 3 and extend downwards to include Donovan, the preferences of middle class pupils are centred on Donovan and extend upwards to include Stevie Wonder. There is thus a degree of overlap in preference. However, if we take the two groups' evaluations of Lennon and Jagger as touchstones, it is evident that there are also considerable differences of emphasis which are entirely congruent with the patterns of musical taste discussed earlier. The divergences in pupils' evaluations of pop singers become even clearer if they are regarded in terms of differential commitment to school and involvement in pop.

Table 37 Selected fourth year pupils' evaluations of various pop performers: net scores (overall rank order in brackets)

School commitment	High		Low	
Orientation to pop	Low		High	
Group	1		3	
Cliff Richard	+50	(1)	−07	(7)
Val Doonican	+38	(2)	−37	(10)
Frank Sinatra	+25	(3)	−33	(11)
Donovan	00	(7)	+19	(4)
John Lennon	−31	(9)	+11	(5)
Mick Jagger	−69	(11)	00	(6)

Table 37 indicates that the patterns of preferences of pupils in Group 1 tend to follow quite closely the pattern of parental approval shown in Table 35. That is, pupils who orientate themselves around the school culture tend to like the singers whom they see as being approved of by adults as represented by their parents (i.e. Val Doonican, Frank Sinatra and Cliff Richard); and tend to dislike singers such as Mick Jagger and John Lennon whom their parents disapprove of. The Group 3 pupils, who are oriented around pop on the other hand, tend to show almost the reverse pattern. They tend to dislike the singers their parents approve of and to like those they disapprove of. Among this group, even Mick Jagger finds as many supporters as detractors, giving a zero score.

The degree of divergence between pupils' preferences and parents' approval can be expressed numerically by means of a statistic known as Spearman's Rho, which is a correlation coefficient based on the rank ordering of the two groups. The closer the rankings of parents' approval and pupils' liking, the higher and more positive the correlation coefficient. As might be expected, the correlation between liking and approval among Group 1 pupils is very high (+0·83). What is interesting, however, is the difference between the school rejectors of Groups 3 and 4. The rank order correlation of the non pop-oriented rejectors of Group 4 is +0·51 which indicates that there is a considerable measure of agreement between them and their parents, so that by and large they tend to like the performers whom they perceive their parents as approving of. Among the pop-oriented rejectors of Group 3, however, there is a considerable measure of disagreement indicated by a coefficient of −0·68. These findings tend to lend further support to our main argument, that pupils whose access to street cultures is restricted will tend to turn to the pop media as a source of alternative values and meanings; whereas pupils who do have access to street cultures already have alternative articulations and hence do not need to turn to pop.

This concludes our analysis of the pattern of pop preference among different groups of pupils, and other aspects of their leisure environment—fashion clothes, television and magazines—will now be examined briefly.

References

1   Horton, Donald, 1957 'The Dialogue of Courtship in Popular Songs' *American Journal of Sociology* Vol. LXII, pp. 569–70.

2   Jackson, Brian, 1968 *Working Class Community* London, Routledge and Kegan Paul, Chapter 8.

3   Coleman, James, 1961 *The Adolescent Society* Glencoe Free Press, p. 23.

4   Parkin, Frank, 1968 *Middle Class Radicalism* Manchester University Press, pp. 146 and 167.

5   Melly, George, 1970 *Revolt into Style: The Pop Arts in Britain* London, Allen Lane, The Penguin Press, p. 171.

6   Alderson, Connie, 1968 *Magazines Teenagers Read* London, Pergamon Press, p. 8.

7   Robinson, John P. and Hirsch Paul M., 1970 *Teenage Response to Rock and Roll Protest Songs* University of Michigan, Survey Research Centre unpublished research report.

8   Blum, L. H., 1966 'The Discotheque and the Phenomenon of Alone-togetherness' *Adolescence* Vol. 1, pp. 351–66.

9   Cleaver, E., 1968 *Soul on Ice* London, Cape Editions, p. 147.

9 The pervasiveness of pop: fashion, television and magazines

Interest in fashion clothes

Adolescence is the period during which young people are attempting to come to terms with their body image and construct a viable personal and sexual identity, and clothes provide an important medium for expression and experiment with various individual and social identities. This experimentation does not take place in isolation, however, but within the context provided by the wider leisure environment. Clothes are the most immediately visible signal of the group with which an individual identifies, and with which he shares his basic values and activities. Indeed it is for exactly this reason that clothes and hair styles are such a source of contention both between adolescents and adults, and between various adolescent groupings. They are an emblem of deep differences of outlook, values and life experience.

As noted in the last chapter, developments in fashion have tended to coincide with developments in pop music so that the two elements coalesce to form a distinctive style which is adopted by particular adolescent groupings. Clothes provide a means of publicly expressing many of the values, attitudes and preoccupations of various segments of the pop media. Consequently, involvement in pop music tends to be associated with interest in fashion clothes; but this is not invariably the case. A number of working class boys for example are more interested in fashion than they are in pop music. The 3N boys at Northlawns for example, took a very great deal of care over their 'uniform' but as we have seen were not particularly interested in pop music. For them, clothes were an expression of values which derived not from the pop media but from the local street culture. Overall, however, as Table 38 shows, there was a general relationship between pop music and fashion clothes among our fourth year sample.

Table 38 indicates that the more familiar pupils are with the current pop music the more likely they are to enjoy buying clothes and to spend extra money on clothes. Although girls tended to show a greater interest in clothes than boys, the difference between the sexes was probably less than most people would expect: 96% of girls and 73% of boys said that they liked buying clothes.

Table 38   The relationship between interests in fashion clothes and knowledge of the Top Twenty (fourth year pupils)

	Knowledge of the 'Top Twenty'		
	High	Medium	Low
Percentage who like buying clothes	97%	85%	67%
Percentage who would spend part of a £5 windfall on clothes	65%	57%	44%
n =	73	47	46

Not only does involvement in pop tend to be associated with differences in interest in clothes, it also appears to be connected with different ways of knowing about fashion and different ways of actually going about buying clothes. Interviewees were asked where they got ideas about what sorts of clothes to buy, how they knew what was 'in fashion'. Answers fell almost entirely into five categories: window shopping (mentioned by 48%), what friends are wearing (41%), what people in the street, at dances, etc., wear (24%), magazines (33%) and television (16%).* Different groups, however, placed varying emphases on these various sources. Nearly two-thirds (64%) of the non-pop oriented school rejectors mentioned that they got their fashion ideas from seeing what their friends were wearing. This reflects the importance attached to group solidarity among street peer groups. The pop oriented rejectors on the other hand, were most likely to mention window shopping (59%) and noticing what other young people seen in the streets and at dances were wearing as their main source of fashion ideas. Only 38% mentioned their friends. Again this stress indicates that these pupils are oriented around a wider, pop based culture, rather than around the culture of the immediate local neighbourhood. It also reflects the more general difference in outlook noted in connection with the Northlawn groups. Thus, whereas the 3A girls were oriented around the West End discotheques and boutiques, the 3N boys were very much rooted in the local neighbourhood. Magazines also provided girls with another important source of fashion ideas. Altogether 51% mentioned this as one of their sources.

Television

When studying a visual medium such as television, it is important to consider not only the content of a particular programme, but also how this content is

* These percentages do not add up to 100% as most interviewees mentioned two or three sources of ideas.

presented. Once this second element is recognized it is noticeable that some programmes are presented in a particular style which stresses speed, action, youthfulness, glamour, contemporary clothes, and general up to the minute 'with-it-ness'. This style was primarily developed to present pop music and the best contemporary example remains *Top of the Pops*, where the visual style is fused with the pop and fashion content. But, and this is the important point, elements of this *pop style* can also be found in a number of programmes that do not feature pop music to any great extent, and consequently, although they are nominally categorized as science fiction or comedy, they may also be linked to the world of pop by this stylistic thread. One piece of research into people's perceptions of television programmes, for example, has found that viewers quite definitely saw certain programmes as forming coherent clusters.[1] One of these clusters included not only *Top of the Pops* but also the crime series *Man from UNCLE* and the domestic comedy *Bewitched*. What these programmes had in common with *Top of the Pops* was not their content—as they clearly did not feature pop music—but rather their overall style, which respondents described in such words as 'trendy', 'fast,' 'youthful' and 'much action'. Among contemporary comedy programmes for example, *Rowan and Martin's Laugh-In* and *Monty Python's Flying Circus* have elements of the pop style whereas such situation comedies as *For the Love of Ada* do not. Among thrillers, *The Avengers* and, among documentary programmes, *World in Action*, may be included as examples of pop style.

Unfortunately, pressures of time prevented the gathering of systematic information on this aspect of pupils' evaluation of television programmes, but it was apparent from the interviews that a number of the older pupils do attach considerable importance to style. Quite frequently the idea of a well produced programme came up, by which the majority meant a programme which held their interest by its movement and visual inventiveness. Although there was no firm evidence, these intimations might help to go some way towards explaining why some pupils do not respond to schools television. Certainly it seemed that this whole question of visual style would be well worth further investigation. With this stated, let us look briefly at pupils' television programme preferences.

Table 39 indicates that, whereas the second year pupils most frequently select either a comedy programme or else a programme produced especially for children as their favourites, the fourth years tend to opt for pop music programmes. Since the 'childrens' and 'pop music' categories are dominated by two particular programmes, we can say that interest in *Blue Peter* has given way substantially to interest in *Top of the Pops*.

In many ways *Blue Peter* represents the antithesis of *Top of the Pops*. It is largely concerned with adult approved activities such as hobbies, pets and sports. It is presented by 'uncle' and 'aunty' figures who, while young, are certainly not teenagers, and who tend to wear casual non-fashion clothes

Table 39 The types of television programmes most frequently mentioned as favourites by interviewees (figures in percentages)

Type of programme	Second year pupils	Fourth year pupils
Comedy	24%	18%
Children's	21%	4%
Investigation	13%	12%
Science Fiction	11%	10%
'Pop' Music	10%	24%
$n =$	67	167

rather than the latest fashion. Similarly, while there is always a considerable variety of items in the programme, the visual presentation tends to be rather orthodox. *Top of the Pops* on the other hand is pure pop. Its *raison d'être* is the ephemeral, gimmicky world of the current Top Twenty; it features an audience of dancing, fashionably dressed teenagers and, above all, it has a very distinctive visual style in which static talking-head shots are kept to a minimum and there is maximum movement, both in terms of the individual cameras (tracking shots, zooms, etc.) and in terms of the speed with which the shots change (jump cuts, fade-outs, superimposition, etc.) The fact that *Top of the Pops* was the most frequently nominated programme among fourth year pupils was not particularly surprising. Indeed, in view of the findings of a number of previous studies, it would have been somewhat surprising if this had not been the case. A study commissioned by the ITA in 1965, for example, found that *Top of the Pops* was the first or second favourite of 14–15 year olds. Having established that this remains the most popular programme with third and fourth year pupils as a whole, it is now necessary to ask the further questions: who are the most frequent viewers, and what do they get out of it?

Table 40 Fourth year pupils in each group who watch *Top of the Pops* regularly and who nominated the programme as their favourite (in percentages)

	Group 1	Group 2	Group 4	Group 3
% who regularly watch 'Top of the Pops'	48%	89%	73%	87%
% who nominated 'Top of the Pops' as their favourite programme	0%	24%	20%	38%
$n =$	21	25	15	29

Table 40 shows that the majority of children from three of the four groups defined by school commitment and pop involvement are regular viewers. Not surprisingly though, Group 1 children, who are highly committed to school and have a low pop orientation, are less likely to watch than other children. However, simply to be a regular viewer does not necessarily imply a high level of involvement in the programme, for as has already been suggested television viewing behaviour is subject to a number of influences. A clearer indication of the true fans is provided by the proportion in each group who nominated *Top of the Pops* as their favourite programme. These figures follow the pattern already familiar from our previous discussion of record listening, with Group 3 containing a relatively high percentage of *Top of the Pops* fans, Group 1 containing none, and Groups 2 and 4 coming in between. One slightly puzzling aspect of these findings is why only 38% of the pop-oriented school rejectors nominate the programme as their favourite. The most likely explanation lies in the nature of the music with which *Top of the Pops* is chiefly concerned. The programme policy is to concentrate almost solely on the Top Thirty records. It features either records already in this list of best sellers or ones considered likely to get there. It is therefore rooted firmly in mainstream pop and only occasionally plays records that could be considered progressive. As such, it has only a limited appeal to the minority of pop fans who favour this type of music and who were nearly always Group 3 children. They were much more likely to prefer the rather more specialist BBC2 programme *Disco* 2 which was running when this study was made. All the children who mentioned this programme as their favourite were in Group 3. In fact a considerable number of the young people interviewed who were highly involved in pop music expressed their dissatisfaction with *Top of the Pops*, frequently describing it as 'too teeny-bopper'. More often than not these were boys for, while girls are more generally interested in pop than boys (for instance 84% of girls claimed to watch *Top of the Pops* regularly as against 71% of boys), a minority of boys take pop very seriously indeed, more so than the most involved girls. Further, boys seemed to be more appreciative of the visual aspects of the programme, for, as Table 41 indicates, while both sexes found the music and the performers the most obvious attractions, boys placed the visual style next while girls emphasized the secondary features—fashion and dancing.

Magazines

Adolescent girls have considerably more magazines to choose from than boys of the same age. Once boys have finished reading children's comics such as *Beano*, *Whizzer and Chips*, and the adventure comics such as *Victor* and *Wizard*, the only publications available to them are those dealing with sports—especially football, with special interests such as pop music, or with hobbies such as photography, modelling or collecting. The adolescent girls of today,

Table 41 Aspects of *Top of the Pops* enjoyed by fourth year pupils
(figures in percentages)

		Boys	Girls
Musical Aspects	The music	50%	56%
	The singers and groups who appear	54%	52%
Visual Style	Lights and special effects	38%	15%
	Bits of film	27%	23%
Secondary Features	Dancing	25%	39%
	Clothes	20%	25%
n =		49	66

Note: Percentages do not add up to 100 as pupils could select more than one aspect.

however, will soon be the housewives of tomorrow and consequently, the large publishing concerns such as the International Publishing Corporation, attempt to provide a series of logical stepping stones which will help girls to graduate from the group's girls' comics to their women's magazines. Thus, adolescent girls are offered a whole series of publications which revolve around the three basic components of romance, fashion and pop. The 'teenage interest' magazines tell girls how to get their man, the women's magazines—to which they will eventually graduate—will tell them how to keep him.

Table 42, shows the types of magazine most frequently mentioned as favourites by our fourth year interviewees.

Table 42 Magazines mentioned as favourites by fourth year interviewees
(figures in percentages)

Boys		Girls	
Football magazines	19%	'Jackie'	51%
Boys' comics	17%	Romance magazines	16%
Hobbies magazines	9%		
Pop music	5%	Pop music	9%
Don't read any	29%	Don't read any	7%
n =	79	*n* =	88

As table 42 shows, a number of boys do not read comics or magazines at all and those who do mainly read magazines whose content is more connected with street culture than the pop media—i.e. football magazines or boys' adventure comics such as *Victor, Jag* or *Lion*. Girls' reading at this age, however, is dominated by romance, pop and fashion. Table 42 shows those magazines mentioned by girls as their favourites, but in fact many regularly read more than one—some girls answering our earlier questionnaire listed six or seven that they see most weeks. These questionnaire responses show that the four most read magazines are *Jackie* (58%), *Valentine* (23%), *Judy* (18%) and *Fab 208* (16%). Of these only *Judy*, which is aimed at rather younger readers than the others, does not deal with the pop world to any extent. *Fab 208* on the other hand consists almost entirely of news and gossip about pop stars with numerous photographs and a little bit of fashion thrown in. *Valentine* is a survivor of a whole group of similar magazines that were introduced in the 'fifties (coinciding with the advent of rock and roll). They consisted largely of comic strip stories about young girls and their romantic problems together with 'information' about pop stars, most of it clearly straight from publicity handouts. The style of *Valentine* has changed very little and it now looks rather dated in comparison with other publications. Not surprisingly, its readership has consistently fallen over recent years; its circulation is now only half the 375 000 it was as recently as 1964. A survey in 1966 found that *Valentine* was read by 43% of girls in the 13–15 age range;[2] our figures show that this percentage has fallen to 23%.

Jackie which was first published in 1964 and, as an updating of the 'love comic' formula, remains popular in a way that *Valentine* has failed to emulate. The 1966 survey mentioned above found that 52% of 13–15 year old girls read *Jackie*, as compared with our figure of 58%. In fact its circulation has risen steadily from 450 000 per week in 1968 to over 600 000 in 1971. Apart from its generally more up to date format and style, this popularity may be to some extent a function of its greater emphasis on fashion. When interviewees were asked which parts of their magazines they liked, three items dominated girls' answers: 46% mentioned fashion, 45% stories and 40% letters from readers.* Stories and letters receive great attention in both publications, but fashion is covered much more fully in *Jackie*, which devotes 12% of its space to fashion compared with only 4% in *Valentine*. As has already been suggested, magazines are an important source of ideas about fashion; 51% of girls claimed to get some of their ideas about what clothes to buy from magazines.

Summing up

From the findings discussed in this, and the two previous chapters, some tentative conclusions can be drawn regarding the nature of the relationship between pupils and the mass media. Firstly, it is evident that, in any discussion of the role of the mass media in the lives of adolescents, a prominent place should be

* Other items were: articles (12%), advice columns (11%), photos (10%), strip cartoons (6%) and advertisements (3%).

assigned to the pop media. Secondly, the evidence tends to indicate that pupils actively choose both the sorts of programmes, magazines and records they will look at or listen to, and the particular components of this material which interests them most. Rather than allowing media material simply to wash over them, they actively evaluate and classify what they are offered according to consistent sets of critical criteria. Thirdly, the sorts of choices and evaluations which pupils make are not arbitrary or random; rather they appear to be strongly related to their experience of the school system, to their social class and background, and to the neighbourhood milieu in which they spend their leisure time. In short, pupils tend to take from the media both what they want and what they feel they need.

Having said this, it now remains to bring together the various threads in our discussion of the pupils' study and to present an overview of the relationship between pupils' commitment to school and their involvement in pop. This then is the subject of the next chapter.

References

1   Frost, W. A. K., 1969 'The Development of a Technique for TV Programme Assessment' *Journal of the Market Research Society* Vol. 11, No. 1, pp. 25–44.
2   Alderson, Connie, 1968 *Magazines Teenagers Read* London, Pergamon Press.

10 Overview: pupils, peers and pop fans

It has been argued that the way in which adolescents come to terms with the demands of the school will depend firstly on how they regard their school experience and secondly on their degree of access to alternative cultures. It was then postulated that grammar school pupils with a low commitment to school—particularly girls—will have only a limited access to the largely working class street culture, and consequently tend to gravitate towards the pop media as a source of alternative ways of defining themselves and their situation. The evidence gathered in the course of this study tends to suggest that this argument is substantially correct. There is some peripheral ambiguity, but the basic pattern is clear. However, as was pointed out at the very beginning of this report, in order fully to understand the situation not only must the general shape of statistical patterns be considered, but also the way in which these patterns are experienced by particular individuals and groups. Accordingly, this chapter rounds off the discussion of the pupils' study with a general overview of the relationship between school commitment and pop involvement followed by detailed case studies of particular peer groups besed on intensive interviewing.

The pupil—pop fan polarization

In Chapter 6 it was mentioned that each of the pupils who had answered our first questionnaire had been allocated to one of nine groups, according to the degree of both their school commitment and pop involvement—both these dimensions being divided into high, medium and low categories. In the analysis presented so far, attention has been focused on the four groups at the corners of our nine cell diagram, but it is now necessary to look at the overall distribution of pupils among all nine of the groups. Table 4.13 in Appendix 4 shows this distribution for each of the three main types of school.

If our basic argument is correct and the pop media culture is more likely to provide an alternative to school culture for grammar school pupils, then one would expect to find that there is a greater degree of mutual exclusivity be tween school commitment and pop involvement among grammar school pupils than among those at other types of schools.

Table 43 shows the varying degrees of pop orientation shown by pupils with a high commitment to their schools. It can be seen that, in grammar schools, 45% of those with a high school commitment have a low orientation in pop, and only 17% appear to be able to maintain both a high school commitment

Table 43 The percentage distribution of pop involvement among pupils with a high commitment to school: by type of school

| Type of school | n | Percentage of pupils with high school commitment who are involved in pop | | |
		To a high degree	To a medium degree	To a low degree
Grammar	58	17%	38%	45%
Comprehensive	112	26%	37·5%	36·5%
Secondary modern	135	30%	40%	30%

and a high orientation to pop. In secondary modern schools on the other hand, the degree of polarization does not appear to be so great, and the same proportion of pupils (30%) manage to maintain a high level of interest in both school and pop as find the two incompatible. Comprehensive schools show an intermediate pattern.

Table 44 The percentage distribution of school commitment among pupils with a high degree of involvement in pop: by type of school

| Type of school | n | Percentage of pupils with a high degree of involvement in pop who are committed to school | | |
		To a high degree	To a medium degree	To a low degree
Grammar	54	18%	41%	41%
Comprehensive	118	25%	47%	28%
Secondary modern	136	29%	49%	22%

The figures in Table 44 also lend some support to our argument. In this case 41% of the grammar school pupils with a high involvement in pop have a low degree of commitment to school, whereas the corresponding proportion for secondary modern pupils is 22%. Again comprehensive pupils fall between the two.

In summary, these results tend to indicate that, in terms of our four basic groups, grammar school pupils are likely to be over-represented in Groups 1 and 3, whereas pupils at secondary moderns and to some extent at comprehensives are likely to be more evenly distributed among all four groups. Further, as the results of the analysis shown in Table 4.13 in Appendix 4 indicate, this difference in the degree of polarization is statistically significant as measured by chi-squared.

This same basic pattern is also evident if the relationship between degree of school commitment and degree of pop involvement is expressed in terms of the correlation coefficients between the two measures. The two schools that represent the biggest contrast in terms of the social class backgrounds of the pupils, Park Road and Dockstreet, show this difference quite clearly. Among the third year pupils at Park Road there is generally an inverse relationship between school commitment and pop involvement indicated by correlation coefficients of -0.30 for boys and -0.47 for girls, a relationship which is statistically significant at the 0.01% level. At Dockstreet, on the other hand, the correlation coefficients for both boys $(+0.18)$ and girls $(+0.11)$ are positive. Whereas at Park Road high school commitment tends to imply a rejection of leisure activities which are not approved of by the school, at Dockstreet the demands of the school culture are not so all embracing, and consequently a number of pupils appear to be able to divide their involvement between school and leisure without experiencing a conflict. Similarly, because the school rejectors at Park Road generally do not have such ready access to street cultures they are obliged to turn to pop as the most available alternative point of orientation, whereas the school rejectors at Dockstreet do have a street culture to fall back on and consequently do not need to rely so heavily on pop. This last point is illustrated very clearly by the correlation coefficients for the two groups with the least and the greatest access to street culture. The correlation for the middle class Park Road girls is -0.85 (significant at 0.01% level) and that for the working class Dockstreet boys $+0.68$.

Another way of looking at the relationship between pop involvement and school commitment is to consider the way in which the pupils themselves relate the various roles which they play both in and out of school. For example, to what extent do they see the roles of good pupil and pop fan as being mutually exclusive?

On the original questionnaire, pupils were presented with a series of cameo descriptions of various social roles, and asked to indicate on a five point scale, how much they thought they were like each of the young people described. Some of the role descriptions were presented to both boys and girls, others were sex specific.* The third year boys' and girls' results are presented separately.

Figure 9 shows the main intercorrelation between the various self images

* This measure is fully described in Appendix 3.

presented to boys. To simplify the presentation only those product moment correlation coefficients which reached the ·01 level of significance or better are shown. The actual numerical values of the correlation coefficients are also shown, although again, in order to simplify the presentation, the decimal points have been omitted.

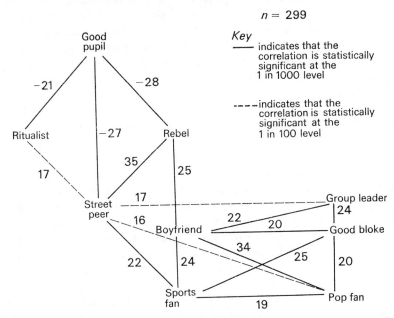

Fig. 9   Intercorrelations of the third year boys' self images

Within the overall pattern of role interrelationships depicted in Fig. 9, it is possible to distinguish two main clusters of self images. The first of these is the triangular relationship between the roles of good pupil, rebel and street peer, which appears to indicate that the rejection of the pupil role and the acceptance of the school rebel role tends to be associated with the adoption of the street peer role. The second main cluster is formed by the four leisure oriented roles of boyfriends, sports fan, pop fan and good bloke. These two main clusters are not entirely separate—indeed, they are linked through the correlation between the rebel and boyfriend roles on the one hand and the street peer and sports fan roles on the other. If, however, one goes beyond the general pattern and look at the results of the factor analysis of the role intercorrelations of middle class and lower working class boys shown in Table 4.13 in Appendix 4, it is apparent that the relationship between the two main role clusters is more complicated than it first appears.

The factor analysis of the middle class boys' replies revealed two principal factors. Factor 1, which is mainly defined by the high loadings of the boy-friend (−72) and sports fan (−71) roles, can be described as a basically leisure oriented cluster. The pop fan role with a loading of −58 also forms part of this cluster. The leader (−65) and good bloke roles (−64) have relatively high loadings, but the loading of the street peer role (−43) is rather lower, which indicates that although these boys select peer oriented roles they tend not to see themselves as members of an informal 'muck about' street peer group. The school role with the highest loading on this first factor is that of rebel, which suggests that participation in leisure activities such as taking girls out, following football, or listening to the latest pop music tend in a number of cases to be associated with a rejection of the self definition offered by the school.

The second principal factor for middle class boys is defined by the high loading of the good pupil role (76). In fact, the only other role to load at all on this factor is that of leader, which tends to suggest that the pupil role provides a number of middle class boys with an almost total definition of themselves and their place in the social order. From these results then, it appears that middle class boys are faced with a relatively clear choice; either to see themselves primarily in terms of the pupil role or else to orientate themselves primarily around the various roles offered by the leisure environment.

The factor analysis of the lower working class boys' results yielded three main clusters of roles. The first factor is defined by the loadings on the ritualist (81) and sports fan (73) roles, and also to a certain extent by the loading (53) on the street peer role. This pattern tends to suggest that some working class boys who have settled for a mediocre level of academic achievement may orientate themselves around watching and playing sports, especially football, usually within the social context provided by the street peer group, where the relevant criterion is physical skill rather than intellectual ability.

Factor 2 is defined by the loadings on the leisure roles of boyfriend (−76) and pop fan (−74). However, whereas among the middle class boys this leisure cluster was unambiguously associated with the rebel role, the pattern for the lower working class boys is a little more complicated, and in fact the school role with the highest loading on Factor 2 is that of good pupil (−35). Further, the street peer role (−34) also appears to be part of this cluster. With the relatively small numbers involved in this analysis and the correspondingly considerable chances of random error, any interpretation of this pattern must remain tentative. However, the configuration of the loading does seem to suggest that a number of working class boys are able to keep the areas of work and play relatively separate and that consequently, unlike the middle class boys, they do not experience any necessary contradiction between playing the pupil role in school and orienting themselves around pop music and dating during their leisure time.

The third factor which emerged from the analysis of the lower working class boys' results is defined by the high loading on the rebel role (84) and to a lesser extent by the loading (50) on the street peer role. That is, the adoption of the rebel role tends to be associated with the adoption of the street peer role. In some ways the pattern of the loadings on this third factor is similar to those of Factor 2 among the middle class boys. There is, however, an important difference. Whereas among the middle class boys the rebel and street peer roles were also associated with the pop fan role, among the lower working class boys the pop role is not associated with the rebel/peer cluster. A possible explanation for this difference in terms of our previous argument, might be that the working class boys' street peer groups are able to provide more or less self sufficient alternative definitions to the essentially middle class roles sponsored by the school, because they are rooted in patterns of values and meanings derived from the ongoing situational culture of the working class neighbourhood. The middle class boys' peer groups, on the other hand, lack such a situational base, and consequently they tend to gravitate towards the pop media and pop music in particular as a source of alternative definitions.

Because they have fewer role options available to them than the boys, the pattern of the girls' role intercorrelations is less complicated.

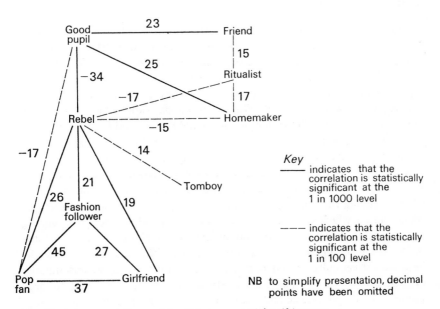

Fig. 10   Intercorrelations of the third year girls' self images

The pattern shown in Fig. 10 suggests that, among girls as a whole, those who reject the good pupil role and accept the rebel role will tend to gravitate towards an expressive role set rooted in the patterns of leisure activity sponsored by the pop media. The pivot of this role set is the pop fan role which is in turn significantly associated with a high degree of interest in contemporary fashion clothes, coupled with success with boys. The central preoccupation of this role set, romance, glamour and being up to date with the latest pop music, are among the most prominent themes of much pop media output, especially those sectors aimed specifically at girls. As has already been seen, the subject matter of *Jackie*, the most widely read magazine among adolescent girls, reflects these dominant preoccupations very accurately. However, magazines like *Jackie* not only reflect the central values of the pop role set, they also actively help to disseminate styles and meanings and to define what is meant by a teenager. By consistently holding out an image of a leisure world where glamour and personality will ensure immediate gratification and success, they serve to provide alternative patterns of meaning and interpretation to those sponsored by the school culture and encapsulated in the good pupil role. Quotations such as the following from an interview with a successful girl pop singer are very frequent:

I went to Waverley Grammar School in Birmingham which I left as soon as I could. I didn't like school very much. I've been singing ever since. (*Jackie* 6 June 1970)

The pop media help to define an anti-school culture, which is about having fun while you can and freely expressing your physical and emotional capacities.

Figure 10 presents a clear picture of the general pattern of role clustering among third year girls. However, because it is based on an analysis of the replies of all the girls, it does not show the interesting variations in clustering among girls from different social class backgrounds. Table 4.14 in Appendix 4 presents the principal factors for girls from middle class and from lower working class backgrounds.

Table 4.14 reveals some interesting and important differences in the relationship between the two main anti-school roles shown in Fig. 10; the pop fan/fashion follower on the one hand, and the tomboy on the other. Thus, whereas among the middle class girls it is the pop fan/fashion follower/girl friend cluster which is most strongly related to the school rebel role, among lower working class girls it is the tomboy and girl friend roles. Once again these differences lend support to our argument about differential access to neighbourhood street cultures. Thus, it might be postulated that, because middle class girls have little or no access to street cultures, they gravitate towards fashion clothes, pop music and dating as a means of articulating their disengagement from school. Working class girls, on the other hand, are not so cut off from local street cultures.

As was suggested in a previous chapter, some working class girls are likely to spend some of their leisure time with predominantly male street peer groups, and it now appears that—among lower working class boys—the street peer and rebel roles tend to be associated. A girl in this social situation is therefore quite likely to be part of an anti-school culture, which accounts for the high loading of the school rejector role on Factor 4. At the same time, she is likely to play a double role within the street peer group; she may engage in group activities and 'pass for male' (i.e. the tomboy), and she may be an object of sexual attention (i.e. the girl friend). Among lower working class girls, therefore, the tomboy—street culture milieu appears to represent the main alternative to the school culture. The school rebel role does load on the pop/ fashion cluster of Factor 2, but not so highly as on Factor 4—the tomboy cluster.

Patterns of school rejection: case studies

The most important distinction that has been made is between those groups who are alike in rejecting the value system of the school, but who are distinguished by their social class background and by the type of school they attend. To illustrate this point in a more concrete way, let us look at a middle class peer group from a grammar school and a working class group from a secondary modern.

THE PARK ROAD AND MIDDLETON BOYS

The middle class group has been chosen from Park Road school and consists of three members, Alec Wilkinson, Roger Carr and Paul Dickens.* Although they have all successfully reached grammar school, none of these boys is well integrated into the school ethos. In general they reject what the school is offering. Paul Dickens is typical in remarking that he hates school. He also volunteered that he never does the homework set for him and intends to leave school immediately after 'O' level. He is less sure what he wants to do after he has terminated his education, suggesting only that he is quite interested in becoming a photographer—not a realistic hope since this intention was not reflected in his reported leisure activities. No doubt the supposed glamour of this 'trendy' occupation is the main attraction.

Our working class group consists of four boys—Jeff Brown, Leyton Dale, Andy Munk and John Russell, who are pupils at Middleton school. Like most of their classmates this group are very disenchanted with school life, which seems to them to have little to offer. John Russell made a chance remark which summarized the lack of rapport between this school and many of its pupils. A keen football fan, John was asked whether he played in any school team. The sarcastic reply was, 'No, it's all rugger here. I was picked once, but of course I didn't turn up'.

The leisure patterns of these two groups show very striking differences

* All names are fictitious.

resulting from their social background. The working class groups are firmly rooted in the local street culture. 'Mucking about with mates' was the reply which most often answered queries about their activities. John Russell, for instance, had spent the whole of the previous Sunday, much of the Saturday afternoon and all the Friday evening 'mucking around' in the streets. Andy Munk had little time for anything but a friend's motorbike. Nearly all his time was spent either washing it, maintaining it or going out on it, and if he had any extra spending money Andy would spend it on additional motorbike parts. Jeff Brown also spends much of his spare time with his mates, wandering around town, going swimming or watching football. Occasionally he goes to the local working men's club with his father. Leyton Dale's leisure pattern is similarly based on his male peer group but, unlike the other three, he did have some contact with the pop media in his visits to the Locarno dance hall, although this is a more typically working class location than the newer discotheques. Apart from this, none of this group had made any use of the media during the previous weekend apart from watching the television.

This pattern contrasts markedly with the behaviour of the middle class group from Park Road. All three had been to the cinema over the weekend and Alec Wilkinson is a regular cinema-goer who is prepared to visit the local cinema whatever film is showing. Two of the three, Alec Wilkinson and Paul Dickens, had been to a discotheque within the previous week. Alec had been to the local one, but Paul had travelled several miles to a neighbouring town in order to go to a rather superior place which featured not only the usual disco material—Negro dance music—but also progressive pop which Paul found more to his taste. He had spent the whole of a weekday evening there, not leaving until the discotheque closed at 10.30 p.m. All three also mentioned listening to music either on radio or records, and all possess sizeable record collections including a number of LPs. These records largely fall into the category of progressive or underground music, and their latest acquisitions had been records by George Harrison and Led Zeppelin. This taste is reflected in their choice of favourite performers and favourite records, while the reasons they gave for these selections fell into two clusters. Firstly, they tended to mention instrumental prowess as being a commendable feature of their records—Roger Carr picked out the electric violin featured by his favourite group as outstanding. Secondly, the sheer volume and energy characteristic of this type of music was clearly important—adjectives such as 'loud', 'lively' and 'wild' were used to describe the appeal of these records.

Radio and television do not provide many programmes that cater for their tastes, so Alec, Roger and Paul make limited use of these media. Only Alec watches *Top of the Pops* every week, and it is the style more than the content which appeals to him—his favourite feature of the programme was its use of lighting and special effects. Paul occasionally watches this programme, but said that he doesn't like it very much and particularly dislikes the sort of music which it presents. A programme more to his liking was *Disco 2* which the BBC used to screen late on Saturday evenings and which consisted mostly of underground music. Similarly, Paul doesn't listen widely to Radio One, except for one specialized programme which features his preferred type of music. This is *Sound of the Seventies*, which was broadcast each weekday evening and to which Paul listened regularly. Alec and Roger are less selective, and Alec in particular listens to quite a lot of radio.

The working class boys at Middleton showed much less involvement in pop, and their use of the media was quite different. Although all listen extensively to Radio One (some 10–20 hours a week each), they regarded it very much as aural wallpaper and preferred the sort of programme which features the hit records of the moment—such as *Pick of the Pops* on Sunday afternoon. *Top of the Pops* is also popular with these boys and all four watch it regularly—three of them adding that the type of music played is one of the programme's greatest merits. Their favourite performers reflect this general interest in undemanding Top Twenty music. Jeff and Leyton expressed interest in the Negro Tamla Motown stars Stevie Wonder and the 'Four Tops'. Leyton explained that this is good music to dance to, while John said that he often dances along with records on the radio. Andy preferred all round family entertainers such as Cilla Black and Lulu, and John chose the Beatles as his favourite group, although he expressed some reserve in regard to their recent development and preferred them 'like when they started'. The attitude of the group to underground music was expressed by Jeff who said that 'I don't like that "progress" music—there's nothing to it'. All four chose as their favourite record one that was in the top three records of that week but, significantly, none of them owns a large record collection.

When asked whether they thought that teachers should be more aware of the mass media, introduce them in lessons and be prepared to talk about them, all four felt that this would be a good idea. Not only did they feel that this approach would make lessons more interesting, they also suggested that it would create greater understanding between teachers and pupils and so help in the teaching-learning process. John remarked that teachers could 'teach us more if they knew our interests' and Jeff that present lessons did not have enough to do with the life experiences of the pupils: 'We're always learning the same old things, not about real life.'

This distinction between school and non-school activities has already been seen to be a feature of teachers' definition of their role. It is thus not surprising that their pupils also should separate the learning situation from that of real life, and the same distinction was also made by the middle class group at Park Road. They, in fact, felt that teachers should not involve themselves in the media. Although rejecting school values, they share the same definition of the function of school as their grammar school teachers. Unfortunately this leads them to believe that there is no possibility of communication between pupils and teachers; their two worlds are too far apart. Paul said, 'Teachers should stick to teaching. It's up to us what we do out of school'. Alec was rather less dogmatic and thought that it *might* be useful to discuss the media in lessons, 'but only as long as it doesn't interfere with work'. Education for these pupils has become a purely instrumental experience; they are in school to pass the necessary exams and then they will leave. As far as possible they do not allow it to affect their leisure time activities.

The two distinct sets of interests and leisure activities that have been illustrated here are shared by other groups in similar structural positions. The same patterns can be found among school rejectors who are distinguished from the cases studied both by sex and by the sort of school they attend. To illustrate this let us look at two groups of girls, one from wealthy middle class backgrounds in North London, and the other made up of working class northern girls.

THE NORTHLAWNS AND WOOLTON GIRLS

Girls' peer groups tend to be smaller than those of boys and not infrequently consist simply of a pair of very close friends. Joan Moss and Maureen Cooper are one such pair who attend the largely working class Woolton grammar school. Working class girls do not have the access to street culture of their male counterparts, so their leisure patterns are necessarily rather different and their involvement in the pop media is correspondingly greater. But like the boys, they spend much of their time—whether in or out of the house—in the company of their peers. Often Joan and Maureen are together, sometimes in a larger group of friends. Most of the remaining time they spend with their respective boyfriends. They prefer to be away from home if possible. Joan has a part time job in the local market which keeps her busy for much of the weekend. Her evenings in the previous few days had been spent dancing at the Mecca dance hall, drinking in the pub, or listening to records with her friends. Maureen also likes to listen to records when she is at home, usually in the company of Joan or her boyfriend. She goes to the cinema every week, not because she particularly enjoys films, for she goes irrespective of what is showing, but because it is 'a good way of getting out of the house'. Usually she goes on Sunday evenings when the rest of the family are gathered around the television. She enjoys being at school about as much as being at home and is eager to leave at Easter, when she is fifteen, because she is bored by the lessons which she finds repetitive. Typically, she was absent from school when we tried to talk to her. When she reappeared next day she told us that she had been down in the town buying a new pair of shoes.

Our middle class group are equally disillusioned with school, although they all come from affluent backgrounds (one has three television sets at home, of which one is in colour) and are in the top stream at Northlawns school. All three—Sally Johns, Margaret Robinson and Vanessa Spencer—hope to leave at sixteen. Vanessa had wanted to stay on at school but had become 'fed up with teachers and school'. Although hoping to pass 'O' level in seven subjects she wants to leave, with vague hopes of combining secretarial training and modelling.

Like their working class peers, these girls are very much oriented towards their friends and spend nearly all the time with one or more friends of the same age. Their behaviour over the previous weekend showed a very similar pattern. Friday night was bath and hairwashing night, accompanied by records or television, preparation for the two days of freedom ahead. Saturday morning and afternoon was spent in the West End and Kensington boutiques where all three bought hot-pants, which were just coming into fashion at the time. Saturday evening (and part of Saturday night) was the climax of all the preparation when the three descended on the clubs of the West End. 'Samantha's' which features a discotheque seemed to be the favourite of the moment and all three—passing for seventeen year olds—were there with friends and boy friends. The music, which includes both Negro pop and progressive rock, and the opportunity to meet people are the chief pleasures of these clubs to which the girls go most weekends. Margaret and Vanessa spent Sunday morning recovering, but Sally was up early to go to a part time job. The lure of the West End claimed Sally and Vanessa again on Sunday evening. This time they went for a drive around in the car of one of their boy friends. Margaret went to a local youth club where there was dancing and also a group discussion on fashion.

The leisure patterns of these two groups reflect their different social backgrounds, although geographical location is also an important variable. The facilities and entertainments available to the London girls are much more numerous and varied than those to which the northern girls have access. Metropolitan life also gives the London group a sophistication and superficial maturity that makes them seem much older than their counterparts in other parts of the country. But by no means all London girls develop in this way. Those in our sample who lived in the East End were much more like working class adolescents in other areas than they were like the Northlawns girls. They rarely leave the area around their homes and as a result do not lead a metropolitan life.

As their leisure activities have indicated, both groups of girls are highly involved in the pop media, but the use they make of them is very different. While the working class girls were both very interested in clothes and would spend any spare money they had on them, fashion is not as central to their lives as it is to the Northlawns group. All three of the latter are fashion conscious to a very high degree. We have already seen that Vanessa Spencer has aspirations towards modelling, but Sally Johns and Margaret Robinson also hope to pursue careers connected with the fashion world. Sally would like to be a beautician while Margaret, who wants to be a fashion designer, already designs and makes a lot of her own clothes. This preoccupation with fashion is reflected in their magazine reading. Whereas Joan and Maureen from Leeds choose the highly popular adolescent magazine *Jackie* as the favourite, Sally and Vanessa read the more sophisticated publications such as *Honey* and *19*, which deal almost entirely with fashion and which are aimed at a rather older readership. Margaret has a rather wider taste and reads magazines as diverse as *Valentine, Jackie, Fab 208* and *Petticoat*, but all of them are chosen primarily for their fashion interest.

Sally, Vanessa and Margaret all share the middle class school rejectors' interest in progressive music that we noticed among the boys. All chose artists such as Jimi Hendrix, George Harrison and Leonard Cohen among their favourite performers. This taste was also reflected in their record collections. Both Sally and Margaret have large collections, consisting mostly of LPs, among which are examples of records which had been thought to appeal only to the most advanced musical taste—pop music equivalents to Stockhausen. However, the interest of all these girls in dancing means that they also appreciate Negro pop music—particularly Tamla Motown. It is this sort of music that has the greatest appeal for the working class girls. Motown, Reggae and soul records make up the bulk of their relatively modest collections which consist primarily of 45 r.p.m. singles, although Joan does have a more catholic taste than the majority of such girls and also appreciates some of the more accessible and easily understood progressive music. Both she and Maureen rely heavily on the radio as a provider of music, each listening to about ten hours a week, whereas the London girls are more likely to listen to their records. Similarly, Joan and Maureen are keen fans of *Top of the Pops*, while only Sally of the Northlawns girls watches it regularly. Vanessa and Margaret watch occasionally if they happen to be at home but in general they find the programme 'too teenybopper'.

Unlike their male counterparts, Sally, Vanessa and Margaret agree with their working class peers that teachers should be more prepared to talk about the media in class. The girls' involvement in pop music and fashion is so intense that it outweighs their rejection of teachers and they felt that introducing such material could alleviate the boredom they feel in many lessons and might improve teacher-pupil relationships. Vanessa thought that teachers should definitely be more aware of the mass media and this would act as common ground on which to build a new sort of relationship between teacher and taught. Maureen also felt that there was a gap which needed bridging from both sides. 'We could get to understand teachers more and get to know them. At the moment we seem far apart from them. On the other hand, they could judge us better out of class.'

The grammar school ethos came over in Joan's and Maureen's responses to this question. While agreeing that teachers could usefully take greater account of the media, they both qualified their agreement, adding that the introduction of special lessons 'would take up too much time'. Once again, the division between school and leisure is discernible.

These examples should have helped to give an impression of the differing degree to which certain groups of adolescents who reject the school culture are involved in the pop media. Again different patterns of involvement are displayed by those groups who are more committed to the value system of the school and who therefore have less need of an alternative system of meanings. Study reveals that working class groups of this sort make very little use of the pop media. They have little interest in clothes or fashion and are usually either indifferent or positively hostile towards pop music. They tend to be more oriented towards their home and family and consequently the mass medium they use most is television—but not for programmes like *Top of the Pops*. Naturally they do not consider that teachers should make any concessions to the mass media—'they're meant to teach us subjects, not what's on the telly'.

Middle class adolescents who accept the school's culture do make use of the pop media, but it is in no way central to their life style. They read the most popular magazines such as *Jackie*, watch the most popular television programmes like *Top of the Pops* and admire the most popular performers, such as Cliff Richard, but their involvement does not extend beyond this relatively superficial level. They also are very much home-based and, besides watching a good deal of television, they read widely, spend a lot of time on their homework and pursue other activities which the school system adjudges to have cultural value.

It may be concluded from our study of these cases that a number of factors are relevant in ordaining what use adolescents make of the pop media and what meaning they have for them; and that the most important are class, sex and evaluation of the school culture. If these things are known, the media use of most secondary school pupils can be predicted with some accuracy.

This concludes the presentation of the substantive findings of this study and a brief discussion of their implications follows in the final chapter.

11 Implications

The brief of this project was to investigate the present state of mass media based teaching in English secondary schools, and to explore the part played by the media in the lives of pupils. The preceding chapters have set out the results of this research. However, in the course of the study, we investigators have formed our own opinion as to what should be happening. In this final chapter, therefore, we intend to set out our own personal summary of the implications of this research for the development of the secondary school curriculum. We would stress however, that these are our personal opinions.

The most widely quoted statements of recent years on the subject of the place of media based teaching in secondary schools are undoubtedly, paragraphs 473 to 476 of the Newsom Report. While we agree substantially with these statements we would wish to add some points of clarification, elaboration, and reservation.

In the first place, the Newsom Report was concerned explicitly with pupils in secondary modern schools and in the low ability bands of comprehensives who are predominantly working class and who constitute the bulk of early leavers. Consequently, the proposals are made with this group specifically in mind. While we would agree that media oriented activities should find a place in any curriculum developed for this group, we would want to extend this point and argue that media based teaching should be an integral part of the middle school course in all secondary schools, for, as we have seen, some of the pupils who are most deeply involved in various aspects of the mass media are in grammar schools and in the high ability bands of comprehensives. The Newsom Report was prepared in the early 1960s before the rise of the British pop groups led by the Beatles. It is therefore understandable that the Committee should have singled out film and television for particular attention. They are certainly not alone in this stress. A very great deal of academic research has concentrated almost exclusively on television, while many of the most vocal proponents of media based teaching have been explicitly concerned with film appreciation. Again, while not denying the importance of film and television, we would point out that our results indicate that the media experiences of a considerable number of pupils are dominated by pop. Hence, in our view, any attempt to come to terms with the contemporary mass media in the teaching situation must be prepared to address itself to the phenomenon of pop in all its various dimensions.

Having argued that media based teaching should be an integral part of all secondary school courses, we are now faced with the much more difficult question of what form this teaching should take.

Towards the curriculum

In our view, media based teaching should aim to do three things, firstly, to encourage pupils to be discriminating in their role as consumers; secondly to give them some insight into the development and workings of the contemporary mass media; and thirdly, wherever possible, to give pupils the opportunity to originate and produce their own mass media materials. Let us take each point in turn.

The evidence we have been able to gather indicates that most pupils have an active rather than passive relationship with the mass media. The important question to ask therefore is not, what are the mass media *doing to* adolescents, but what are adolescents *doing with* the mass media. Far from accepting what they are offered wholesale, or just letting the material wash over them, most pupils are constantly making judgements and discriminations, selecting those elements which in some way speak to them and rejecting those that do not. Instead of ignoring these judgements, and with them the life experiences from which they stem, teaching should take them as a necessary starting point and attempt to build upwards from this base, encouraging pupils to have more confidence in their own judgements and to extend the range and depth of their critical capacities. Elements of so-called 'high culture' should be introduced, not as an implicit condemnation of the material which pupils spontaneously enjoy, but in order to introduce them to ways of codifying and expressing experience of which they might not otherwise be aware. As Michael Marland put it, 'the basis of all our teaching must be adding, enriching and encouraging—not deleting, criticizing and inhibiting'.[1]

In order to encourage pupils to be more aware and articulate in their role as consumers of mass media material, it is essential that they should be given some insight into the process of production and some understanding of how the mass media work. The material which is finally offered to us as consumers is the end result of a cumulative process of selection during which certain elements are emphasized, others played down, and others still cut away altogether. For example, what is finally shown on a television news broadcast represents only a tiny fraction of the material that could have been shown. Who decided what to show, and on what basis did they make their decisions? An awareness and understanding of these and other similar questions is essential if pupils are to be members of an informed audience which can actively challenge the adequacy of what is offered to them.

In addition to giving pupils an understanding of the present, media based teaching should also provide some perspective from the past, for the present situation cannot be understood apart from an analysis of the way in which the mass media developed. Until very recently, however, most commentators either ignored the development of the mass media and popular culture altogether, or misrepresented it. Most accounts of the rise of the popular press, for example, lay great stress on the foundation of the *Daily Mail* by Lord Northcliffe in 1896,[2] but very few devote much attention to the radical newspapers of Cobbett, Carlisle and Hetherington, or to the 'gallows ballads' of Jemmy Catnach. Yet, the present popular press owes as much to these sources as it does to Lord Northcliffe. Fortunately, this forgotten social and cultural history is now beginning to be written. It is the history of industrial England written from the bottom up rather than the other way around. It represents an attempt to recreate the texture of the daily life and thought of ordinary people. Nor is this history simply confined to contemporary documents. Although these are indispensable, a surprising amount still survives in the memories and recollections of people who were there at the time. The Second World War for example, was not only manoeuvres and battles; it was also the Blitz and the Black Market. Recording this oral history should form an integral part of any attempt to recreate the everyday past. Without this awareness of the past, and the distinctive sense of time and place which accompanies it, any understanding of the contemporary situation must necessarily remain partial.

The next few years are likely to be particularly important for the future of the British mass media. The introduction of local radio and the development of video cassettes and cable television provide potential opportunities for greater participation and more democratic forms of control. However, the extent to which these possiblities will become realities depends firstly on how forcefully audience members and consumers can press their claims, and secondly on whether or not people feel that they are capable of participating. In order to bring about this second situation it is necessary to go beyond the training of critical and informed consumers and to encourage pupils to become aware of their ability to originate and produce material which expresses their own distinctive view of their situation and of the world around them. As often as possible, therefore, pupils should be provided with the opportunity to make their own films, print their own magazines, perform their own songs, transmit their own radio shows, and run their own advertising campaigns. Nor should these be merely academic exercises. They should be produced with a real audience or public in mind—either the school community or, even better, the local neighbourhood. In this way links can be established between school and the environment that are not simply a one-way process of bringing street experiences into the classroom. Insights and initiatives from the classroom can be taken back into the streets—perhaps in the form of a neighbourhood news-paper, perhaps as an advertising campaign for a local cause or charity.

Implications

Any proposals for innovations in the curriculum sooner or later raise questions about what schools ought to be teaching and how they should go about this task. In the case of media-based activities these questions are thrown into particularly sharp relief. What then are the wider implications of our proposals?

1   Our findings suggest that one of the main reasons why pupils gravitate towards the patterns of meaning and expression offered by the pop media is because they find few opportunities to explore their social and personal experience within the school. The introduction of media-based activities therefore immediately raises the question of the place of the emotional and expressive dimensions of adolescence as against the cognitive and intellectual. This in turn implies a major reassessment of the place of arts subjects and of creativity within the curriculum. There is already a good deal of experiment within art, music and English teaching and in our view media-based activities should be seen as a logical extension of these existing trends rather than as a completely separate and self-contained subject.

In addition to encouraging pupils to explore their responses to the contemporary mass media and to originate their own material, we have suggested that pupils should also be aware of how the modern communications media developed and how they work. Again these activities should not be hived off as a separate course in media studies, but should be integrated into a more general rethinking of history and social studies courses.

Media-based activities therefore present a challenge to conventional subject divisions and point towards the constructing of courses which would create sustained links both within creative arts and social studies and between these two curriculum areas. This in turn implies a move towards team teaching.

2   Our findings also suggest that pupils from different social class and neighbourhood backgrounds, with different school experiences, differ very considerably in the amount of interest they take in the mass media and in the particular elements they select for attention. In view of these differences, therefore, it would—in our view—be counterproductive to design a single course for all pupils, or even for all pupils in the same sort of school. Rather, if media-based activities are seen as a necessary part of a more general attempt to create links between the school and the surrounding community, they must relate to the particular environment from which the pupils come. The necessary change is not therefore in the direction of providing all pupils of a certain age with common educational fare, but rather of developing a common intention towards pupils. This requires that all preconceptions about individual

capacities be laid aside and that attention be concentrated on 'leading each adolescent as far as he or she can be got to go. This means less emphasis on the assimilation of a predetermined content and more on the development of various processes of thought and sensitivities of feeling'.[3] This in turn raises the question of assessment and suggests that attention should be given to extending the use of the more flexible procedures presented by CSE Mode 3. But this approach has certain repercussions for the organization of the learning situation.

3   Unlike conventional school subjects such as mathematics, the knowledge and experience offered by the contemporary mass media is potentially open to everyone. Consequently, the teacher involved in media-based activites is likely to find that he is no longer in possession of a discrete body of knowledge, skills and techniques, which he dispenses to the pupils and which they gratefully collect. Indeed, in some cases, the roles may be reversed and the teacher may find that the pupils possess more knowledge and information than he does. Again this situation challenges conventional chalk and talk methods and points towards the more frequent use of discussion not only between teacher and pupils, but more importantly between the pupils themselves. For, as Patrick Creber has pointed out:

It is probably only in the pupil-to-pupil talk of small groups that the adolescent can feel safe enough to think aloud in a way that enables him to 'realize' and recognize aspects of his experience, his emotion, his personality that he has hitherto kept private even from himself. In this context, the teacher's role may be largely confined to making such situations feasible, and to offering some initial stimulation.[4]

In this process pupils discover their own experience and cast around for a language that will do it justice. Indeed, it can be convincingly argued that providing pupils with a series of language environments in which they can discuss and try out their judgements and ideas may be the most important innovation of all.[5] Discussion presents only one avenue through which to explore experience; other equally important means of discovery are provided by individual and collective creative work and by social action within the community. Nor are these necessarily mutually exclusive. An advertising campaign planned and conducted by pupils on behalf of a local cause, for example, would involve discussion, creative work and community action. Such activities imply a deemphasis on the classroom as the central learning environment and a corresponding consideration of the possibilities of individual and group project work.

4   Very rapidly, as two teachers taking part in a secondary school mathematics project discovered, such changes in the content and presentation of lessons can raise fundamental questions about the school's organization.

Information and instruction are given by staff who see themselves (and apparently they are accepted by the children) as members of the team, guiding the work rather than pontificating. This change of role in the teacher has established a change in the relationship between teacher and pupil. There is increased communication . . .

The influence of the project on school organization has been significant. Through our work with mixed-ability groups in mathematics we learned to question the formal streaming of our classes for all subjects.[6]

Again, media-based activities are much more likely than mathematics to raise such questions. Our findings suggest that the formal academic divisions between pupils, and the assumptions upon which they rest, play a considerable part in creating and sustaining the sense of alienation which a number of pupils experience. Labelling children either failures or successes, serves both to alienate a large sector of those at the bottom and to place those at the top under considerable pressure. The result is disengagement at both ends of the spectrum. Our findings, in common with those of others, indicate that the more rigorously a school differentiates between pupils on the basis of supposed ability, the greater is the likelihood that an anti-school peer culture will emerge at the bottom and that a proportion of those at the top will become 'mental migrants'. Further, as we have seen, for some pupils, involvement in the pop media provides a way of articulating this experience of disengagement.

Introducing media-based activities into the school without a corresponding change in the formal organization, therefore, simply tackles the symptoms while leaving the basic causes untouched. Ultimately, therefore, media-based teaching along the lines suggested here implies a move away from streaming towards more flexible internal grouping systems, and beyond that—at a more general level—the development of genuinely comprehensive schools.

We have raised these implications in order to indicate that any discussion of the place of media-based teaching in secondary schools must inevitably concern itself not only with this particular problem but also with wider questions of educational policy. This does not mean that no attempt can be made to introduce media-based activities until these general issues have been resolved. On the contrary, successful changes are the result of continuing attempts to experiment and adapt to changing circumstances and—exactly because they touch on so many important issues—experiments with media-based activities are likely to prove particularly fruitful and illuminating. They do, however, present a number of difficulties—both for the pupils and for the schools.

DIFFICULTIES—THE PUPILS

The first question which arises is, do pupils want the sort of course that we have described?

Towards the end of the interviews pupils were asked if they wanted teachers to talk about the mass media, particularly the pop media, in lessons. Of the 146 fourth formers who answered this question, 59% said 'yes'. The reasons given in support of this opinion were most revealing.

M.S.—6*

The great majority of these pupils criticized both the content and structure of existing lessons, saying that they found the lessons boring and repetitive and that most teachers made little or no attempt to introduce variety into their presentation or to relate the material to the situations of everyday life. But a considerable number of pupils also had some positive proposals to make. Of these, by far the most frequently mentioned was a general suggestion that there should be more discussions in which pupils would have an opportunity to talk with each other and with the teacher, rather than just being talked at. In view of the proposals for specific media-based courses such as film apprecia- tion, it is interesting that only 17% of our respondents said that they would like this sort of separate consideration.

Not all the pupils we spoke to were in favour of change, however, and in fact 41% said that they did not want teachers to introduce mass media material into the classroom. The majority of these pupils had a very 'instrumental' attitude to education. In their view, schools exist to provide examination passes which will hopefully secure a well paid job, and that consequently time should not be wasted listening to pop records or looking at films. Others added that teachers should 'stick to teaching' and that 'what you do out of school is none of their business'. Pupils holding these opinions were more likely to be working class than middle class; in fact almost half (49%) of the working class pupils said that they did not want their teachers to talk about the mass media in lessons compared with 28% of the middle class respondents. Clearly, then, the introduction of more mass media material into lessons is not likely to pro- vide an immediate solution to the problem of finding a curriculum which work- ing class children find relevant and interesting. Nor, judging by our findings, is media-based teaching likely to prove equally attractive to all school rejectors. Certainly, the majority (71%) of the pop-oriented rejectors said that they would welcome such a change, but 60% of the non pop-oriented rejectors were hostile or indifferent to the idea. This is not particularly surprising, because, as we have indicated, the pop media are not a central part of the culture of all working class school rejectors. We have thus arrived at a paradox, in so far as the so-called 'Newsom' children (who are usually considered as the primary target for curriculum innovations) appear to show the least enthusiasm for this particular proposal, while those in grammar schools and in the top half of comprehensives, where innovations are much less likely, would apparently very much welcome the idea of more media-based teaching.

These findings indicate that a number of pupils, particularly those from working class backgrounds, have internalized the schools' stress on preparing for work roles and that consequently they regard their leisure experience as something completely separate. Thus, in the short run, attempts to alter this definition and to reduce the gap between schools and the surrounding environ- ment—through introducing media-based activities—are likely to meet with a certain amount of resistance from these groups of pupils and more particularly from their parents, whose only reference point is their own schooling. It takes time to break through this kind of resistance, but it can be overcome if the school is open both in the sense of actively encouraging parents and prospective employers to visit and participate and in the sense of involving the school in the life of the local community. Nevertheless, our results suggest that about half the working class pupils and almost three-quarters of the middle class children are, in varying degrees, discontented with the present situation and would like to see some changes made. Given that a number of pupils would like more of the sort of teaching that we have outlined, the question now arises as to whether or not the schools can provide it.

DIFFICULTIES—THE SCHOOLS

The major difficulty facing schools is lack of resources. Many of the suggestions recommended in this chapter must have made a large number of teachers smile in despair. There are still many schools which do not even have an adequate supply of books, let alone such equipment as portable tape recorders, film cameras and video-tape facilities. Without a substantial increase in funds many of the more adventurous media-based creative work called for here cannot be put into practice. Nevertheless, there is still some scope in this area by, for example, making greater use of some relatively inexpensive techniques.

The classroom consideration of mass media material presents fewer resource problems, since children can be encouraged to bring magazines, newspapers and their own records from home. Similarly, pupils can be asked to watch a particular television programme with a view to discussion and follow-up work the next morning. Films present the greatest problem, as they are expensive. A visit to the cinema would make a sizeable hole in most pupils' pocket money, and hiring films for showing within the classroom is often beyond the school budget. But, this cost factor can be alleviated to some extent. In the first place, a number of important cinema films are now being shown on television. Secondly, the cost of showing films within the school can be reduced by forming a film club open to all pupils and to their parents. Cost, although important, is not the only factor in the situation. For, as we have seen, the frequency with which teachers introduce mass media material into lessons depends not only on the availability of the necessary material and equipment, but also upon their attitudes towards the media.

According to the result of our survey, only 20% of grammar schools, 26% of comprehensives and 28% of secondary modern actively support the sort of approach suggested here (i.e. Approach 4 described in Chapter 5). The remaining schools either do not see media-based teaching as part of their job, or else introduce media material into lessons in order to denigrate it. We have argued that these attitudes are based on too rigid a differentiation between media material and the products of so-called 'high culture', and that this division in turn reflects the basic division between the school and the environment.

Reclassifying selected media products (such as the films of Ingmar Bergman, or certain songs by Bob Dylan and the Beatles) as art or culture does nothing to challenge the basic assumptions on which this division rests. If as we have suggested, media-based teaching should start from the pupils' interests and experiences, then we must come to terms with the material which is an integral part of their daily life, and we could do worse than begin by re-examining our own experience.

The gap between schools and the environment permeates not only the relationships between teachers and pupils but also the experience of teachers themselves. The process of becoming a professional teacher requires that students, particularly students of English, should cut away or suppress large areas of their personal experience and replace an involvement with popular culture with a commitment to high culture. In this the universities and training colleges are fairly successful. Consequently, as Richard Hoggart has pointed out:

> Each year's group of graduates . . . leave . . . anxious to communicate their heritage in the schools. They soon find that the voices that most readily speak to their school children are very different from the voices heard in that high art they are now trained to teach . . . how many teachers make sense of this split, although many of them listened to those popular voices before they came to university and some might still do so with some part of themselves? In my experience few resolve the contradictions.[7]

A number of teachers, particularly young teachers, therefore live a kind of double life divided between their professional role and their private experience, teaching Shakespeare and Keats to their pupils while returning home to watch *Top of the Pops*. Before teachers can reduce the gap between schools and the environment for their pupils, therefore, they must first resolve the divisions within their own experience. The first step is to re-examine the basis of our own participation in popular culture. For, as Pauline Karl put it in connection with commercial cinema films:

> If we go back and think over the movies we've enjoyed—even those we knew were terrible movies while we enjoyed them—what we enjoyed in them, the little part that was good, had in some rudimentary way, some freshness, some hint of style, some trace of beauty, some audacity, some craziness.[8]

This applies equally well to television shows, magazines, comics and pop music. In even the simplest, most mechanical production that may be something worth salvaging, and it is with this elementary act of salvage that any attempts to encourage appreciation and discrimination must begin. There will of course be a sizeable gap between the tastes and experiences of the pupils and those of the teachers. This is inevitable, given the differences in social class background, age and training. Nevertheless, if teachers are prepared to understand their own experience of popular culture and to take seriously the judgements and discriminations of their pupils, then a constructive dialogue can begin.

It is not that the teacher should try uncritically to accept everything in the teenager's view of his world—in any case this is a self defeating procedure—but that he should have sufficient respect for children and sufficient confidence in his own judgement to recognize what is of value in it. Only when a dialogue has been started through this approach can the teacher hope to relate what he values in his own cultural life to the needs and interests of the adolescent.[9]

The process is therefore a reciprocal one in which the teacher encourages pupils to share his enthusiasms and invites them in turn to share their own preferences and antipathies with him. In this process, both parties open themselves to new experiences and jointly explore their responses.

Changes in attitude of the sort that we have argued are necessary will obviously not take place overnight, but an immediate and constructive start can be made with teacher training. In the first place, the sort of media-based activities which we have outlined for pupils should also be incorporated into the syllabus for all intending teachers, particularly those engaged in arts and social science subjects. Nor should these opportunities be restricted to teachers in training; there should also be more courses offering practising teachers the chance to extend their knowledge and understanding.

We have argued that media-based activities should be geared to the needs and interests of the pupils. This does not mean, however, that there can be no carry-over from one situation to another for, despite important local variations, similar environments present similar kinds of problems. Indeed, it is often the lack of communication between teachers in different schools, and the consequent feeling of isolation, which most often deters experiment. Teachers who have experimented with media-based activities should be encouraged to provide a description of their work, the backgrounds of the pupils involved, the activities engaged on, the materials employed, where they were obtained, how much they cost, how the pupils responded to the various activities, and the difficulties encountered. These reports would then be lodged with a central clearing house, where copies would be available to any teacher contemplating activities with similar groups of pupils. Judging from the frequent requests for information that we have received ourselves in the course of this project, there is an immediate and pressing demand for such a system among teachers at all levels of secondary and further education. At the moment many of the sources available are widely scattered, difficult to obtain, out of date, and insufficiently detailed—particularly as regards practical matters such as cost, access and suitability.

Conclusion

In our view, simply introducing more mass media material into lessons will not help to close the gap between the school and the environment, or reduce the number of alienated pupils, unless it is part of a more general reassessment of assumptions and structures. The example provided by two of the schools in our sample illustrates this point.

Dockstreet and Middleton are both inner urban secondary schools catering for 'Newsom' children. In both schools teachers were found to introduce media material into their lessons quite frequently, but in very different ways. At Dockstreet the use of media material in teaching was part of an overall strategy which attempted to link life in the school to life in the local neighbourhood, and so reduce the gap between the two. To this end, streaming and school uniforms have been discontinued and a more flexible curriculum introduced, stressing team teaching and project work in the surrounding neighbourhood. This situation contrasts markedly with that obtaining at Middleton, where a rigid streaming system is in operation and school uniform is compulsory. (In fact a member of the research team was asked not to wear coloured trousers, as this set a 'bad example' to the children.) This organizational rigidity is reflected in the approach to teaching which stresses the conventional, the compartmentalization of subjects and the primacy of 'chalk and talk' methods. Mass media material was used in lessons almost wholly in a negative way, in an attempt to 'inoculate' pupils against the worst effects of too much exposure to media products.

Our findings suggest that these two approaches do produce different results; that pupils in these schools do feel differently about their school and, on the basis of the evidence gathered in this study, we would argue for an extension of the basic strategy adopted at Dockstreet. Ultimately, the argument is not about techniques or even about content, but about the quality of the relationships between teachers and pupils and the assumptions on which these relationships rest and, beyond that, about the kind of society we want to be members of. A modern education worthy of the name must be an education against alienation.

References

1   Marland, Michael, 1969 *Mainstream* in Denys Thompson ed.

2   See for example; Thompson, Denys, Foreword to; Fred Inglis, ed. *Literature and Environment* London, Chatto and Windus, 1971, pp. 7–10.

3   Holly, Douglas, 1972 *Society, Schools and Humanity* London, Paladin Books, pp. 44–5.

4   Creber, J. W. Patrick, 1971 *Lost for Words* Harmondworth, Penguin Books, p. 63.

5   Barnes, Douglas, Britton, James and Rosen, Harold, 1971 *Language, the Learner and the School* Harmondsworth, Penguin Books.

6   'Mathematics for the Majority' (quoted in) *Dialogue: Schools Council Newsletter* No. 3, June 1969, p. 5.

7   Hoggart, Richard, 1970 'Schools of English and Contemporary Society' in: Richard Hoggart, *Speaking to Each Other: Volume II About Literature* London, Chatto and Windus, p. 253.

8   Kael, Pauline, 1970 'Trash, Art and the Movies' in: Pauline Kael *Going Steady* London, Maurice Temple Smith, p. 107.

9   Hannam, Charles et al., 1971, op. cit. p. 23.

Appendices

Appendix 1

Pupils, teachers and researchers

In my perfect school there would *not* be a lot of visiting people coming to try out experiments on us and, in general, treating us like a lot of human guinea pigs! That sounds a bit biased but that's what I think. [Isabel, aged 11[1]]

Isabel is not alone in holding an unfavourable view of research. She is joined by a number of teachers. This is not to say that the pupils and staff who participated in this particular study were unhelpful or antagonistic; quite the opposite in most cases. In the schools who finally agreed to participate in the study we were greeted with more interest, encouragement and courtesy than we had any right to expect. But in some of the schools where cooperation was refused, the head and some of the staff were often suspicious and sometimes hostile and, judging from a recent report, there are quite a number of teachers who would act similarly.[2] It is worth pausing to ask ourselves why.

The postwar years in Britain have been years of rapid social change during which the goals of education have been constantly reviewed, with the consequence that many of the reference points that secured the daily relationships of teachers and pupils have been called into question. New questions have a habit of creating new forms of expertise to provide the answers, and so it is that sociologists—themselves a product of educational changes within the university—have become a familiar sight in classrooms up and down the country. There is a thread running through some of the research that has been done, parts of which many teachers have recognized. It runs something like this; they came, they observed, they measured, they published, they were promoted. With each step along this line the mental distance between researchers and teachers widens, until it stretches across a space marked 'them' and 'us'. Here are just a few of the things teachers have said:

They came:

I've heard it said in staff rooms. 'What do they know about teaching? They don't come in and face thirty-six children every morning. They haven't got these little problems that rule our lives'.

. . . there is little respect in the teaching profession for people who sit in their offices and pronounce judgement. I should prefer to see research aimed at the restoration of the teacher, i.e. taking power of decision away from sociologists.[3]

They measured:

There is a natural tendency for us to be a little bit suspicious of researchers who are a very long way away, and are apparently doing everything as a result of what I happen to put down on a piece of paper, myself being aware as I put it down that this is a possible answer to the questions and not the only one, and could be interpreted in quite the wrong way.[4]

They published:

The language sometimes is incomprehensible. One has to pause and say 'What the devil does this mean?' Some of it is like an income tax form, or a solicitor's letter![5]

They were promoted:

This is the third survey I have completed lately and I'm wondering what is read into the statistics they all yield, apart from postgraduate awards to the compilers.

Who's going to get a Ph.D. out of this lot then?[6]

These comments apply most forcefully to the particular style of sociological research which C. Wright Mills has characterized as 'abstracted empiricism'.[7] However, a glance into many of the journals and books that pour from the presses is enough to confirm that this style continues to dominate a great deal of research, and it is therefore understandable that many teachers should have formed the opinion that more or less all sociological research is a variety of abstracted empiricism. Happily, this is not the case, but, nevertheless, many of the criticisms expressed in these comments are more than justified, and it is worth pursuing some of the issues in a little more detail.

Practitioners of abstracted empiricism see themselves as detached observers of social reality whose essential task is to collect hard facts (preferably by means of sample surveys), present them in statistical tables, and publish the results in academic journals. Behind this orientation lies a conception of social science which stresses the word 'science'. According to this view, studying human behaviour is essentially the same as studying chemical reactions in a test tube or the behaviour of gas in a vacuum. In the same way that a chemist or physicist is separated from the processes he studies by his gas jar or micro-scope, so the sociologist is distanced by his questionnaires and computers. He is a detached observer, studying human behaviour objectively in the sense that people are treated as objects of study, laid out like T. S. Eliot's patient, 'ether-ized upon a table', waiting to have their private and social anatomies dissected by the surgery of statistics. This stress on the necessity of distance at each stage of the research process, has several important consequences.

If research is regarded as simply a matter of gathering and manipulating facts which are assumed to be already present in the situation, any sort of personal contact between the sociologist and the actors in the situation may be seen as diminishing the researcher's status as a scientific observer. So, in order to avoid the 'contamination' of personal feelings, he is more or less obliged to treat the actors as objects rather than subjects, as things rather than people. Hence the empiricist's preference for objective research techniques which minimize personal contacts. But the impersonal nature of this kind of research means that, for many of those on the receiving end of pre-coded questionnaires, the experience of becoming an object of sociological study is often accompanied by an increasing conviction that researchers are people apart, and that research is an essentially one-way process in which teachers and pupils do all the giving and researchers all the taking.

The initial distance between teachers and sociologists which arises out of the way in which abstracted empiricist research tends to be conducted is further extended during the analysis and presentation of the results. To take one example, adolescents were asked by researchers at Birmingham University to fill in a diary sheet stating how they spent their time on three separate days. The data from the completed forms was fed into a computer and the resulting statistical analysis provided the basis for an article in an academic journal describing how secondary modern pupils typically spend their leisure time.[8] This process serves to widen the gap between teachers and researchers in two ways. Firstly, the results are likely to be inaccessible to the teacher, being published in a specialist academic journal which is not generally available at bookstalls or public libraries and which will almost certainly never find its way on to the staffroom table. This inaccessibility tends to reinforce the idea that sociological researchers are a race apart who are interested only in talking to each other. Secondly, the results may be largely unintelligible to the teacher in the sense that they appear to describe a 'world elsewhere', a world of tables, percentages, and technical jargon, which has very little to do with the daily experience of teaching adolescents. In the Birmingham study, for example, we are told the following facts about how fourth year girls spend their evenings; 'With TV she spends 2 hours 56 minutes; radio 15 minutes; records 13 minutes'.[9] This series of statements simply describes atomized aspects of behaviour without attempting to relate them to the contexts of daily life within which they took place, or trying to understand what the experience of watching the television or listening to records might mean to the girl herself. As a result, all the life is wrung out of the material. In the next sentence, for example, one of the most important and deeply felt aspects of adolescent experience is reduced to a single phrase and a simple statistic; 'She associates with a boy for 1 hour 7 minutes'. Small wonder that teachers picking up such a report are often unable to recognize anything of themselves or their pupils among the tables and erudite footnotes. Reading this sort of research is like visiting a museum of

dentistry and seeing the extracted teeth clearly displayed in bottles of preserva-
tive. It may look very impressive but it does not say very much about the
state of the jaws from which the teeth were taken, and nothing at all about
how the patients felt.

Abstracted empiricism may therefore be considered as a process of reification, through which people's life experiences are turned into thing-like
objects.[10] People are presented with a questionnaire asking for information
about those aspects of their thinking and behaviour—hours of television
watched, newspapers read—which can be relatively easily expressed in the
form of ticks on paper. This procedure results in a series of atomized items of
information about the person, which are totally abstracted and divorced from
the overall context of his daily life. These items are then analysed and the
results presented in the form of statistical tables which tend to give them an
air of finality. The outcome of this process is the creation of statistical and
administrative categories which people may come to see, not as descriptions or
summaries of their personal experiences or social situation, but—on the contrary—as thing-like objects which have been created by 'them' (the sociologists and powers-that-be) and which are therefore in some way opposed to
'us' (the pupils and teachers) and 'our' experience.

The comments quoted above suggest that quite a few teachers have, in one
way or another, grasped the nature of this process and have come to resent it.
Unfortunately, however, many teachers fail to distinguish between the techniques employed in collecting and analysing the data, and the overall perspec-
tives underlying research. Consequently, there is a tendency to see all research
that makes use of questionnaires, computers and statistical analysis as a variety
of abstracted empiricism. This is a mistaken view. Although the present study
also employs these techniques, it differs from abstracted empiricism in two
very important ways. Firstly, we took every opportunity to supplement the
information gained from the questionnaires by talking to as many individual
teachers and pupils as possible, both formally in interviews, and informally
through chance meetings and discussions in corridors, dining halls and staff-
rooms. Secondly, and more importantly, the whole study was planned and
conducted within a framework provided by a view of social science directly
opposed to that underlying abstracted empiricism.

In our view the stress on social science should be on the word 'social'.
People just do not behave in a vacuum, and you cannot bottle up someone's
life in a test tube. People will laugh, learn and fight whether or not a sociologist
is there to record the scene. But if he is present, although he is not necessarily
of the situation, he is most certainly in it, and it is thus a part of his own life
experience—albeit a small part—as well as being the pattern of daily life for
the people he is studying. Although he is 'down there on a visit' and he will
return to the university, the fact that he has made the visit may in some way
alter both his perception of himself and his view of the situation. The research-

er should not try to suppress this possibility; on the contrary he should accept it and make it a part of his research strategy. Through involving himself in a continuing series of dialogues with teachers and pupils, both during and after the fieldwork period, the researcher is gradually able to reach some under-standing of the situation and to contribute a distinct perspective which will hopefully encourage those involved to look again at the things that they usually take for granted and to reconsider the possibilities of change. The basic ideas behind this study are therefore not distance and objectivity, but dialogue, reciprocity and understanding.

All social situations may be viewed from two basic vantage points; by a detached observer looking in from outside, and by a participant looking out from inside. The deficiency of abstracted empiricism is that because it is only capable of looking at social situations from the outside, it completely ignores the interior meanings that situations have for those directly involved in them. According to the German sociologist, Max Weber, sociology's distinctive con-tribution is to view the situation from both these viewpoints and to relate one to the other. In order to do this he argues, it is necessary to employ the approach of 'verstehen'—understanding.[11]

The role of understanding has been very well described by Brian Jackson and Denis Marsden in the introduction to their book, *Education and the Work-ing Class*, in which they explain why they chose to do their study in the town where they themselves went to school.

Marburton is a real city in the north of England. It is a place where we were born ourselves, and the place where we grew up and where we went to school . . . We were formed by the grammar school world of Marburton.

To have gone elsewhere to do the research would have strengthened our claims to distance and 'objectivity' . . . But against this there seemed so much to be gained by facing the paramount fact that we were dealing with people and not things; and that any 'objectivity' to which we could lay claim must always conceal areas of 'relationship' which, though they might threaten to divert or swamp the social observer, were also, in potential, the richest source of vital *understanding*.[12] (our italics)

The fact that Jackson and Marsden had experienced the 'grammar school world' of Marburton from the inside was a great help to them in grasping the possible interior meanings of this experience for the working class pupils whom they studied. At the same time, however, as they themselves point out, personal experience may also serve to 'divert or swamp' the researcher in his role as sociological observer. If this happens, he may begin to see the situation entirely from the point of view of the actors inside it, and consequently lose sight of an overall sociological perspective. An example of this sort of foreshort-ening is provided by the purely autobiographical approach of Edward Blishen's documentary novel, *Roaring Boys*, in which he describes his own experience of becoming a teacher.[13] From his vivid descriptions of people and incidents we gain a real sense of what it felt like to be at 'Stonehill Street', down to the smell of chalk dust and utility floor polish. But, because he looks at the situation entirely through the eyes of a teacher the action tends to be concentrated in the classroom, and consequently the possible effects of the kinds of environments the pupils came from, or the impact of wider social changes, are only glimpsed in passing. This sort of approach exhibits the opposite deficiencies to abstracted empiricism. Whereas abstracted empiricism is too distant from the situation and grasps only the exterior dimension, pure autobiography is too close to the action and can only grasp aspects of the interior meanings.

If the researcher allows his personal experience to 'divert or swamp' him entirely he may begin to find himself in the same position as the hero of Richard Farina's novel who claimed that he had 'been down so long it looks like up to me'. There are, however, several ways in which the sociologist can avoid this.

One way is to abandon the attempt to understand interior meanings and to fall back on abstracted empiricism with its twin concepts of objectivity and distance, as Ronald King did in his study of the values and involvement of grammar school pupils.[14] He returned as a teacher to the same school at which he had earlier been a pupil but, instead of using his personal experiences as a means of understanding, he opted to conduct his study through pre-coded questionnaires, thus throwing the baby out with the bath water. Other researchers have attempted to strike a balance between involvement and detachment by assuming the dual role of participant-observer. Thus, David Hargreaves studied the pupils at a secondary modern school by teaching them himself and by observing other teachers' lessons. This Jekyll and Hyde stance is, however, a hazardous one to adopt, for, as Hargreaves points out, the researcher inevitably finds himself in an ambiguous position. He is likely to be distrusted by both staff and pupils and consequently a lot of his time may be taken up with the 'conscious manipulation of roles to avoid conflicts at different levels', and as a result there will be 'severe limitations on material obtained and bias in its interpretation'.[15] Our own particular solution to the problem of balancing involvement and detachment, which was by no means ideal, followed from our final choice of research strategy. Before describing this solution, therefore, it is necessary briefly to sketch some of the ideas and considerations which helped to form that strategy.

Our general view of the nature of the research process, together with many of our ideas on how actually to go about things in the research situation itself, owed a great deal to the work of Brian Jackson, Denis Marsden, and David Hargreaves. We were particularly impressed by the way in which these authors used 'case studies' of particular individuals and groups in specific situations as a means of illustrating and illuminating general processes. Certainly this attention to the details of unique circumstances can provide an invaluable source of insight, but paradoxically it can also become a weakness.

Because both these pieces of research concentrate on the pupils in one sort of school located in one particular area, neither is able to demonstrate how far their analysis applies to pupils in other schools, in other areas.

In choosing our own research strategy, we were in a slightly different position from many researchers, including Jackson and Hargreaves, for our research was primarily oriented not towards illuminating problems of academic interest, but rather towards contributing information to a crucial ongoing debate about public educational policy—the raising of the school leaving age and the shape of the future secondary curriculum. Naturally the immediate subject matter of the present research, the nature of the relationship between school cultures and the cultures provided by the mass media, touches on a number of interesting academic debates and our results throw light on several old controversies. But, in the final analysis, this research was not undertaken for the benefit of other academics, but to provide those responsible for making policy decisions, and those involved with making them work on the ground, with some sort of map of the situation and some definition of the dimensions of the problems facing them. Hence we needed a research strategy which would to some extent enable us both to eat our cake and have it. We wanted to produce a general overview of the present situation in a wide variety of English secondary schools, while at the same time retaining the illustrative richness of the kind of case study material employed by Jackson and Hargreaves, and to present the whole thing in such a way as to be intelligible to readers besides professional academics. Our search for indications of how this might be done led us rapidly to the Newsom Report, *Half Our Future*.

A number of pieces of policy oriented research appear to have modelled themselves on the census, and consequently statistical completeness has become a goal in itself. Unfortunately, this sort of research exhibits exactly the same deficiencies as we noted earlier in the case of abstracted empiricism. Once again people's life experiences are converted into statistics and not translated back again, and once again what is lost 'is the sense of life itself, the pattern of varying emotional pressures which is different from the pattern made by statistical comprehensiveness'.[16] The Newsom Report, however, does attempt to translate the statistics back into the experiences from which they were derived. In Chapter 22, the general survey findings are presented in terms of the actual case histories of 'individual boys and girls who were included in the sample' in order to 'give some idea of how great may be the differences between human beings—included for teaching purposes in the same category'.[17] Admittedly, this attempt has the appearance of being conceived more as an afterthought than as a necessary and integral part of an overall research strategy. Nevertheless, in recognizing that a grasp of the various ways in which particular individuals perceive and experience a situation is an essential part of any adequate sociological understanding of that situation, it represents a considerable step in the right direction.

The present research is an attempt to build on the framework of the Newsom Report and on the work of Brian Jackson and David Hargreaves, in order to develop a research strategy which will enable us to find consistent and systematic links between the interior meanings which situations may have for participants, and the general social and cultural environments within which these situations are experienced.

The way in which we finally decided to approach the task of integrating these two levels of analysis owed a very great deal to the vision of C. Wright Mills and what he called the 'sociological imagination'. Here is how he describes the potential role of this perspective;

... the individual can understand his own experience and gauge his own fate only by locating himself within his period ... The 'sociological imagination' enables us to grasp history and biography and the relations between the two within society. That is its task and its promise. It is the capacity to range from the most impersonal and remote transformations to the most intimate features of the human self—and to see the relations between the two. Back of its use there is always the urge to know the social and historical meaning of the individual in society and in the period in which he has his quality and his being.[18]

This perspective implies a certain distance. The sociologist cannot live all the time with close-ups, he must often stand back and see how the details form patterns. In the final analysis, he is an observer and chronicler, trying to make sense of what he can see. This does not mean that he does not try to get inside the viewpoints of the actors in the situation; on the contrary, this is an essential part of his task. But his basic contribution is to point out the links between these 'intimate features of the human self' and the 'impersonal and remote transformations' of the social structure and, in order to achieve this, he must be able to stand back from the action and to look at the situation from a series of vantage points. As Max Weber pointed out, although one should 'be able to put one's self in the place of the actor', 'it is not necessary to *be* Caesar in order to *understand* Caesar'[19] (our italics).

Therefore, although both of the authors of this report have been pupils in secondary schools and one of us has done a little teaching at one time, we have not conducted the research from within; either from inside one particular school or from inside our personal experience of the education system. Consequently, while our recollections of similar situations may perhaps have helped us to understand the viewpoints of the participants, our essential task has been to relate the biographical experiences of the teachers and pupils in the schools we have studied to the changes which are taking place within the education system, and indeed throughout contemporary society. At the same time we have tried to remain open to details, especially to those that do not fit, and not to let generality become superficiality.

Our underlying research perspective can be compared to the opening shots of the film, *West Side Story*. The film begins with an almost abstract pattern of lines, which are gradually defined as the Manhattan skyline. The camera moves slowly across the city until it reaches the tenements of the lower west side. It hovers for a moment, then cuts to an image of snapping fingers. Gradually, the camera moves out to show a group of youths playing basketball in a concrete playground surrounded by high rise blocks and wire fences. This attempt to view the problem from a series of vantage points in order to relate particular images, incidents, and personal experiences to a general overview of the social environments within which they take place, has guided this research throughout its various stages.

Our research design (illustrated in Fig. 1.1) attempted to put into practice the theoretical perspective offered by Mills' idea of the sociological imagination.

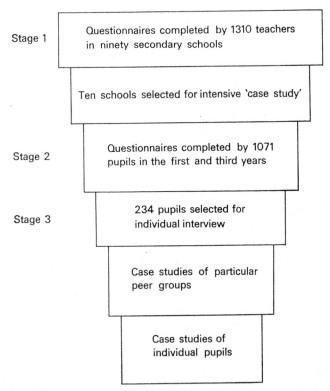

Fig. 1.1 Research design

At Stage 1 we started with a general survey of teachers in ninety widely different sorts of secondary schools in various parts of England, concentrating particularly on their attitudes towards the mass media and their approach to using media material in the classroom. On the basis of the questionnaire returns we selected ten schools which represented the diversity of attitudes and approaches, for more intensive study at Stage 2. These case studies were intended to provide concrete illustrations of the general structures revealed by the survey. Within these ten schools we gave a self completion questionnaire to pupils in the first and third years, and on the basis of these returns we selected a number of pupils for intensive personal interview at Stage 3. Again the interview material was seen as a way of building up a series of case studies of particular groups of pupils and of individual pupils who occupied specific positions with the school's social structures as revealed by the questionnaire. We further supplemented the survey data with a short test designed to elicit pupils' pop music preferences, conducted with classroom groups. We also took every opportunity to talk to the staff and to observe the patterns of social relationships within the schools.*

However, the various stages of the research should not be seen as a rigidly demarcated set of separate steps. Rather they are a series of Chinese boxes, which can be extended or collapsed according to the level of generality of the analysis at a particular time. Thus, the first level contains all the other levels and these can be extended to provide concrete illustrations of general structures. Alternatively, the boxes can be collapsed in order to relate particular case studies to the general survey findings.

Fred Inglis has recently expressed a hope that researchers may move 'nearer the magician and poet' than 'the sociologist (as we know him)'.[20] By this we take him to mean that sociology should move away from the sterile and unimaginative approach of abstracted empiricism and nearer perhaps to the poetic vision of William Blake; to see the world in a grain of sand.

It is a noble aim and one which we share to some extent but, as with all visions, it is partial. Certainly the sociologist should look beneath the surface and try to understand the levels of meanings contained within the seemingly insignificant particles of everyday social behaviour and, like the poet or magician, his work should jolt people out of their conventions and clichés, and encourage them to look again at things they take for granted. There is a crucial and permanent difference, however, between the aproach of a poet or magician on the one hand, and the sociologist on the other. Poetry deals essentially with the unique interior of personal experience, and it is largely left to the reader to draw his own generalizations. Similarly, a magician may be able to pull a surprising white rabbit out of an everyday hat but he never reveals how the rabbit got into the hat in the first place, or how it remained concealed for so long. Yet, it is exactly this attempt to demonstrate the nature of the relationships between the hat and the rabbit, between the interior content of human behaviour and the overall social and historical context within which it takes place, that constitutes the distinctive task and promise of sociological research. Our hope is that teachers and others interested and involved in education, who read

* A full account of how each stage of the research was planned and conducted may be found in Appendix 2.

the results of this particular piece of research, may recognize at least something of themselves and their pupils and be encouraged to continue to search for a fuller understanding of the present situation and of the possibilities of change.

References

1   Blishen, Edward, ed., 1969 *The School That I'd Like* Harmondsworth, Penguin Education Special, p. 165.

2   Crane, Brian and Schroeder, Colin, 1970 *The Teacher and Research: A Study of Teachers' Priorities and Opinions on Educational Research and Development* National Foundation for Educational Research in England and Wales.

3   Crane and Schroeder, op. cit., p. 40 and p. 48.

4   Crane and Schroeder, op. cit., p. 55.

5   Crane and Schroeder, op. cit., p. 39.

6   A headmaster and an English teacher in a mixed comprehensive, commenting on our questionnaire.

7   Mills, C. Wright, 1970 *The Sociological Imagination* Harmondsworth, Penguin Books, Chapter 3.

8   Curr, W., Hallworth, H. J. and Wilkinson, A. M., 1964 'Patterns of Behaviour in Secondary Modern School Children' *Educational Review* Vol. 16, No. 3, pp. 187–96.

9   Curr, W. *et al.*, op. cit., p. 191.

10   Berger, Peter and Pullberg, Stanley 'Reification and the Sociological Critique of Consciousness' *New Left Review* No. 35, January-February 1966, pp. 56–71. For a fuller discussion of the concept of 'reification'.

11   Weber, Max, 1962 *Basic Concepts in Sociology* (Translated and introduced by H. P. Secher) London, Peter Owen, pp. 29–55.

12   Jackson, Brian and Marsden, Denis, 1962 *Education and the Working Class* London, Routledge and Kegan Paul, pp. 3–4.

13   Blishen, Edward, 1966, op. cit.

14   King, Ronald, 1969 *Values and Involvement in a Grammar School* London, Routledge and Kegan Paul.

15   Hargreaves, David, 1967 *Social Relations in a Secondary School* London, Routledge and Kegan Paul.

16   Hoggart, Richard, 1959 'We Are The Lambeth Boys' *Sight and Sound* Vol. 28, Nos.3–4, p. 164.

17   *Half Our Future* (The Newsom Report) London, HMSO, p. 194.

18   Mills, C. Wright, 1970, op. cit., pp. 12–14.

19   Weber, Max, 1960, op. cit., p. 30.

20   Inglis, Fred, 1969 *The Englishness of English Teaching* London, Longman's Curriculum Reform Series, p. 15.

Appendix 2

The planning and conduct of the research

Stage I: The teachers' study

SELECTING THE SAMPLE

The basic aim of the initial sampling procedure was to include representatives of the whole range of English state secondary schools. This basically meant selecting grammar, comprehensive and secondary modern schools, both single sex and mixed, which drew their pupils from contrasted local environments.

Although comprehensives seem likely to be the schools of the future, at the present time they account for only about one third of the secondary school population and consequently, in order to obtain an accurate picture of the current situation, it was necessary to include both grammar and secondary modern schools in the sample. In addition to school type, we also selected schools with differing sexual compositions. This seemed essential both because it is known that sex is an important determinant of mass media preference and use, and also because much previous educational research has tended to concentrate on boys' schools, with the consequence that much less is known about the attitudes and behaviour of pupils at either girls' schools or mixed schools.

It is evident that media use is to some extent a function of supply, and this supply is not constant over the whole country. London provides a much fuller and wider range of media possibilities than any other area, whilst the provinces vary considerably amongst themselves. Rural areas offer the poorest selection and a child from such a neighbourhood may have great difficulty in getting to a cinema, record shop or large newsagent. We therefore attempted to choose schools in contrasting environments. In order to maximize the contrast between urban and rural conditions, urban areas were defined as cities with a population of at least 200 000, while rural areas were not to include any town with more than 20 000 inhabitants. A further distinction was also drawn between small country towns and more truly rural areas. Within the urban areas schools were further subdivided into those catering predominantly for middle class pupils from suburban areas and those serving mainly working class areas. This distinction coincided with a further factor that appeared relevant to the design—the character of school buildings and facilities. It is almost a truism to note that schools in middle class areas generally provide better physical conditions and are most extensively equipped. Schools in working class districts are likely to be older, being often in the decaying city centre rather than the newly created suburbs, and to a greater extent unsuited to modern teaching methods. This correlation between social class and school facilities is by no means perfect, however, and care was taken to include both poor middle class schools and newer schools in working class areas.

We felt that the maximum number of schools that we could handle would be about one hundred, and these we intended to find in six areas—four urban and two rural. Discovering that rural single-sex comprehensives are rare, we decided to eliminate this category. Consequently, at the end of the preliminary planning stage we arrived at the ideal sample illustrated in Table 2.1 below.

Table 2.1   The ideal sample

School			Urban		Rural	
	Boys	8		4	
Grammar	Girls	8	24	4	12
	Mixed	8		4	
	Boys	8		0	
Comprehensive	Girls	8	24	0	4
	Mixed	8		4	
	Boys	8		4	
Secondary modern	Girls	8	24	4	12
	Mixed	8		4	
		TOTAL	72	+	28 = 100

Selecting education authorities
It is the nature of ideal plans that they cannot be perfectly translated into practical form, and this one was no exception. In the first place, it was found that the number of education authorities whose schools conformed to our requirements was strictly limited. Many areas were either already fully comprehensive or else had not yet started reorganization, and a number of authorities who had all three types of school could not assure us that the status of their schools would not change during the three years in which field work was to be

done. Many education officers were uncertain about the future of their schools, especially where the return of Conservative majorities at local elections had cast doubts on how far the Government Circular 10/65 was to be implemented.

Four urban and two rural authorities were finally located which both satisfied our selection criteria and were able to give us assurances about the stability of the schools; these were Coventry, Leeds, Liverpool, the Inner London Education Authority, Gloucestershire and Derbyshire. Unfortunately, Liverpool and the ILEA were unable to offer cooperation, both feeling that they already had as many research commitments as they could reasonably manage. It seemed essential to include some London schools in our sample if it was to be in any way representative of the country as a whole, so we approached a number of Outer London Boroughs. Newham, Haringey and Barnet agreed to help us. To replace Liverpool, we approached Newcastle-upon-Tyne which fulfilled our requirements in all respects except that its secondary modern schools are denominational.

Selecting schools

Two forms of approach to schools were employed depending on the wishes of the Education Authorities. Gloucestershire and Coventry preferred the research staff to make the initial approach, helped by a note to schools informing them that the project had the approval of the Authority. The other Authorities sent outlines of the project design to those schools we had selected and then passed on to us the names of head teachers willing to take part. A small number of schools declined to help us and nearly all of these were replaced by similar schools from the same area. We then visited all these schools and explained the project more fully to head teachers.

A fairly well balanced sample had emerged except for a shortage of mixed schools. To make good this deficit the Lancashire Education Authority was approached and consented to help. This area did not fully comply with our requirements as the towns involved do not have populations of 200 000 but it was felt that the urban sprawl in which the schools were situated gave the area a thoroughly urban character which corresponded to the spirit, if not the letter, of our specifications. The final sample, as illustrated in the table below, does not differ markedly from our ideal except for a lack of single sex comprehensives. Since these are in any case relatively rare, no attempt was made to compensate for this deficiency.

ADMINISTERING THE TEACHERS' QUESTIONNAIRE

Every effort was made to utilize maximally the returns from these ninety schools. The questionnaires were delivered to all schools by the research staff who, wherever possible, spoke to teachers about the questionnaire and the research in general. A questionnaire was left for every member of the teaching staff, together with an envelope in which to seal up the completed form in

Table 2.2 The final sample for Stage I: the teachers' questionnaire

School		Urban		Rural	
Grammar	Boys	7		3	
	Girls	8	25	3	10
	Mixed	10		4	
Comprehensive	Boys	3		0	
	Girls	2	15	0	4
	Mixed	10		4	
Secondary modern	Boys	8		4	
	Girls	9	25	4	11
	Mixed	8		3	
	TOTAL	65		+ 25 = 90	

order to ensure privacy. Teachers were free to sign their name at the end of the questionnaire or not, as they wished. On a prearranged date, some three weeks later, the researcher returned to the school to collect the completed forms and to discuss the project with teachers. These discussions varied from seminars with almost the whole staff to talks with a few teachers who showed interest, or with one teacher delegated to represent the staff. It was hoped that these personal contacts would both stimulate interest in the research and add to our knowledge of the schools and of the attitudes of their staffs.

The response rate varied widely from school to school, with a low of 9% and a high of 100%, with an overall mean of 43·0%. The most important determinant was size of school. Large schools with greater administrative problems, a higher degree of decentralization of authority and less personal contact between the head teacher and his (or her) staff tended to produce relatively low returns. The few very large schools, in fact, significantly depressed our overall return rate. The other factor was the attitude of the head teacher and his relationship with his staff. Autocratic heads, whilst usually unsympathetic towards our study, put pressure on their staffs to complete their forms. More liberal headteachers were less inclined to act in this way, so that, ironically, those heads who were most interested in our study and keenest to help, often produced the poorest returns. Secondary modern schools were more forthcoming (52·2%) than grammar schools (44·2%) or comprehensives (34·7%), differences largely explicable in terms of size. Boys' schools produced higher returns (47·6%) than either mixed (41·9%) or girls' schools (40·2%). Mixed schools include the large comprehensives, but the poor response from girls' schools may well be some reflection on the nature of head teachers and staff. Among areas, the highest response rate was obtained in Gloucestershire (58·1%), and the lowest in Lancashire (31·4%). The Lancashire return rate is low because, as the last addition to the sample, questionnaires were not distributed until the summer terms, whereas other areas were completed during the more convenient Christmas and Easter terms. The remaining five areas all had response rates between 40% and 44%.

Stage II   The pupils' questionnaire

SELECTING THE SCHOOLS

The first aim in selecting the schools for the second stage was to preserve the variety of school types employed at Stage 1. Thus, we aimed to select a grammar, comprehensive, and secondary modern in each of the three principal sorts of catchment areas—inner urban, suburban and rural—giving a total of nine schools in all. However, as we felt that we should pay particular research attention to the so-called 'Newsom' pupils, the rural grammar school cell was left unfilled and replaced by a second inner urban secondary modern. In addition to ensuring a spread of school types we also wanted to include schools which represented the main sorts of pedagogic response to the mass media. The second major criterion governing the selection of the second stage schools was therefore the media orientation and attitude scores of the staff derived from the replies to the teachers' questionnaire. If these scores were to have any meaning, they had to be computed from a sufficiently large proportion of the staff in the school. Schools with poor response rates were therefore avoided.

Fig. 2.2 Sample schools for Stage II

School Type	Catchment area		
	Inner Urban	Suburban	Rural
Grammar	Woolton (Leeds)	Park Road (Lancashire)	—
Comprehensive	Brownhill (Newcastle)	Northlawns (London)	Woodfields (Gloucs)
Secondary modern	Dockstreet (London) Middleton (Coventry)	Churchgate (Leeds)	Minedale (Derbyshire) Peakside (Derbyshire)

Note: All schools in the sample were assured of anonymity and consequently each has been given a fictitious name.

Of those finally selected, only the largest comprehensive had a response rate of less than 60%. An attempt was also made to include at least one school from each of the five research areas. Finally, a tiny rural secondary modern school was added to give a complete range of school sizes. The final sample is represented in the diagrams below.

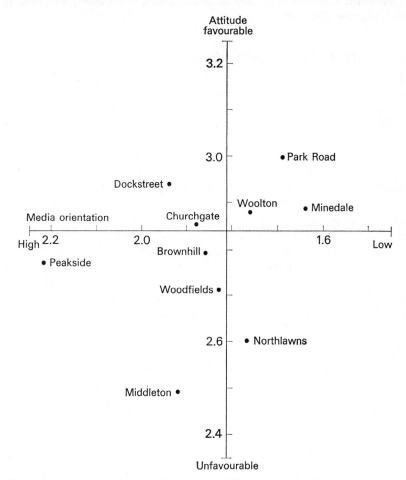

Fig. 2.3 Attitude and orientation scores of the ten study schools

Note: The attitude and orientation scores intersect at the overall means for all the schools in the Stage I sample.

SELECTING THE PUPILS

All the headmasters allowed us to select any pupils we needed. Since interviewing was to be carried out in the academic year following the questionnaire stage, it was not possible to include fourth year pupils as many of those in comprehensive and secondary modern schools would have left before the final stage. The third year pupils were therefore the oldest group completing the questionnaires. A first year sample was also included for comparative purposes. In the smaller schools the entire first and third years were sampled, while in the larger ones a random sample of high and low ability groupings in each year was obtained.

ADMINISTERING THE QUESTIONNAIRE

This phase of the project was conducted during February and March 1970. The research team visited each of the ten schools for a day or two and personally supervised the procedure. In order to minimize disruption, the questionnaires had been designed to be completed in 35–40 minutes (i.e. during one school lesson). The researchers explained to each class just what they had to do and were then present throughout the lesson to advise pupils who had difficulties. Nearly all children managed without any trouble and problems were encountered only with classes containing a large proportion of slow or nonreaders. Since this could be anticipated, wherever it was felt necessary two lessons were allocated for the completion of the questionnaire and, with assistance, even the most backward pupils were able to finish.

Altogether, 1071 pupils completed the questionnaires, of whom 437 were in their first year and 634 in their third. There were 522 boys and 549 girls. The number of pupils at each of the ten study schools who completed the questionnaire, together with the number who were subsequently interviewed during stage three, is given in Table 2.3 below.

Table 2.3   Number of pupils who participated in Stage II

School	Completing the Questionnaire (No. of pupils)	Interviewed at Stage III (No. of pupils)
Park Road	85	28
Woolton	105	29
Northlawns	161	33
Brownhill	154	24
Woodfields	98	—
Churchgate	183	30
Dockstreet	73	23
Minedale	87	27
Middleton	93	28
Peakside	32	12
TOTAL	1071	234

Stage III   Interviewing the selected pupils

From the total questionnaire sample of 1071 a smaller number of pupils were selected for intensive interview. Unfortunately, Woodfields dropped out at this point. The headmaster had taken up another appointment without warning us of his departure and his successor could not be persuaded to let us continue our work. This was a serious blow, leaving us with a less well balanced sample, but it was then too late to add an eleventh school.

The basic aim of the interviews was to examine in more detail the relationship between pupils' school commitment and their involvement in pop. On the basis of their replies to the questions on school commitment and pop involvement on the questionnaire, pupils were allocated to high, medium and low groups along each dimension. (The questions are discussed in Appendix 3.) The basic unit of comparison was the form group. If a pupil's score fell in the top third of his form he was allocated to the high group. The bottom third constituted the low group, and the middle third the medium group. This procedure was carried out separately for both school commitment and pop involvement and resulted in the nine basic groupings of respondents shown below.

Table 2.4   Basic groupings: pop involvement/school commitment

Pop involvement	School commitment		
	High	Medium	Low
Low	Group 1		Group 4
Medium			
High	Group 2		Group 3

Within each school, boys and girls representing all nine groupings were selected for interview, but particular attention was paid to pupils occupying the cells at the four corners of the matrix, i.e. groups 1–4. We aimed to interview about 30 children in each school, except at Peakside where we necessarily had to be satisfied with a smaller number. Of the 234 pupils who were interviewed, 111 were boys and 123 girls—67 were in their second year, and 167 in their fourth. Each pupil was interviewed individually, and in private, by a member of the research team in whatever vacant rooms the schools could provide. Interviews lasted 25–60 minutes, depending on the attitude of the interviewees. Pupils' replies were noted by the interviewer on a schedule, most of which was precoded. Each of the nine schools was visited for a complete week during the period between October 1970 and February 1971.

In addition to the interviews, the research team during this period also conducted a further pencil and paper test with class groups—as far as possible the same groups that had completed the questionnaire the year before. This test, which was designed to gather supplementary information about pupils' pop music tastes, is described in Appendix 3.

Appendix 3

Notes on specific measures

The majority of the measures and questions employed in the various question-naires and interview schedules were quite straightforward, e.g. 'How often do you buy a pop record?' 'When you go to buy new clothes, whom do you usu-ally go with?' Consequently, we do not feel that it is worthwhile to print the research schedules in full. However, a number of the central measures, which we used as a basis for selecting the second and third stage samples and which played a prominent part in the subsequent analysis, were constructed specific-ally for the project. This appendix is therefore devoted to describing these measures and to explaining the rationale behind them.

Stage I   The teachers' questionnaire

TEACHERS' GENERAL ATTITUDE TOWARDS THE MASS MEDIA

A number of statements about the mass media and their possible effects were derived from pilot work with practising teachers and from the standard cur-rent criticisms of the mass media. A selection of these statements was then presented to a sample of teachers in the form of a Likert-type scale. Respond-ents were asked to indicate the extent of their agreement or disagreement with each of the statements by ticking one of the five points on the scale which ranged from, 'I strongly agree' at one end, to 'I strongly disagree' at the other. Each tick was assigned a score ranging from 1 to 5, so that a high score indi-cated a favourable attitude towards the media, and a low score an unfavour-able attitude. A Principal Components analysis of the resulting scores revealed that eight of the statements selected loaded quite highly on a single central factor which could be characterized as a general attitude towards the mass media. These eight statements were thus selected for inclusion in the final scale. Table 3.1 presents the factor loadings for each of the eight statements in the scale based on the questionnaire returns from the final teachers' sample. On the basis of this analysis we can be reasonably sure that the scale is valid, that it does in fact measure what it is supposed to measure—a general attitude towards the mass media.

By summing the scores of individual members of staff on this question and

Table 3.1 Media attitude scale: loadings of each item on the principal factor (decimal points omitted)

Item	Factor Loading
The blame for many of society's troubles today may be justly levelled at the mass media	63
On the whole, the information provided by the mass media gives children a distorted picture of the world	68
The range of children's interests is enlarged by mass media	42
Pupils should devote to the reading of books much of the time they spend with the mass media	52
Exposure to mass media reduces children's capacity to concentrate	64
The quality of fictional material in the mass media reduces children's capacities to come to terms with real life	67
The treatment of sex in the mass media impedes the growth of civilized values in pupils	69
Mass media encourage superficiality	69
Percentage of total variance accounted for	39

dividing the resulting totals by the number of staff in school who completed the questionnaire, we arrived at a mean attitude score for the staff of the school as a group. In this way it was hoped to gain some indication of the overall climate of opinion among the teaching staff of a school, whether—as a group—they were generally favourably disposed towards the mass media or not. Group means varied between 2·4 and 3·2. Of course, this measure confronts the problem of all measures based upon the arithmetic mean—that it may in fact conceal more than it reveals. It is quite possible that there is as much, if not more, variation of attitude between staff members within the same school as there is between the staff of two entirely different schools. However, if we take the standard deviation as an indicator of the degree of variation between staff members in the same school, we find that this internal variation is not sufficiently great to invalidate comparisons between schools.

For example, if we take the two inner urban secondary modern schools which were later selected for inclusion in the pupil phase of the study, we find that the group attitude score for Middleton is 2·49 with a standard deviation of ·43, while the group mean for Dockstreet is 2·94 with a standard deviation of ·40. Thus, in both schools there is a similar degree of variation, so that in both cases the scores of the great majority of individual staff members fall within a range approximately four points either side of the group mean. Hence, as the degree of internal variation in both cases is approximately the same, the comparison between the two groups remains valid. Of course, it is possible for individual teachers to achieve scores outside the four point limit but, as a general rule, it appears that there is a tendency towards consensus regarding the mass media among the staff at a particular school. Hence it is possible to characterize the climate of opinion at Middleton as being generally unfavourably disposed towards the mass media, and that at Dockstreet as being generally more favourable. Certainly, this impression was very strongly confirmed when the researchers talked at greater length to the staff at both these schools during the fieldwork for the pupil phase of the study.

To facilitate presentation, two items designed to elicit teachers' attitudes towards the specific relationship between the mass media and teaching were also included in the format of the media attitude scale. (Viz: 'On the whole, mass media make my job as a teacher easier' and 'It is not the teachers' responsibility to encourage children to be more discriminating in their use of mass media'.) The replies to these two items were considered separately, and consequently they were excluded when computing the general attitude towards media scores.

TEACHERS' 'ORIENTATION' TOWARDS THE USE OF MASS
MEDIA CONTENT IN LESSONS

11   This question refers to mass media to which pupils are exposed in their leisure time. Do you ever deliberately introduce such mass media content as material for lessons? If so please indicate the frequency with which you use this approach by placing a tick in the appropriate column opposite each medium.

	never	about once a term	several times a term	once a week or more
newspapers				
television				
pop records				
radio				
comics				
magazines				
the cinema				

Fig. 3.4 Item 11—Teachers' questionnaire

This item attempted to assess the extent to which teachers were oriented towards introducing mass media content into their lessons. This question was not concerned with the utilization of audio-visual aids (this aspect of media usage had been dealt with in the question immediately preceding), but with those elements of the mass media which pupils were most exposed to during their leisure time—how often did teachers bring newspapers or magazines into class? Did they ever discuss last night's television programmes or the current Top Twenty pop records? Answers were assigned a numerical score ranging from 1 for 'never' to 4 for 'once a week or more'. Group orientation scores were again calculated by summing the scores of individual teachers and dividing by the number of staff. As in the case of the attitude scores described above, there were variations in the degree of orientation among staff in the same school. This is not surprising, as some subjects afford many more opportunities for the teacher to introduce material from the mass media into lessons. This is certainly the case for English, as compared with subjects like woodwork. In fact our results showed quite clearly that English teachers tend to have higher orientation scores than other subject specialists. In addition, it appears to be the case that the degree of orientation of the English staff is also reflected in the rest of the staff, so that, in schools where the English department provides a dynamic centre of media-oriented classroom teaching, the rest of the staff also tend to have a higher general interest in the classroom possibilities of media material. Conversely, where the English staff have a low orientation, the rest of the staff also tend to be relatively uninterested. It is therefore possible to characterize the general orientation towards media displayed by the staff of particular schools as either high or low.

The overall correlation between the attitude and orientation scores for the sample as a whole is only 0·07, and we can therefore be reasonably sure that these scores are measuring two relatively independent dimensions of the possible range of relationships between teachers and the mass media.

Stage II The pupils' questionnaire

SCHOOL COMMITMENT

Recent research suggests that pupils' overall orientation to school is made up of at least four or five separate dimensions. Roma Morton-Williams and Stewart Finch (1968),[1] for example, isolated five main factors which they called interest of school, subject curriculum, acceptability of school behaviour, identification with school, and attitude to school discipline. Similarly, Bromley Kniveton (1969)[2] found four dimensions: liking for school, interest in subjects, education and life goals, and education and personality development.

It is by no means the case that these dimensions are always highly interrelated. For example, according to Kniveton, pupils at grammar schools tend to score lower than pupils at secondary moderns on 'liking for school', but higher on other dimensions. Grammar school pupils may therefore be very interested in specific subjects, and they are likely to recognize that it is necessary to have good examination results and a good report from the headmaster in order to go on to university or to get a good job when they leave, but they do not necessarily actively enjoy school or accept its values.

Unfortunately many researchers do not take this complexity into account, and consequently they attempt to assess pupils' commitment using measures that are far too crude. For example, Robert Witkin[3] presented pupils with four statements about school and asked them to pick the one which came nearest to the way they felt. Unfortunately, a statement such as: 'I like school because I enjoy my lessons but I don't have many friends here', for example, includes the three distinct dimensions; 'liking for school', 'enjoyment of lessons' and 'degree of integration into a peer group' and Witkin has no way of assessing its validity, i.e. the degree to which it actually measures what it purports to measure. Thus, although he asserts that the item measures pupils' 'general orientation to school' he cannot demonstrate statistically that this is in fact the case. However, even if it were a valid measure of commitment, this sort of single choice item severely limits the possible range of statistical analysis. In the absence of a numerical score, arithmetical means cannot be derived, which in turn rules out the possibility of using correlational analyses.

Previous researchers have isolated a general factor in pupils' orientation to school which Morton-Williams calls 'interest' and Kniveton 'liking', and the statements employed in the present research correspond very closely to items in both these scales. What we are measuring, therefore, is pupils' general orientation towards school—whether they actively enjoy the experience of going to school and find it interesting. This general factor we call 'school commitment', and the results both of previous research and of our own pilot studies indicate that it is relatively independent of more specific aspects of school experience such as attitudes towards discipline or uniforms.

On the basis of the results of our pilot studies we selected seven statements which appeared to measure school commitment. On the final questionnaire these were presented in the form of a Likert-type scale with five points, so that for each statement pupils could indicate the degree of their agreement or disagreement. The direction of the points was alternated in order to avoid response set. Each statement was scored 0 to 4, so that a pupil's total score could vary between 0 and 28. The validity of the scale was ascertained by a Principal Components analysis of the final questionnaire returns, the results of which are presented in Table 3.2.

Table 3.2 indicates that all the items load quite highly on the principal factor, and we can therefore be reasonably sure that the scale is valid and does in fact measure school commitment.

Table 3.2 School commitment scale: loadings of each item on the
principal factor (decimal points omitted)

Item	Factor Loading
1 Most of the lessons you do at school are a complete waste of time	79
2 On the whole I quite enjoy school	81
3 School is the same, day after day, week after week	85
4 Most of the time at school they treat you like a kid	75
5 I am usually glad to get back to school after the holidays	63
6 Teachers at school don't really try hard enough to make the lessons interesting	80
7 I can't wait to get out of school for good and start work	72
Percentage of total variance accounted for	59

POP INVOLVEMENT

The degree of pupils' orientation towards the culture surrounding pop music
was one of the key variables in this study and so, in order to make comparisons
between pupils both individually and in groups, we needed a single numerical
score that would indicate the degree of their orientation towards pop.

Although the situation is now changing with the rapid growth of the LP
market, the weekly chart of the Top Twenty best selling single records still
figures prominently in a number of Radio 1 programmes, and is the basis of
Top of the Pops, the most popular television programme with secondary school
pupils. Thus, in order to know the current Top Twenty, a pupil would have
to be a regular user of these pop based sectors of the mass media. Hence, it can
be argued that a good knowledge of the current hit records is an indication of
considerable involvement in the world of the pop media. Respondents were
therefore presented with a completely open ended question asking them to
list as many records as they could which were in the current Top Twenty.
They were further instructed verbally by the researchers that an entry would
be considered correct if it listed either the record title, the performer, or a
recognizable part of the lyric. The number of correct entries constituted the
pupil's score. All three of the research staff who subsequently coded the
questionnaire returns had a very full knowledge of the current hits, which
enabled them to recognize correct entries despite the often bizarre spelling
('HMS MTS', for Herman's Hermits, for example). In this way it was hoped
to reduce the effects of differences in writing ability.

Nevertheless, it may still be the case that differences in pupils' scores can be
explained by variation in their ability to remember titles and write them down,
and by differences in their performance in pencil and paper tests administered

in the classroom. The very crowded research schedule meant that we were unable to test these factors independently, and consequently we were obliged to infer them from the IQ scores recorded in the school records, together with pupils' performance in the last internal school examination.

Intelligence quotient—In most schools the records were either not readily available or else incomplete, and comparison between schools was further hindered by the fact that not all the scores were of the same type. Some were for Verbal Reasoning Tests (VRT), for example, while others were derived from more broadly based IQ tests. Two schools (Park Road and Minedale) however, did have reasonably complete records, and the general conclusion to be drawn from an examination of the IQ scores is that IQ does not appear to affect significantly the scores on the Top Twenty question.

According to the school records, the two most intelligent third year pupils in our Park Road sample both had VRT scores of 140+, yet one correctly identified fifteen out of the current Top Twenty, while the other failed to identify any at all. The pupil with the lowest VRT score (105), on the other hand, correctly identified thirteen titles. Similarly, at Peakside, the third year pupil with the highest IQ (113) scored nine on the Top Twenty question, while the pupil with the lowest IQ (76) scored eight. The evidence we have been able to obtain, therefore, points to the fact that IQ does not significantly affect pupils' score on the Top Twenty question.

Ability in school examination—Some of the schools in our sample either did not have a formal system of internal academic assessment, or else the mode varied between different ability groups, thus making inter-form comparison extremely difficult. The school with the most complete set of examination marks was Churchgate, where they constitute a necessary part of the 'streaming' system.

On the basis of the last set of examination results we divided the pupils in each of the third year forms at Churchgate into two groups, depending upon whether they were placed in the upper or lower half of the form. If we take the two groups most differentiated by examination ability, the top half of the top stream (studying for GCE), and the bottom half of the lowest stream (the early leavers) we find that the top group have a mean Top Twenty score of 8·4, while the bottom group have a score of 6·0. At first sight this difference seems to indicate that examination ability does affect the Top Twenty score. However, the difference is not statistically significant and can easily be explained in terms of the operation of chance. If we take the individual pupils at the top and bottom of the GCE stream, we find that they score five and seven respectively on the Top Twenty question, while the pupils at the top and bottom of the early leaving stream each score six. This provides another indication that ability in examination does not significantly affect pupils' scores on the Top Twenty question.

Taken overall then, there is no evidence that high scores on the Top Twenty question are significantly related to memory or writing ability as measured by IQ scores or performance in school examinations, and we can therefore be reasonably sure that differences in the Top Twenty scores do indicate real differences in pop involvement.

PUPILS' SELF IMAGES

The self image question was principally conceived as a way of looking at relationships between school commitment and pop involvement from the point of view of the pupils themselves. Was it the case, for example, that the roles of 'pop fan' and 'good pupil' were seen by them as being mutually exclusive, and how was the pop fan role related to other leisure time roles?

On the basis of previous research we drew up a list of the main roles which adolescents could play in various social situations, expressed in the form of short cameos of fictitious boys or girls. During the pilot stages of our research we experimented with various forms of presentation and discussed the content and wording of the cameos with pupils until eventually we arrived at a set of nine descriptions which seemed to have meaning for them. Some of the cameos were common to both boys and girls, others were sex specific. Boys' names were used with boys, and girls' names with girls. The actual descriptions are presented below:

Descriptions presented to both boys and girls
John (Hilary) gets good marks in most things and usually comes top in at least one subject. The teachers like him because he always pays attention in class. John wants to stay on and pass some exams.

Mick (Sheila) feels that most of the things you do in school are a waste of time. He is always mucking about in class and being cheeky to the teachers. He can't wait to start work.

Pete (Mary) never comes top in anything but works hard and always does the best he can. On the whole he enjoys lessons.

Bob (Joan) is the sort of person who gets on well with everyone. He can take a joke and always shares things with his friends.

Paul (Carol) is a keen pop fan. He spends a lot of time listening to the radio or playing his own records. He always knows what's in the Top Ten and can usually say whether a new record will be a hit or not.

Descriptions presented to boys only
Phil is naturally good at sports. When he is not playing for his team he usually goes to a match or watches sport on the television.

Andy is pretty good looking. He never has any trouble picking up girls and he spends a lot of his time taking them out.

Charlie is never stuck for things to do or places to go. He is a natural leader and the rest of the group usually follow him.

George spends most of his time out with his mates just mucking around doing nothing in particular.

Descriptions presented to girls only
Diana likes to wear trendy clothes. She spends a lot of time window shopping or browsing through fashion magazines and pattern books to find out what the latest styles are.

Pat is pretty good looking and knows how to make the best of herself. Boys find her attractive and she is always being asked out.

Janey is a bit of a tomboy. She loves swimming and really looks forward to gym lessons. She doesn't like dressing up and would rather wear her old jeans all the time.

Liz likes to spend most of her spare time at home. She is pretty good at cooking and makes quite a lot of her own clothes.

The idea of presenting pupils with cameo descriptions had been tried in an earlier piece of research conducted by the Rileys[4] in New Jersey, in which pupils were simply asked whether or not they wanted to be like a particular person. In this case we wanted some measure of the strength of pupils' attachment to or rejection of particular roles, and consequently we asked them to indicate how much they thought they were actually like a particular person along a five point scale which ranged from, 'a lot like me' to 'nothing like me at all'. Answers were given a numerical score from 0 to 4, which enabled us to utilize correlation techniques during the analysis.

Stage III   The pupils' interview schedule

KNOWLEDGE OF POP ARGOT TEST

Recent research undertaken by Paul Lerman[5] in America and H. B. Gibson[6] in Britain has demonstrated that knowledge of delinquent slang or argot is a strong indicator of association with delinquents and involvement in delinquent activities. We attempted to apply the same principle to the special vocabulary of the pop world as displayed in the patter of disc jockeys and in articles in pop magazines.

On the basis of pilot tests we selected twelve pop argot terms and arranged them in order of the frequency with which they were known to the pupils we tested. The words in Group 1 were very widely known, those in Group 2 quite well known, while those in Group 3 were only known among those most highly involved in pop. Thus, the higher a pupils' knowledge of argot, the greater his involvement in pop.

The argot terms used in the final interview, together with their meanings, are listed below.

	Argot term	Meaning
Group 1	Chart	List of top twenty best selling records of the week
	Album	Long playing record
	D.J.	Disc jockey
	Number One	Top selling record of week
		Number one in the chart
Group 2	Flip	Reverse side of a 'single' record
	Tranny	Transistor radio
	Follow up	The record released by a performer immediately after a hit
	Stateside	America
Group 3	Groupie	A girl who follows pop groups
	Gig	A paid performing date
	Roadie	The road manager for a pop group
	'A & R' man	The Artists and Repertoire man in a record company

PUPILS' PERCEPTIONS OF POP PERFORMERS

Pupils' perceptions of pop performers were assessed by an item based on the *Repertory Grid* method developed by the American psychologist, George Kelly.[7] According to Kelly, everybody has a repertoire of constructs which they use to classify and make sense of their world, or particular parts of it at least. In a pilot study we attempted to elicit pupils' repertoire of constructs concerning popular heroes such as pop singers, footballers, film stars and television personalities, but we rapidly discovered that pupils saw these various personalities as belonging to different mental universes. Consequently we decided to confine our attention to one particular range of media personalities —male pop performers.

On the basis of pilot tests we selected eleven pop stars who represented a wide range, both of types of pop music and of life styles. They were: Val Doonican, Stevie Wonder, Donovan, Engelbert Humperdinck, Mick Jagger, John Lennon, Elvis Presley, Cliff Richard, Tom Jones, Ringo Starr, Frank Sinatra.

Figure 3.5 shows the completed Grid schedule from an interview with a fourth year girl. This was arrived at as follows:

1   The respondent was presented with eleven white cards, each bearing the name of one pop performer, and asked if she recognized all the names. Any names respondents failed to recognize were removed.

Constructs (Emergent pole /)	(1) Val Doonican	(2) Stevie Wonder	(3) Donovan	(4) Engel. Hump.	(5) Mick Jagger	(6) John Lennon	(7) Elvis Presley	(8) Cliff Richard	(9) Tom Jones	(10) Ringo Starr	(11) Frank Sinatra	Contrast (X) pole
(a) Smart clothes like a 'bopper'	/	/	X	/	X	X	/	/	/	X		more freaky clothes
(b) Typical commercial person	/	X	X		X	X	/	/	/	X		not out for money
(c) Short hair	/	/	X	/	X	X	/	/	/	X	/	long hair
(d) Follows trends		X	X		X	X	/	/	/	X		plays what he likes
(e) Takes drugs	X		/	X	/	/	X	X	X	/		lives clean
(f) Very simple music	/	/	X	/	X	X	/	/	/	X		more involved music
(g) Just a singer	X	/	X	X	X	X	X	/	/	X	/	does other things
(h) I like	X	X	/	X	/	/	X	X	X	/		don't like
(i) Parents approve	/	/	X	/	X	X	X	/	/	X	/	parents disapprove

Fig. 3.5 Completed grid schedule of a fourth year girl

2   The respondent was then shown two cards, Mick Jagger and Cliff Richard on the assumption that as these two performers were diametrically opposed in every way, they would be likely to elicit some of her basic constructs concerning pop stars.

3   The respondent was asked to say whether she thought Mick Jagger and Cliff Richard were similar or different. She replied that they were different. She was then asked to say in what way they were different. She replied that they wore different sorts of clothes. She was then asked to describe Cliff Richard's clothes. Her reply, 'Smart, like a "bopper" ', constituted the 'emergent' pole of the first construct, indicated by a tick (√) in the column under Cliff Richard's name. Her description of Jagger's clothes as 'freaky' constituted the contrast pole of the first construct, indicated by a cross (X) in the Jagger column.

4   The respondent was then asked to say if Mick Jagger and Cliff Richard differed in any other respects and these replies provided the 'emergent' and 'contrast' poles of several other constructs.

5   When the respondents' repertoire of constructs concerning Jagger and Richard were exhausted the interviewer returned to the first construct offered (clothing) and asked her to sort the remaining nine cards into three piles depending upon her perception of these performers as being similar to Richard (indicated by a tick), similar to Jagger (indicated by a cross), or in between (indicated by a blank). This procedure was repeated with all the constructs offered.

6   The respondent was then presented with a new pair of performers, John Lennon and Tom Jones, and the same procedure was repeated.

7   When the respondent's repertoire of constructs was finally exhausted, a line was drawn across the paper and further questions asked using all the cards simultaneously: 'Which of these do you personally like?' (ditto ' . . . . . dislike?') and 'Which do your parents approve of?' (ditto ' . . . . . disapprove of?')

An identical procedure to that outlined above was followed in every case.

The Grid method combines the advantages of open endedness, in the sense that respondents are asked to express themselves in their own words, while at the same time arranging the information in such a way as to facilitate the maximum possible use of statistical analysis.

In the example given in Fig. 3.5, for instance, it is immediately apparent that the respondent saw a basic division between singers such as Mick Jagger, John Lennon and Donovan on the one hand and Cliff Richard, Tom Jones and Engelbert Humperdinck on the other. It is also apparent that this difference applies equally to music, appearance and life style, and that this particular girl identifies herself with Mick Jagger and John Lennon, in opposition to her parents. It is most unlikely that the range and density of the information elicited by the Grid format could have been obtained by a series of conventional questions occupying the same amount of time.

Stage IV   The supplementary group testing

PUPILS' EVALUATIONS OF POP MUSIC

Within particular social groups particular concepts have particular meanings which the members of the group share. The *Semantic Differential* method developed by Professor Charles Osgood is a way of plotting the position of a concept in 'semantic space'.[8] If this space were two dimensional, any concept could be pinpointed on a graph, its position in space being described by its relationship to the axes, as in the diagram below. Concept 'A' in this example

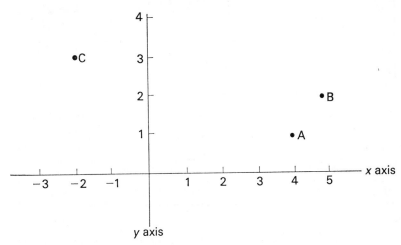

Fig. 3.6 Plotting the position of a concept in 'semantic space'

is situated in semantic space at 4 on the X axis and 1 on the Y axis. It can be said to have a similar meaning to concept B which is at 5X and 2Y, but to be quite different from concept C (3Y and −2X) Both A and B are high on the X dimension but lower on Y, whilst C is high on Y but has a negative X value.

Semantic space is, of course, much more complex than this and has many dimensions. Osgood's research has enabled him to identify the most important of these dimensions, so that we can say in what respects A and B are alike and different from C. His method was to get people to respond to concepts in terms of a series of bipolar adjective pairs. Thus they would be asked to decide whether the concept seemed to them to be good or bad, beautiful or ugly, clean or dirty—and so on. Each respondent would run through a long list of such pairs and indicate his feeling about the concept by putting an X between each pair on a seven point scale.

Osgood found that, when analysed, the adjective pairs fell into clusters. These clusters are the semantic dimensions and Osgood identified three major ones which he called evaluative, potency and activity. The evaluative factor includes adjective pairs like those in Fig. 3.7, the potency cluster has adjectives involving some idea of strength, while activity pairs express motion and action. Osgood argues that most of the meaning attached to many words or concepts is made up of these three factors, although he also found several others of lesser importance. Osgood developed a long list of adjective pairs which correspond to these factors and this list still forms the basis of most

	Very*	Quite*	I can't decide*	Quite*	Very*	
Interesting						Boring
Unoriginal						Original
Gentle						Powerful
Easy to understand						Hard to understand
Unexciting						Exciting
Beautiful						Ugly
Simple						Complicated
Old fashioned						Up to date
Sad						Happy

Fig. 3.7 The semantic differential schedule employed in final testing

* It is not usual, or scientifically ideal, to label the columns in this way, but it made the form more intelligible to pupils of low ability. It is also more usual to use a seven point scale, but we limited ours to five for the sake of clarity and ease of response.

semantic differential studies. We used the technique to study the meanings that certain sorts of pop music have for pupils. Each concept was a record which we played to children before asking them to respond in terms of nine bipolar adjective pairs. This process was repeated eight times with eight records (concepts). The adjective pairs were selected to provide information along four dimensions:

1 *Evaluative:* Osgood's main factor which was measured by the adjective pairs, interesting/boring, beautiful/ugly.

2 *Potency/Activity:* In terms of music it was thought that these two dimensions would be very similar and this assumption was supported by a study by Tucker (reported by Osgood), which studied the meaning of paintings. Tucker found that exciting/calming and violent/gentle scored high on both factors. We substituted unexciting for calming and powerful for violent.

3 *Novelty:* This was one of Osgood's minor dimensions but a pilot study showed it to be highly relevant to pop music. We used the pairs original/unoriginal and old fashioned/up to date.

4   *Understandability:* This factor was identified by Nunally[9] in a study of conceptions of mental health, and pilot work showed it to be relevant. We used simple/complicated and easy to understand/hard to understand as our adjective pairs.

The dimensions and associated adjective pairs finally chosen were those which pupils in a series of preliminary trials had found most relevant and meaningful. Ideally more than two pairs per dimension should have been used, but we were obliged to keep the music test as simple as possible. The Semantic Differential schedule employed in the final testing is reproduced above. Respondents were asked to tick one box for each adjective pair. A full rating sheet was completed for each of the first eight record extracts.

Pilot work also guided our final selection of records, and we attempted to present examples of the whole range of pop music which adolescents of school age listen to. The records finally selected included an example of a ballad (Andy Williams) and several examples of the sort of records which form the basis of the Top Twenty (e.g. Jackson Five, Beatles, Creedence Clearwater Revival and The Brotherhood of Man). It also included examples of the major styles of Negro music currently popular: soul (Aretha Franklin), Tamla Motown (Martha Reeves) and Reggae (Owen Gray) together with examples of the work of contemporary singer-songwriters (Simon and Garfunkel and Leonard Cohen) and excerpts from 'progressive rock' records (Rolling Stones, Johnny Winter). A full list of the records used in the final study, in the order they were heard by pupils, is given below.

Fig. 3.8   Records used in final study (in order heard by pupils)

Performer	Title
1 Aretha Franklin	*Come Back Baby*
2 The Jackson Five	*The Young Folks*
3 The Beatles	*The Two of Us*
4 Simon and Garfunkel	*Song for the Asking*
5 Owen Gray	*Girl What You Doing to Me*
6 Brotherhood of Man	*Living in the Land of Love*
7 Rolling Stones	*Let it Bleed*
8 Leonard Cohen	*That's No Way to Say Goodbye*
9 Johnny Winter	*I Love Everybody*
10 Creedence Clearwater Revival	*Cross Tie Walking*
11 Andy Williams	*Sweet Memories*
12 Martha Reeves and the Vandellas	*Girl You've Been in Love too Long*

Titles were selected in such a way that although the style would be immediately recognizable, pupils were unlikely to have heard the actual records themselves many times. Thus, excerpts were taken from long playing records or from the reverse side of hit 'singles'.

The final tape contained twelve excerpts lasting for from one-and-a-half to two minutes each. For each extract, pupils were asked to indicate how often they had heard it before and how much they liked it. In addition, for each of the first eight records, they were required to complete a semantic differential schedule.

References

1   Williams, Roma Morton and Finch, Stewart, 1968 *Schools Council Enquiry I. Young School Leavers* London, HMSO, Appendix 3, p. 372.

2   Kniveton, Bromley H., 1969 'An Investigation of the Attitudes of Adolescents to Aspects of Their Schooling' *British Journal of Educational Psychology* Vol. 39, pp. 78–81.

3   Witkin, Robert W., 1971 'Social Class Influences on the Amount and Type of Positive Evaluation of School Lessons' *Sociology* Vol. 5, p. 175.

4   Riley, M. W., Riley, T. W. and Moore, M. E., 1961 'Adolescent Values and the Riesman Typology: An Empirical Analysis' in: S. M. Lipset and L. Lowenthal eds. *Culture and Social Character* Glencoe Free Press, p. 370.

5   Lerman, P., 1967 'Argot, Symbolic Deviance and Subcultural Delinquency' *American Sociological Review* Vol. 32, pp. 209–24.

6   Gibson, H. B., 1964 'A Slang Vocabulary Test as an Indicator of Delinquent Association' *British Journal of Social and Clinical Psychology* Vol. 3, pp. 50–55.

7   Kelly, G. A., 1955 *The Psychology of Personal Constructs: Volume One* New York, W. W. Norton and Co. Inc., esp., pp. 280–91.

8   Osgood, C., Suci, G. and Tannenbaum, P., 1957 *The Measurement of Meaning* Urbana, University of Illinois Press.

9   Nunally, J., 1961 *Popular Conceptions of Mental Health* New York, Holt, Rinehart and Winston.

Appendix 4

Supplementary tables: the pupils' study

Table 4.1 Percentages of third year pupils wanting to stay on after 16: by type of school and social class

	Social class		
Type of school	Middle	Upper working	Lower working
Grammar	64% $n=55$	46% $n=53$	31% $n=16$
Comprehensive	65% $n=57$	39% $n=87$	9% $n=41$
Modern	37% $n=59$	26% $n=108$	13% $n=71$

Table 4.2 Mean disagreement with parents' score: by year and social class

	Social class			
Year	Middle	Upper working	Lower working	Significance level
First year	9·0	9·2		NS
	9·0		9·5	NS
Third year	9·1	9·5		NS
	9·1		9·7	NS
	NS	NS	NS	

Table 4.3 Third year pupils' mean disagreement with parents' scores:
by sex and social class

| | Social class | | | |
	Middle	Upper working	Lower working	Significance level
Boys	9·8	9·4		*NS*
	9·8		10·5	*NS*
Girls	8·4	9·5		*NS*
	8·4		8·7	*NS*
	**	*NS*	*	

Table 4.4 Pocket money and part time earnings of third form pupils

		% receiving 50p or more pocket money each week	% having part-time jobs	% of those with jobs who earn over £1 each week
Dock Street, inner urban Secondary Modern	(n = 47)	70	34	82
Northlawns, suburban Comprehensive	(n = 80)	56	33	77
Middleton, inner urban Secondary Modern	(n = 71)	44	34	50
Brownhill, inner urban Comprehensive	(n = 71)	39	17	33
Woolton, inner urban Grammar	(n = 77)	34	21	13
Churchgate, suburban Secondary Modern	(n = 115)	32	31	25
Park Road, suburban Grammar	(n = 54)	30	19	10
Minedale & Peakside, rural Secondary Modern	(n = 70)	25	27	37
Woodfields, rural Comprehensive	(n = 49)	24	33	50
TOTAL: all third year pupils	(n = 634)	38	27	42

Table 4.5 Frequency with which third year pupils go to discotheques or dances (figures in percentages)

	Not at all in last month	Once or twice in last month	Three or more times in last month	Numbers responding
Boys	71	17	12	301
Girls	47	34	19	330
Grammar	65	22	13	131
Comprehensive	57	21	22	199
Secondary modern	56	31	13	301

Table 4.6 Frequency with which third year pupils buy pop records (figures in percentages)

	Never	Less than one a month	About one a month	About one a fortnight or more	Numbers responding
Boys	33	40	14	14	303
Girls	23	36	22	18	325
Grammar	27	44	23	5	129
Comprehensive	21	38	23	18	198
Secondary modern	32	35	14	19	301

Table 4.7 Amount of time third year pupils spend listening to pop radio over the weekend (figures in percentages)

	None	Less than one hour	Two or three hours	Over four hours	Numbers responding
Boys	14	34	31	22	303
Girls	8	21	38	32	329
Grammar	11	24	32	33	131
Comprehensive	12	31	30	27	200
Secondary modern	11	25	39	25	301

Table 4.8 Amount of time third year pupils spend listening to pop radio on an average weekday evening (figures in percentages)

	None	Less than 1 hour	Two or three hours	Over four hours	Numbers responding
Boys	19	51	23	7	302
Girls	15	48	27	10	327
Grammar	17	50	28	5	131
Comprehensive	16	52	23	9	199
Secondary modern	17	47	26	10	299

Table 4.9 Radio access of third form pupils (figures in percentages)

	Have own radio	Share radio with family	No radio at home	Numbers responding
Grammar	65	34	1	131
Comprehensive	61	37	2	199
Secondary modern	52	45	3	291

Table 4.10 Mean number of days each week that homework is set for third year pupils, and the percentage who do over and under one hour each night

	Mean days of homework per week	Percentage doing under 1 hour of home-work a night	Percentage doing over 1 hour of home-work a night	Numbers responding
Boys	4·0	38	62	304
Girls	3·9	32	68	334
Grammar	5·0	17	83	131
Comprehensive	4·2	34	66	200
Secondary modern	3·2*	44	56*	303

* These figures are probably rather high. One secondary modern in our sample—Churchgate—seemed to give pupils 2 hours of homework 5 nights a week. The other four expected very much less than this.

Table 4.11 Time spent watching television on an average weekday evening at home: third year pupils (figures in percentages)

	Less than 1 hour	About 2 hours	About 3 hours	Over 4 hours	Numbers responding
Boys	8	22	33	37	304
Girls	12	25	32	31	330
Grammar	14	32	33	21	131
Comprehensive	12	21	31	36	200
Secondary modern	8	21	33	38	303

Table 4.12 General distribution of school commitment and pop involvement by type of school

(a) Grammar school pupils ($n = 190$)

		Commitment to school		
		High	Medium	Low
Involvement in pop	Low	26	19	8
	Medium	22	40	21
	High	10	22	22

$$\chi^2 = 16 \cdot 835 \ (p < 0 \cdot 01)$$

(b) Comprehensive school pupils ($n = 413$)

		Commitment to school		
		High	Medium	Low
Involvement in pop	Low	41	54	28
	Medium	42	96	34
	High	29	56	33

$$\chi^2 = 6 \cdot 77 \ (NS)$$

(c) Secondary rnodern school pupils ($n = 468$)

		Commitment to school		
		High	Medium	Low
Involvement in pop	Low	40	58	29
	Medium	55	94	56
	High	40	67	29

$$\chi^2 = 2 \cdot 23 \ (NS)$$

Table 4.13 Third year boys' self images: loadings on the principal factors (Varimax rotation, decimal points omitted)

Self image	Middle class boys (n = 81)		Lower working class boys (n = 69)		
	Factor 1	2	1	2	3
Good pupil	16	76	20	−35	−66
Group leader	−65	28	07	−17	−004
Good bloke	−64	−01	28	−35	−27
Sports fan	−71	−10	73	02	07
Boy friend	−72	−20	02	−76	15
Pop fan	−58	−34	−02	−74	−06
Street peer	−43	−49	53	−34	50
School rebel	−20	−74	−21	−24	84
Ritualist	−06	−59	81	03	−15
Percentage of total variance accounted for:	26·98	21·69	18·27	17·48	16·97

Note: Due to the relatively small numbers involved in these calculations, there is a considerable probability of random error, and consequently factors are identified in terms of the highest loadings.

Table 4.14 Third year girls' self images: loadings on the principal factors (Varimax rotation, decimal points omitted)

Self image	Middle class girls (n=86)				Lower working class girls (n=59)			
	Factor							
	1	2	3	4	1	2	3	4
Good pupil	-03	79	19	33	-34	-38	74	33
Home maker	02	72	-10	-08	-81	-10	-03	06
Ritualist	02	-05	-85	-19	-82	03	11	06
Good friend	-48	29	-58	30	-08	-27	-85	23
Pop fan	-78	-31	13	07	11	86	08	-04
Fashion follower	-66	-004	42	-20	-03	88	-02	01
Girl friend	-66	-003	-09	-21	23	-06	20	-50
Tomboy	20	-07	07	82	-29	02	-20	-81
Rebel	-25	-68	08	23	45	21	09	-69
Percentage of total variance accounted for:	19·98	19·78	14·69	11·77	20·06	19·95	15·28	17·27

Note: Due to the relatively small numbers involved in these calculations, there is a considerable probability of random error, and consequently factors are identified in terms of the highest loadings.